Coding Ockham's Razor

Lloyd Allison

Coding Ockham's Razor

Springer

Lloyd Allison
Faculty of Information Technology
Monash University
Melbourne, Victoria, Australia

ISBN 978-3-030-09488-1 ISBN 978-3-319-76433-7 (eBook)
https://doi.org/10.1007/978-3-319-76433-7

Softcover re-print of the Hardcover 1st edition 2018

Printed on acid-free paper

This Springer imprint is published by the registered company Springer International Publishing AG part of Springer Nature.
The registered company address is: Gewerbestrasse 11, 6330 Cham, Switzerland

To Sally, Bridget, Jean, Yeshi, Nyima, and Lhamo.

Preface

The minimum message length (MML) principle was devised by Chris Wallace (1933–2004) and David Boulton in the late 1960s [12, 93] initially to solve the unsupervised mixture modelling problem—an important problem, a mathematical analysis, and a working computer program (Snob) that gives useful results in many different areas of science, a "complete" research project.

The Foundation Chair of Computer Science at Monash University, Chris is also particularly remembered for his work on the "Wallace multiplier" [85, 86], pseudo-random number generators [14, 89], and operating systems [6, 99].

MML was developed [91, 92] in practical and theoretical directions and was applied to many inference problems by Chris, co-workers, postgraduates, and postdocs. One of my personal favourite applications is Jon Patrick's modelling of megalithic stone circles [65, 66].

I first heard about MML over lunch one day which led to applying it to biological sequence alignment [3] and related problems [15], and eventually after many twists and turns to protein structural alignment [17] and protein folding patterns [83].

Unfortunately much MML-based research that led to new inductive inference programs resulted in little shared software *componentry*. A new program tended to be written largely from scratch by a postgrad, postdoc or other researcher and did not contribute to any software library of shared parts. As such the programs embody reimplementations of standard parts. This phenomenon is not due to any special property of MML and actually seems to be quite common in research but it is rather ironic because, what with the complexity of models and of data being measured in the same units, MML is well suited to writing components that can be reused and supplied as parameters to other inductive inference software.

The first MML book is the one written by Chris Wallace [92] but published posthumously; it is the reference work for MML theory. This other MML book is an attempt to do a combined MML and Software Engineering analysis of inductive inference software. Sound programming skills are needed to write new application programs for inductive inference problems. Some mathematical skills, particularly in calculus and linear algebra, are needed to do a new MML analysis of one's favourite statistical model.

Melbourne, Victoria, Australia Lloyd Allison

Acknowledgements

Chris Wallace was a great inspiration and always generous with ideas. He is sadly missed. This book was begun largely at the urging of Arun Konagurthu who at times shows aspects of both an irresistible force and an immovable object. He also contributed to the content and examples and fought valiantly in the typesetting wars.

Leigh Fitzgibbon, Josh Comley, and Rodney O'Donnell deserve special mention for contributions [18, 34, 61] to early attempts to create and use *general* MML software.

Many thanks go to Dianna Kenny for sharing her data on musicians and mortality (Sect. 7.5).

I am indebted to those who read parts, a little or a lot, of drafts of the book and who suggested improvements, a few or many, in alphabetical order: Rohan Baxter, Minh Duc Cao, Trevor Dix, Rodney O'Donnell, Arun Konagurthu, Francois Petitjean, Joel Reicher, Daniel Schmidt. But, as they say, the mistakes are all my own.

Contents

Chapter 1
Introduction

This book is about inductive inference using the minimum message length (MML) principle and a computer. It is accompanied by a library of software (Chap. 13) to help an applications programmer, student or researcher in the fields of data analysis or machine learning to write computer programs of this kind.

Inductive inference is the business of learning something general from a given data-set. The thing that is learnt might be a parameter estimate, probability distribution, hypothesis, statistical model, explanation or theory, and the data-set is sometimes called examples, observations, evidence or training-data. Over-fitting is a well known danger in which a complex model is liable to fit data better than a simpler model yet may not be justified—the improvement in fit may not be worth the added complexity of the model. MML [92, 93] relies on Bayes's theorem [8] and Shannon's information theory [76]. It quantifies a model's complexity and allows it to be traded off against the model's fit to data. It is a realisation of Ockham's razor [78] (or Occam's razor).

Inductive, "characterized by the inference of general laws from particular instances."

Inference, "a conclusion reached on the basis of evidence and reasoning."[1]

---

[1]OED.

L. Allison, *Coding Ockham's Razor*, https://doi.org/10.1007/978-3-319-76433-7_1

pr(H)	prior probability of H
pr($H\|D$)	posterior probability of H given D
pr($D\|H$)	probability of D conditional on (given) H, also likelihood (of H (given D))

Fig. 1.1 Standard definitions

An inference is an answer to some question about a process that gives rise to data and that we are interested in. The question assumes some aspects of the process that are taken to be common knowledge, some aspects that are unknown but of no interest, and some aspects that are unknown but of interest and that are to be inferred. It specifies the form of an answer—what unknowns or parameters have to be filled in. It is important to be clear about exactly what question is being asked and about the form of an answer—what it includes and does not include.

An inference can be something modest such as an estimate of a parameter of a probability distribution, or something grand such as a theory of fundamental particles in physics, say. People tend to use the terms estimate, distribution, hypothesis, model, explanation, and theory in rough order of increasing grandeur although in reality there are no hard divisions between them. Regardless, an inference may well be wrong in that it is possible for it to be invalidated by future data, although it may be good enough to be useful until that day [13].

Q: What is the difference between a hypothesis and a theory?
A: Think of a hypothesis as a card. A theory is a house made of hypotheses.[2]

For hypotheses $H, H_0, H_1, \ldots$ and data D, common terminology (Fig. 1.1) includes, *prior* and *posterior* which refer to before and after seeing the data D. If X is a random variable that may take one of the values $x_1, x_2, \ldots$, we often write $\text{pr}(x_i)$ for $\text{pr}(X = x_i)$.

Bayes's theorem [8], in a form [52, 81] that is relevant here, states that the probability of hypothesis H and data D equals the probability of H times the probability of D given H:

$$\text{pr}(H\&D) = \text{pr}(H).\text{pr}(D|H) = \text{pr}(D).\text{pr}(H|D) \tag{1.1}$$

$\text{pr}(H)$ is given by a prior probability distribution over hypotheses and represents general ideas about what might typically be inferred from real data before that has been sighted. $\text{pr}(H|D)$ is given by a posterior distribution over hypotheses and is to be calculated. $\text{pr}(D)$ and $\text{pr}(D|H)$ are given by distributions over data; the former is often not known in practice and the latter follows from the specification of a model. It follows from Bayes that the posterior odds ratio of two hypotheses H_1 and H_2 is $\frac{\text{pr}(H_1|D)}{\text{pr}(H_2|D)} = \frac{\text{pr}(H_1).\text{pr}(D|H_1)}{\text{pr}(H_2).\text{pr}(D|H_2)}$.

[2]Marilyn vos Savant.

Shannon's mathematical theory of communication [76] tells us that the length of a message transmitting event E using an optimum code is

$$I(E) = -\log(\text{pr}(E)) \tag{1.2}$$

The letter I stands for information. If the log is the natural log to base e the units of $I(E)$ are *nits*, also known as nats. If the log is to base 2 the units are *bits*. Incidentally, arithmetic coding algorithms [64, 70] can get arbitrarily close to $I(E)$, even in the case of fractional bits! Sometimes $I(.)$ is used to stand for information content and sometimes $msg(.)$ to emphasise message length; they are synonyms,

$$msg(E) = I(E) = -\log(\text{pr}(E)) \tag{1.3}$$

Putting Bayes (1.1) and Shannon (1.2) together gives

$$I(H\&D) = I(H) + I(D|H) \tag{1.4}$$

The length of a message transmitting hypothesis H and data D is the length of first transmitting H and then transmitting D under the assumption that H is true. This two-part message, first H and then $(D|H)$, is the basis of the MML principle [92, 93]. Note that it transmits strictly more than the data D alone; it also transmits an *opinion* H about the data and so will in general be longer than an optimal message transmitting D alone. If anything, the first part H, being an answer, is generally of more interest than $D|H$ which can be thought of as the *noise* after the *structure*, H. A sensible person would choose a good hypothesis H, but she or he is not forced to do so. $I(H)$ is a natural measure of the complexity of hypothesis H. A more complex H_2 may fit D better than a simpler H_1, that is $I(H_1) < I(H_2)$ and $I(D|H_1) > I(D|H_2)$, but if $I(H_1) + I(D|H_1) < I(H_2) + I(D|H_2)$ then H_1 is preferred over H_2. This creates a brake on choosing more and more complex hypotheses, a *stopping* criterion that resists over-fitting.

William of Ockham (c. 1288–1347) was a Franciscan friar who is believed to have been born in Ockham, Surrey, and who is widely remembered for the principle known as Ockham's razor. He wrote "Numquam ponenda est pluralitas sine necessitate" (Plurality is never to be posited without necessity) and made other similar statements [78], although positions in favour of simplicity were taken at least as long ago as Aristotle (384–322BC): "We may assume the superiority ceteris paribus [other things being equal] of the demonstration which derives from fewer postulates or hypotheses—in short from fewer premisses" [58]. In MML inference, we might interpret a reduction in $I(H) + I(D|H)$ as being sufficient need to posit an increase in $I(H)$.

Note that the complexity, $I(H)$, of a hypothesis depends not just on the number of parameters that H has but also on the precision with which those parameters are stated. It is certainly possible that H_1 has more parameters than H_2 and yet $I(H_1) < I(H_2)$.

Also note that making inferences with MML rarely calls for actual encoding and transmission of messages. It is sufficient to compute what would be the lengths of hypothetical messages. A data-compression program can in principle be based on MML plus an arithmetic coder but data-compression programs are almost invariably expected to run quickly, processing mega-bytes of data in seconds or less, and having linear or near linear time complexity—think `gzip` [35] for example. It is indeed a great thing if an inference program also has these properties but we are generally prepared to give it more time, perhaps much more time, in return for a good answer.

In what follows a hypothesis is a fully parameterised model. The word *model* is near the middle of the estimate-theory scale, and it is nice and short.

1.1 Explanation versus Prediction

Predict, "Say or estimate that (a specified thing) will happen in the future or will be a consequence of something."[3]

Inductive inference is a different kind of problem to *prediction*. In prediction we want to know what is likely to happen in the next sample, or in the context of certain observations. In pure prediction we do not care why this is. An inductively inferred model comes complete with its inferred parameter values but in pure prediction we are not interested in them. An inference can naturally be used to make a prediction and the best model does often give good predictions but its *primary* purpose is to explain what has happened, not to predict what will happen. An average over all models, "integrating out" the model, may give better predictions than a single model, and indeed if $H_1, H_2, \ldots$ are all the distinct possible causes of D, Bayes [8] gives

$$\text{pr}(D) = \sum_i \text{pr}(H_i) \cdot \text{pr}(D|H_i)$$

However, the average over models has no structure, has no parameters, and it cannot be examined to explain *why* the source of the data is the way it is. Here we are principally concerned with inductive inference.

A subclass of models, the function-models will be encountered later (Chaps. 5, and 8). They are commonly used to make predictions where an input id is thought to, at least partly, cause an output $od \sim f(id)$. Given an input, a function-model returns a model, a probabilistic prediction, of the possible values of the output conditional on that input. The function-model inferred by an optimal inference algorithm is the best function-model, out of the set of function-models that the algorithm was allowed to choose from, at modelling (explaining) how id influences od. It may not

[3] OED.

be the best function-model of all possible function-models at predicting od, and the best of these may be nothing like a good explanation of how id influences od.

1.2 Models

The main duty of a fully parameterised model over a data-space is to give a probability pr(d) to d where d is a datum, a data value, from the model's data-space. It is sometimes convenient to deal with negative log probability $-\log_e(\mathrm{pr}(d))$ nits, or possibly in bits, $-\log_2(\mathrm{pr}(d))$. Continuous data can only ever be measured to limited accuracy $\pm\frac{\epsilon}{2}$ so even a distribution (model) over continuous data can deliver a probability of such a $d \pm \frac{\epsilon}{2}$, as well as a probability density pdf(d). It is also desirable that a model be able to generate random values according to its idea of what is random.

An unparameterised model needs to be supplied with *statistical* parameters to produce a fully parameterised model. For example, the unparameterised 2-state model over the set {head, tail} requires at least pr(head). (Then pr(tail) $= 1 -$ pr(head).) An unparameterised model may have problem-defining parameters but these are not statistical parameters; problem-defining parameters are given, stated up front, whereas statistical parameters are inferred (estimated, fitted, learned) from data. For example, the 2-state model is a special case of the multistate model (Sect. 2.3) where the bounds on values in the data-space are ⟨head, tail⟩. The bounds are problem defining parameters for this use of the multistate model (Sect. 2.2) and pr(head) is a statistical parameter. The distinction between the unparameterised and fully parameterised model here concerns its statistical parameters.

Ideally, an unparameterised model will have a method of estimating a fully parameterised model from a given data-set, $ds = [d_1, d_2, \ldots, d_N]$. An *estimator* may itself have parameters, perhaps to specify prior beliefs about likely estimates, or to limit how much time a search algorithm is allowed to take.

Sufficient statistics $ss = stats(ds)$ consist of some possibly structured value derived from a data-set ds from which a model M can calculate the negative log likelihood $nlLH(ss) = -\log(\mathrm{pr}(ds|M))$ of the data-set, and from which an estimator can estimate a fully parameterised model. In the worst case ss is just the data-set itself, but often ss is much condensed compared to ds, and $nlLH(ss)$, while mathematically equal to $\sum_i -\log(\mathrm{pr}(d_i|M))$ provided the d_i are independent, is often faster to compute than the sum.

1.2.1 *Implementation*

The notions above can be implemented as unparameterised `UPModel`, `Estimator` and fully parameterised `Model` in a suitable programming language:

```
UPModel            // an UnParameterised Model
 { defnParams()    // UPModel's problem defining
                      parameters
   stats(ds)       // suff stats of data-set ds for
                      estimation
   estimator(ps)   // Estimator of a Model, parameter ps
   ...
 }
Estimator          // an Estimator of Models
 { stats(ds)       // suff stats of ds for estimation
   ss2Model(ss)    // suff stats to Model
   ds2Model(ds)    // data-set to Model
   ...
 }
Model              // a Fully Parameterised Model
 { statParams()    // Model's statistical parameters
   pr(d)           // probability of datum d
   nlPr(d)         // neg log_e probability of d
   nl2Pr(d)        // nlPr in bits
   stats(ds)       // stats of data-set ds for nlLH()
   nlLH(ss)        // neg log likelihood, nlLH(stats(ds))
   random()        // generate, a random datum
   ...
 }
```

In an implementation it is desirable that each `UPModel`, `Estimator`, and `Model` satisfies the relevant standard interface because it can then be used as a component of other structured `UPModels`, `Estimators`, and `Models`.

Note that "unparameterised" and "fully parameterised" are sometimes dropped, and we then use "model" on its own to mean either or both of these as implied by context. Mathematics is written thus, $-\log(\text{pr } d)$, and its implementation in computer code is written in fixed width font thus, `-log(pr(d))`. There is more information on a Java implementation of the models described in Chap. 13.

1.3 Estimators

A fully parameterised model is sometimes just a given. For example, we may have a use for $\mathcal{N}_{0,1}$, the normal (Gaussian) probability distribution (Sect. 4.3) with mean 0 and standard deviation 1. However we are usually more interested in a model inferred from a data-set ds. As touched on earlier, MML judges such a model on its two-part message length $msg = msg_1 + msg_2$ where msg_1 corresponds to the model itself and msg_2 to the data-set from which it was inferred. These are properties of an implementation of a model.

```
Model              // a Fully Parameterised Model
 { statParams()    // Model's statistical parameters
   ...
   msg()           // = msg1() + msg2()
   msg1()          // message length of this Model and
   msg2()          // of data the Model inferred from
   ...
 }
```

In the case of a model that is a given, such as $\mathcal{N}_{0,1}$ above, set $msg_1 = msg_2 = 0$ to indicate that the model is common knowledge and not the result of an inference. There is no need to encode something that everyone already knows.

It can be argued that a message length is the property of the act of estimating a `Model` in some context rather than of the `Model` itself. However, given the way that Models are estimated and compared, in nine times out of ten it is *convenient* to have `msg`, `msg1` and `msg2` directly available from the `Model`. Just make sure that if a `Model` is used twice in a message, it is only transmitted once and is "free" the second time.

Message lengths allow us to compute the posterior log-odds ratio of two models,

$$log\frac{\mathrm{pr}(H_1|D)}{\mathrm{pr}(H_2|D)} = \log \mathrm{pr}(H_1|D) - \log \mathrm{pr}(H_2|D)$$

$$= msg_1(H_2) + msg_2(D|H_2) - msg_1(H_1) - msg_2(D|H_1)$$

and to compare two or more models and choose the best one– the one having the shorter two-part message length. An implemented `Estimator` can do the same thing. However, finding the best `Model`, or even a good `Model`, is sometimes a hard computational problem.

Recall that the sufficient statistic(s), $ss = stats(ds)$, of a data-set, ds, is something computed from the data-set that is sufficient to calculate the negative log likelihood, $nlLH(ss)$, of the data-set and to estimate a fully parameterised model—if we know how to do that. It is convenient in the implementation of many models for the unparameterised model, the `UPModel`, to define `stats(ds)`, and for its estimator `UPModel.Est` and its fully parameterised model `UPModel.M`[4] to use that definition. However, in some models estimation requires more information than does calculation of the negative log likelihood and, in such cases, the estimator's `stats(...)` and the fully parameterised model's `stats(...)` differ.

Some estimators of structured models, for example, a classification tree (Sect. 8.4), also require the ability to compute sufficient statistics not just for a whole data-set but for a sub-range of its elements `[lo, hi)` from `lo` inclusive to `hi` exclusive, and to be able to combine the statistics of two parts of a data-set.

[4]This textual packaging of a `UPModel.M` and a `UPModel.Est` inside a `UPModel` is simply convenient, often. It is not compulsory.

For some classic probability distributions having a small number of statistical parameters it is possible to derive a closed form for an MML estimator. Sometimes numerical approximations are needed. Failing even that, if there are only a few possible models, perhaps they can all be evaluated and compared. Often however, particularly for models with variable numbers of parameters, there is an unlimited number of possible fully parameterised models and a search for a good model, perhaps using heuristics, must be used.

1.4 Information

Tracy and Richard are facing away from each other. Tracy tosses a fair coin and tells Richard that it came up heads. Richard learns one bit of information: $I(\text{head}) = -\log_2(\text{pr}(\text{head})) = -\log_2 0.5 = 1$ bit. Tracy rolls a fair dice with four sides labelled A, C, G and T, and tells Richard that the bottom face (think about it) is a C. Richard learns two bits of information. The dice lies there for a while and Tracy tells Richard it is still C down. Richard learns nothing new, that is zero information, $0 = -\log(\text{pr}(C)) = -\log(1)$. However Robin, who has only just then come into the room and who overhears, learns two bits of information; information depends on what the recipient already knows. Examples like these follow from the definition of Shannon information (1.2).

As remarked before, a continuous datum, d, can only be measured to some limited accuracy $\pm\frac{\epsilon}{2}$, and a continuous parameter θ can only be estimated and stated to some limited precision $\pm\frac{\delta}{2}$. Consequently a model over the parameter can give a non-zero probability, and a finite information value, a finite message length, to an estimate $\theta \pm \frac{\delta}{2}$. And the same goes for a model over data $d \pm \frac{\epsilon}{2}$.

The *entropy* of a model over a discrete data-space is the expected information per member of the data-space $\sum_d \text{pr}(d).I(d)$. The entropy of the fair four-sided dice model is of course 2 bits. A second four-sided dice is biased with probabilities $\frac{1}{2}, \frac{1}{4}, \frac{1}{8}, \frac{1}{8}$, Table 1.1. The entropy of this biased dice model is $\frac{1}{2}.1+\frac{1}{4}.2+\frac{1}{8}.3+\frac{1}{8}.3 = 1\frac{3}{4}$ bits. The model with probabilities 1, 0, 0, 0 has zero entropy ($0 \times \infty$ is taken to be zero). The distribution of a disordered system (Fig. 1.2a) has high entropy, and that of an ordered system (Fig. 1.2b) has low entropy.

The Kullback Leibler (KL) divergence [51], $D_{KL}(,)$, from distribution #1 to distribution #2 is $\sum_d \text{pr}_1(d).(I_2(d)) - I_1(d)))$. It is the expected extra message

	Fair dice	Biased dice
A	00	0
C	01	10
G	10	110
T	11	111

Table 1.1 Binary codes for {A,C,G,T}, DNA

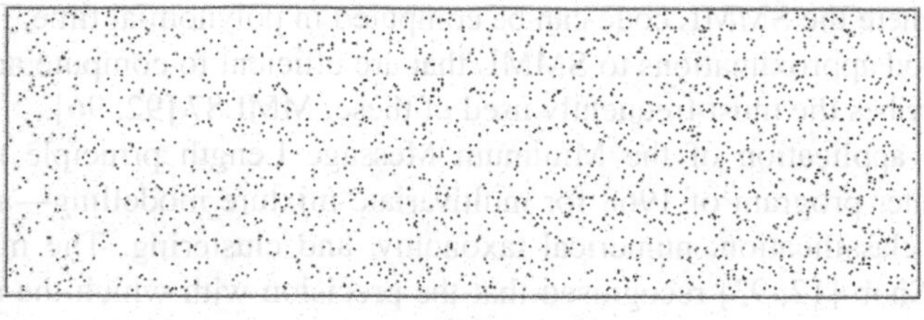

(a)

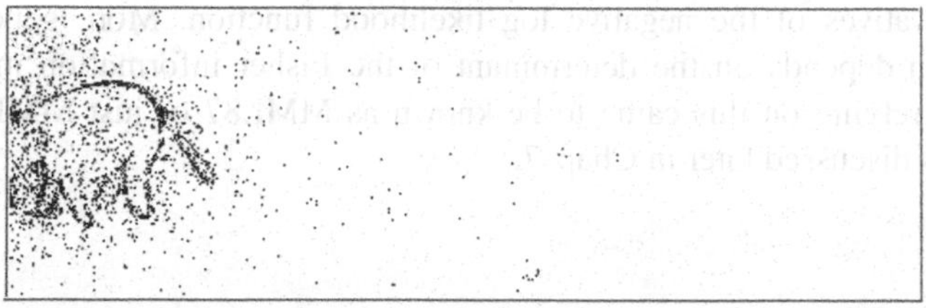

(b)

Fig. 1.2 High (**a**) and low (**b**) entropy (click)

length per datum due to using a code based on the wrong distribution (#2) to encode data sampled from the true distribution (#1). The KL-divergence from the fair dice to the biased dice is $((1-2)+(2-2)+(3-2)+(3-2))/4 = \frac{1}{4}$ bits. KL-divergence is always non-negative. In general it is not symmetric although in the case of the two dice above it happens to be so. The terminology "Kullback Leibler distance" is also sometimes seen.

In the long run, a method of encoding a sequence of data generated by some process cannot encode the data more succinctly per item on average than the entropy of the true model of the process, although most often in the real world we do not know the true model.

1.5 MML

In mathematical terms, an estimator is a many-to-one mapping from data-sets to fully parameterised models. It may be the case, particularly given a small amount of data, that not all possible models can be distinguished one from another. A Strict Minimum Message Length (SMML) code [94] partitions the space of data-sets and nominates a representative model for each part of the partition so as to minimise the expected two-part message length: A message first nominates a representative and then encodes the data as if the representative is the true model. A smaller (larger) subset indicates the representative is more (less) precise. The bad news is that in general, and in almost every case of interest, the design of an SMML code has been shown to be NP-hard [28]. The 2-state model (Sect. 2.2) of the next chapter is a rare exception where the SMML code can be computed in polynomial time. Fortunately there are good approximations to SMML that are efficient to compute and the next section describes the most frequently used of these, MML87 [92, 96].

The first application of the Minimum Message Length principle was in the *Snob* computer program of 1968 for multivariate mixture modelling—also known as intrinsic classification, numerical taxonomy, and clustering. The mathematics supporting Snob [12, 93] recognised that the precision with which the continuous parameters of a probability distribution should be stated depends on the expected second derivatives of the negative log likelihood function. More generally [96] the precision depends on the determinant of the Fisher information matrix[5] and the method relying on this came to be known as MML87 or just MML. Mixture modelling is discussed later in Chap. 7.

1.6 MML87

This section is included for completeness; it closely follows [96] (which generalized [93]) and [92]. You may care to skip it at a first reading but it is important reading when analysing a new probability distribution.

1.6.1 Single Continuous Parameter θ

First consider a model with a single continuous parameter θ. An SMML code would use some estimate $\hat{\theta}$ when transmitting a data set ds. Assuming that the likelihood is nicely behaved as θ varies, the estimate has limited precision $\pm\frac{\epsilon(\theta)}{2}$, or just $\pm\frac{\epsilon}{2}$ for brevity. That is $\hat{\theta}$ is the representative for an interval $\hat{\theta} \pm \frac{\epsilon(\hat{\theta})}{2}$ of possible parameter values. If the prior probability density $h(.)$ varies slowly over the interval $[\hat{\theta} - \frac{\epsilon}{2}, \hat{\theta} + \frac{\epsilon}{2}]$ then $\mathrm{pr}(\hat{\theta}) \approx h(\hat{\theta})\epsilon$ and the length of the first part of the message is $-\log(h(\hat{\theta})\epsilon) = -\log(h(\hat{\theta})) - \log\epsilon$. The quantity $\epsilon(\theta)$ can be chosen to be smaller or bigger as part of optimising the message length. The representative of a different interval may be used for a different data-set. In the design of an SMML code, the position and size of each interval potentially influences every other interval and also the number of intervals. Rather than actually optimise the number, positions and sizes of all intervals, the MML87 approximation [96] considers just one estimate $\hat{\theta}$ and its precision. The estimate and its precision approximate what SMML would do in that region of parameter space.

[5] David [22] attributes the "first (?) occurrence" of the term "information matrix" to Fisher [31, p.184].

For θ close to $\hat{\theta}$, that is $\theta = \hat{\theta} + \omega$ and $|\omega| \leq \frac{\epsilon}{2}$, the negative log likelihood is, by Taylor expansion up to the quadratic term,

$$- \log L = - \log \text{pr}(ds|\theta) \tag{1.5}$$

$$\approx - \log \text{pr}(ds|\hat{\theta}) - \omega \frac{d}{d\hat{\theta}} \log \text{pr}(ds|\hat{\theta})$$

$$- \frac{1}{2}\omega^2 \frac{d^2}{d\hat{\theta}^2} \log \text{pr}(ds|\hat{\theta}) + \ldots \tag{1.6}$$

This depends on the data-set ds which is hypothetical at this stage, and on $\hat{\theta}$ and ϵ which are ours to choose.

The expected negative log likelihood over $[-\frac{\epsilon}{2}, +\frac{\epsilon}{2}]$ is $\frac{1}{\epsilon}$ times the integral with respect to ω

$$- \log L \approx - \log \text{pr}(ds|\hat{\theta}) - \frac{1}{24}\epsilon^2 \frac{d^2}{d\hat{\theta}^2} \log \text{pr}(ds|\hat{\theta})$$

Note that the linear term in ω, being an odd term, has cancelled out, and that the quadratic term comes from $\frac{1}{\epsilon} \int_{-\epsilon/2}^{+\epsilon/2} \omega^2 = \frac{1}{\epsilon} \left[\frac{\omega^3}{3} \right]_{-\epsilon/2}^{+\epsilon/2} = \frac{\epsilon^2}{12}$. A minimum in $- \log L$ is a maximum in L, $\frac{d^2}{d\hat{\theta}^2} \log \text{pr}(ds|\hat{\theta})$ is negative and the expected negative log likelihood above increases with ϵ.

For a given ϵ, the expected total message length is therefore

$$msgLen \approx - \log(h(\hat{\theta})) - \log(\epsilon) - \log \text{pr}(ds|\hat{\theta}) - \frac{1}{24}\epsilon^2 \frac{d^2}{d\hat{\theta}^2} \log \text{pr}(ds|\hat{\theta})$$

The second derivative in the last term has a name: The (expected) Fisher and the observed Fisher are defined as

$F(\theta) = -\text{E}_{ds} \frac{d^2}{d\hat{\theta}^2} \log \text{pr}(ds|\hat{\theta})$ – (expected)Fisher, and

$F(\theta, ds) = - \frac{d^2}{d\hat{\theta}^2} \log \text{pr}(ds|\hat{\theta})$ – observed Fisher for data-set ds.

The former is the expectation, taken over expected data-sets. The latter is variously called the observed Fisher, the empirical Fisher, or the Hessian.

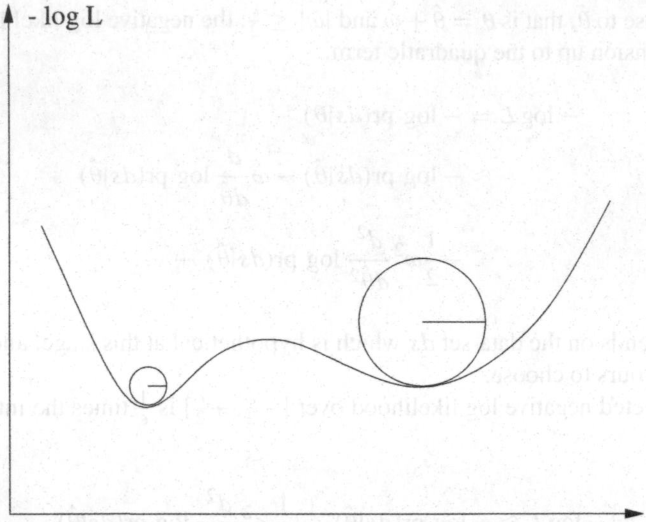

Fig. 1.3 Curvature, $-\log L$ v. θ

The Fisher tells how sensitive the expected negative log likelihood is to changes in θ. A high value at an estimate $\hat{\theta}$ indicates a sharp minimum and such an estimate should be stated to high precision or the average negative log likelihood will blow out over parts of the estimate's range of use that are further from $\hat{\theta}$. You may recall that the second derivative of a function is inversely proportional to its radius of curvature—Fig. 1.3. Big second derivative, small radius. Small second derivative, big radius.

Differentiating the expected message length with respect to ϵ and setting to zero gives the optimum precision, $\epsilon(\hat{\theta})^2 = -12/\frac{d^2}{d\hat{\theta}^2}\log \mathrm{pr}(ds|\hat{\theta}) = -12/F(\hat{\theta}, ds)$. However this depends on the empirical Fisher which depends on the data-set ds which is unavailable when computing the SMML code that MML87 is approximating. But the expected Fisher does not depend on ds so it can be used:

$$\epsilon(\hat{\theta})^2 = -12/F(\hat{\theta})$$

And this gives

$$msgLen \approx -\log(h(\hat{\theta})) + \frac{1}{2}\log\left(\frac{F(\hat{\theta})}{12}\right) - \log \mathrm{pr}(ds|\hat{\theta}) + \frac{1}{2}\frac{F(\hat{\theta}, ds)}{F(\hat{\theta})}$$

Assuming that $F(\hat{\theta}, ds) \approx F(\hat{\theta})$ for the estimate that will be used for ds, the expected message length is

$$msgLen \approx -\log(h(\hat{\theta})) + \frac{1}{2}\log\left(\frac{F(\hat{\theta})}{12}\right) - \log \mathrm{pr}(ds|\hat{\theta}) + \frac{1}{2} \tag{1.7}$$

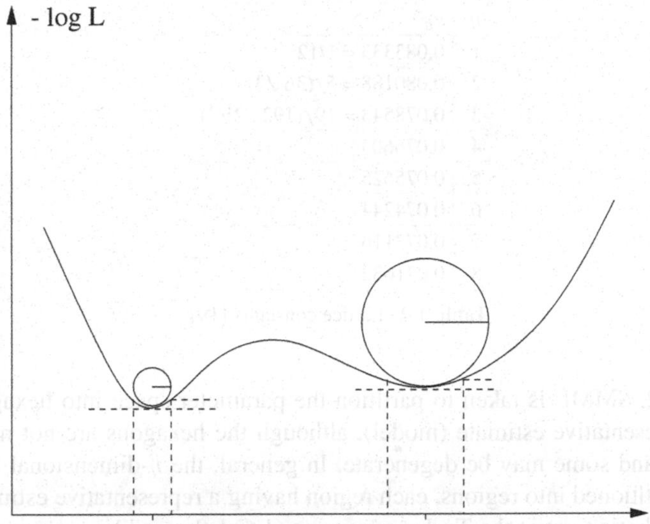

Fig. 1.4 Parameter precision

The first two terms make up the length of the message's first part that states $\hat{\theta}$ to optimum precision. The second two terms make up the length of the message's second part that encodes the data-set ds; the $\frac{1}{2}$ is the expected price borne by the second part using the limited precision $\hat{\theta}$ in return for the first part's saving due to that same limited precision. The more sensitive $-\log L$ is to θ, the more precisely θ is stated (Fig. 1.4) in order to maintain this effect.

An MML87 estimator aims to mininise the expected message length (1.7). In contrast, a maximum likelihood estimator seeks to maximise the likelihood, minimise the $-\log \text{pr}(ds|\hat{\theta})$ term, alone. Of itself, making the negative log likelihood small is no bad thing but, considering the wider picture, MML87 also takes into account the other terms that depend on θ.

1.6.2 Multiple Continuous Parameters

Next consider a model with η continuous parameters, that is a vector $\theta = \langle\theta_1, \ldots, \theta_\eta\rangle$. In this case the Fisher information *matrix* [31] is the symmetric, positive definite, $\eta \times \eta$ matrix of expected second derivatives of the negative log likelihood function

$$\begin{pmatrix} \frac{\partial^2}{\partial\theta_1^2}(-\log L) & \frac{\partial^2}{\partial\theta_1\,\partial\theta_2}(-\log L) & \ldots \\ \frac{\partial^2}{\partial\theta_2\,\partial\theta_1}(-\log L) & \frac{\partial^2}{\partial\theta_2^2}(-\log L) & \ldots \\ & \vdots & \end{pmatrix}$$

and its *determinant* is the Gaussian curvature of the function.

η	κ_η
1	0.083333 = 1/12
2	0.080188 = $5/(36\sqrt{3})$
3	0.078543 = $19/(192 \,.\, 2^{1/3})$
4	0.076603
5	0.075625
6	0.074244
7	0.073116
8	0.071682

Table 1.2 Lattice constants [19]

If $\eta = 2$, SMML is taken to partition the parameter space into hexagons each with a representative estimate (model), although the hexagons are not necessarily symmetric and some may be degenerate. In general, the η-dimensional parameter space is partitioned into regions, each region having a representative estimate.

The quadratic term in the Taylor expansion (1.6) behaves like a squared distance and the selection of a lattice of points in $\mathbb{R}^\eta$ that minimises average squared distances is the business of Voronoi regions, polytopes and quantisation [19]. The quadratic term that was averaged over $[\hat{\theta} - \frac{\epsilon}{2}, \hat{\theta} + \frac{\epsilon}{2}]$ previously when $\eta = 1$, is now averaged over the region containing $\hat{\theta}$. Where ϵ was the length of an interval for $\eta = 1$ it becomes an area (volume, ...) of a region for $\eta \geq 2$, giving $\frac{1}{2}\kappa_\eta\, \epsilon^{2/\eta}$ [92, 96] where κ_η is a *lattice constant* for η dimensions (note that κ_η is called G_η in [19]).

$$msgLen \approx -\log(h(\hat{\theta})) + \frac{1}{2}\log(|F(\hat{\theta})|) + \frac{\eta}{2}\log(\kappa_\eta) - \log \mathrm{pr}(ds|\hat{\theta}) + \frac{\eta}{2} \qquad (1.8)$$

The first three terms give the length of the message's first part that states the estimate $\hat{\theta}$. The second and third terms can be interpreted as the area (volume, ...) of the estimate's imprecision. The last two terms are the length of the message's second part that encodes the data.

Exact values of lattice constants are only known for small η (Table 1.2) but it is known that $\kappa_\eta \to \frac{1}{2\pi e} = 0.05855\ldots$ as $\eta \to \infty$ [103].

1.7 Outline

The following chapters describe MML models roughly in ascending order of difficulty—first models of atomic data and then structured models of structured data. Many of the latter models take other models as parameters.

Chapter 11 discusses models of graphs (networks) as an example of a current research area where there are many unsolved problems. It is included as much for the story of an attempt to solve some interesting problems as for the particular models defined.

The last two chapters examine some practical matters (Chap. 12) and implementation (Chap. 13). The glossary defines terminology and includes short notes on related topics.

Chapter 2
Discrete

Boolean = {false, true}, Coin = {head, tail}, Gender = {male, female}, Politics = {Labor, Liberal, Green}, and DNA = {A, C, G, T} are all examples of *discrete* data types (data-spaces). In computer programming languages they are often called *enumerated*, and in statistics *categorical*. The above examples are all unordered. On the other hand, Quality = {awful, poor, adequate, good, excellent}, Size = {small, average, large}, and Letter = {a, b, ..., z} are also ordered.

A discrete value can be implemented as an integer provided there is a way to turn the external representation into the integer and back again, for example,

head ↔ 0, tail ↔ 1
A ↔ 0, C ↔ 1, G ↔ 2, T ↔ 3

In general for a discrete value `d`, `d` ↔ `d.n()`. The actual integers representing discrete values are arbitrary so they may as well be consecutive.

As before (Sect. 1.3) it is often convenient to have an unparameterised `Discrete` model textually contain a parameterised `Discrete.M` model. Most operations on data within a model of discrete data can be implemented in terms of the integer representing a value leading to `pr_n(n)`, `random_n()` within

```
Discretes.M
 { ...
   pr(d);         // probability of d
   pr_n(n);       // probability of the int (of a value)
   nlPr_n(n);     // -ve log probability of ...
   random_n();    // random int (of a random() value)
   ...
 }
```

where `pr(d)`, the probability of a discrete datum `d`, returns `pr_n(d.n())`, and so on.

L. Allison, *Coding Ockham's Razor*, https://doi.org/10.1007/978-3-319-76433-7_2

Most discrete data types are bounded, in a range $[lwb, upb]$, there then being $upb-lwb+1$ distinct values. This does not necessarily mean that the type is ordered, just that there is a way of stepping through the discrete values in a systematic but arbitrary order as determined by the underlying integers, for example, A, C, G and finally T. Models of unbounded integers are discussed in Chap. 3.

This chapter discusses the Uniform (Sect. 2.1), MultiState (Sect. 2.3), and Adaptive (Sect. 2.4) models of Discrete Bounded data whose implementations fit into the model hierarchies as follows.

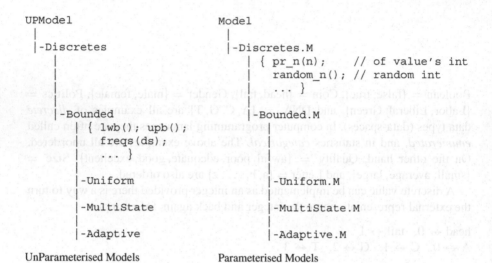

```
UPModel                            Model
 |                                  |
 |-Discretes                        |-Discretes.M
    |                                  | { pr_n(n);     // of value's int
    |                                  |   random_n(); // random int
    |                                  |   ... }
    |-Bounded                          |-Bounded.M
       | { lwb(); upb();                  |
       |   freqs(ds);                     |
       |   ... }                          |
       |                                  |
       |-Uniform                          |-Uniform.M
       |                                  |
       |-MultiState                       |-MultiState.M
       |                                  |
       |-Adaptive                         |-Adaptive.M
```

UnParameterised Models Parameterised Models

Note that there is a correspondence between the MultiState and Multinomial models. The former is a model over a data type of k discrete values so a data-set is a sample of a number of those values. The latter, which should perhaps more correctly be called Multinomial$_N$ where N is a given, is a model over the numbers of *occurrences*—the frequencies—of each of the k values in a sample of size N from the MultiState. As such its data-space consists of k-dimensional vectors of non-negative integers that sum to N. Both models have the same statistical parameters, these specifying the probabilities of the k values being sampled from the MultiState. Because of this correspondence the distinction between the two models are sometimes blurred. The Multinomial is discussed further in Sect. 5.2.

2.1 Uniform

The bounds of a bounded discrete data-space are given, problem definition parameters of models of that data-space; they are not statistical parameters. The simplest possible fully parameterised model of such a data-space is the Uniform distribution where each datum has probability $\frac{1}{upb-lwb+1}$. This model has a trivial estimator—it always estimates the same fully parameterised Uniform model, `Md1`. The estimator, while being trivial, can be useful: It can be passed to a function that *requires* an estimator, such as the estimator of a structured model if and when a component of data happens to be modelled uniformly. The fully parameterised Uniform model has no statistical parameters or equivalently it has the trivial parameter known as `triv` or "`()`". The implementation of the `Uniform` model of discrete data is straightforword.

2.2 Two State

The two-state model is a special case of MultiState where $upb = lwb + 1$. It is discussed here because it is a rare example of a model where the strict MML (SMML) estimator runs in polynomial time [28]. Strict MML is a gold standard for MML inference. The MML paradigm is that a transmitter and a receiver are planning some transmissions of data-sets. Naturally they want the transmissions to be efficient, they want the messages between themselves to be as compact as possible.

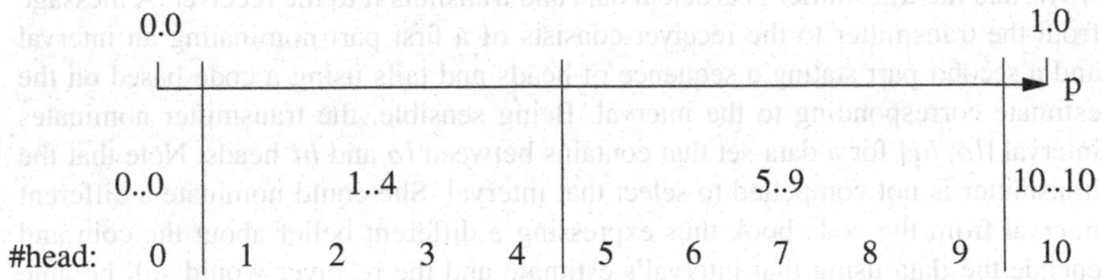

Fig. 2.1 Partitions, $N = 10$

In this example, each data-set is the result of N Bernoulli trials, that is N tosses of a coin, a sequence of N heads and tails where N is common knowledge. The coin may be biased; its $p = \text{pr(head)}$ might not equal $\frac{1}{2}$, in fact it is believed that all values between 0 and 1 inclusive are equally likely. In other words, the *prior* on p is uniform. You can choose another prior if you prefer but uniform is the simplest, blandest prior. The transmitter and the receiver want to learn whatever they can about the p of each coin from the data-set produced by the coin.

Before they have seen any actual data the transmitter and the receiver get together to design an efficient code for this situation. It is obvious that if a coin were known to be fair it would take 1 bit per trial to transmit the data but these coins can be biased. The *question* is, how biased, if at all, is each coin? An *answer* to this question assigns an estimated value to p.

It is intuitively obvious that how much can be inferred about p depends on N and on the number of heads. For $N = 10$, 3 heads and 7 tails, very little can be inferred—except that the coin does have two different faces and does not seem to be extremely biased. But for $N = 100$, 30 heads and 70 tails, it is a good bet that the coin is biased. On the other hand for $N = 100$, 45 heads and 55 tails, the coin could well be fair.

The number of heads, #head, in N trials lies between 0 and N inclusive, that is in $[0, N]$, and all values are equally likely given the uniform prior. It is well known that for a given #head, all sequences containing #head heads are equally likely. Given an estimate of p, $N = \#head + \#tail$ trial results can be transmitted in $-\#head \cdot \log_2(p) - \#tail \cdot \log_2(1-p)$ bits. The SMML code that the transmitter and the receiver design is based on a partition of $[0, N]$ into one or more intervals, $[0, a], [a+1, b], \ldots, [f+1, N]$, Fig. 2.1. In principle there could be as few as one interval, $[0, N]$, as many as $N+1$ intervals, $[0, 0], [1, 1], \ldots, [N, N]$, or anything in between. An interval $[lo, hi]$ corresponds to an estimate of p of $\frac{lo+hi}{2.N}$. It does not express a belief that p necessarily equals $\frac{lo+hi}{2.n}$ but rather that it probably lies between $\max(0, \frac{lo-1/2}{N})$ and $\min(1, \frac{hi+1/2}{N})$. This is the *precision* to which p has been inferred. The prior probability of the interval, and hence of its estimate, is $\frac{hi-lo+1}{N+1}$ which is just the fraction of $[0, N]$ that the interval covers—a small interval has a low probability, a large interval a large probability.

Once the code is designed, the transmitter and the receiver go their separate ways, and the transmitter gets actual data and transmits it to the receiver. A message from the transmitter to the receiver consists of a first part nominating an interval and a second part stating a sequence of heads and tails using a code based on the estimate corresponding to the interval. Being sensible, the transmitter nominates interval $[lo, hi]$ for a data-set that contains between lo and hi heads. Note that the transmitter is not compelled to select that interval. She could nominate a different interval from the code book thus expressing a different belief about the coin and encode the data using that interval's estimate and the receiver would still be able to decode the message. However the greater message length resulting from such a choice would show it to be a poor one.

The design of an optimum code amounts to finding an optimum partition of $[0, N]$, one that minimises the expected message length, *expected* because when the code is being designed there is as yet no actual data. A one-dimensional dynamic programming algorithm (DPA) computes an optimum partition of $[0, N]$.

The Javascript demonstration (Fig. 2.2) calculates expected message lengths for N trials, for the Adaptive code and for the SMML two-part message. It also shows an optimum partition of $[0, N]$; the partition is not necessarily symmetric about the mid-point of $[0, N]$ because there can be ties in which case the algorithm makes an arbitrary choice. The *Adaptive* code which is an alternative to the SMML code is discussed in Sect. 2.4 but the thing to know at this point is that it does not provide

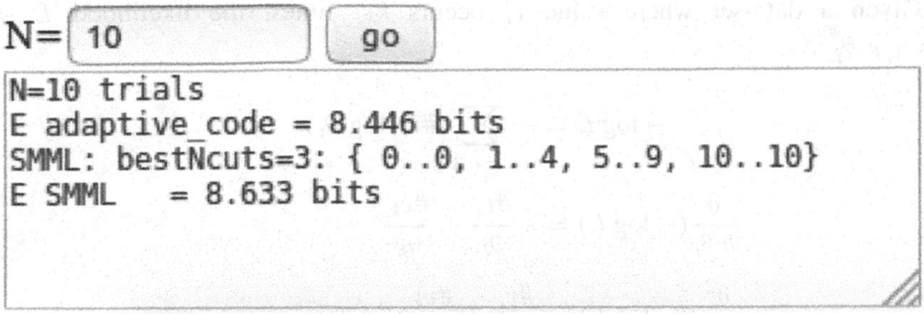

Fig. 2.2 SMML 2-state (click)

an answer to the question of the coin's bias; it only transmits the data. SMML estimates the coin's bias to an optimum precision, states it, and then transmits the data assuming the estimate is correct. As such it transmits strictly more than the data—it also transmits an inference (answer, opinion, estimate, explanation) about the coin—and consequently is slightly longer than the Adaptive code but only by a surprising small amount, just a fraction of a bit.

The DPA runs in $\Theta(N^2)$-time. Farr and Wallace [28] also examined the problem of finding the SMML code for an arbitrary model and its parameter space. They pointed out that essentially the DPA above can be used for other "one dimensional" SMML problems. (Dowty showed how to calculate "the strict minimum message length (SMML) estimator for 1-dimensional exponential families with continuous sufficient statistics" [25].) The complexity of the 3-state model remains open and they gave a good heuristic for this case. However they showed that in general constructing an SMML code is NP-hard. This would seem to be bad news for the MultiState model, let alone anything more complicated, but fortunately there is a good approximation to SMML known as *MML87* [96] (Sect. 1.6), or just as *MML*, which is efficient to compute.

2.3 MultiState

The MultiState model over a data-space of k discrete values has a vector of $k-1$ free parameters, $\langle\theta_{1..k-1}\rangle$ where θ_i is the probability of the ith value. The probability θ_k of the kth value is not a parameter and is, of course, one minus the sum of the other probabilities. Another way of putting it is that $\langle\theta_1, \ldots, \theta_k\rangle$ lies in the standard k-Simplex (Sect. 9.2).

$V = \{v_1, v_2, \ldots, v_k\}$, k-state values
N, number of trials of k-state source
$\#v_i$, number of instances of v_i in a data-set, $\sum_i \#v_i = N$
$\theta = \langle\theta_i\rangle$ where $\theta_i = \mathrm{pr}(v_i)$
note $\theta_k = 1 - \sum_{i=1..k-1} \theta_i$, and $\frac{\partial}{\partial\theta_i}\theta_k = -1$ where $i < k$

Given a data-set where value v_i occurs $\#v_i$ times, the likelihood $L = \prod_{i=1..k} \theta_i^{\#v_i}$.

$$-\log L = -\sum_{i=1..k} \#v_i \log(\theta_i)$$

$$\frac{\partial}{\partial \theta_i}(-\log L) = -\frac{\#v_i}{\theta_i} + \frac{\#v_k}{\theta_k}$$

$$\frac{\partial^2}{\partial \theta_i^2}(-\log L) = \frac{\#v_i}{\theta_i^2} + \frac{\#v_k}{\theta_k^2}$$

$$\frac{\partial^2}{\partial\theta_i \, \partial\theta_j}(-\log L) = \frac{\#v_k}{\theta_k}, where 1 \leq i, j < k, \; i \neq j$$

The expected value of $\#v_i$ is $N.\theta_i$ so the $(k-1) \times (k-1)$ Fisher information matrix is

$$\begin{pmatrix} \frac{N}{\theta_1} + \frac{N}{\theta_k} & \frac{N}{\theta_k} & \cdots & \frac{N}{\theta_k} \\ \frac{N}{\theta_k} & \frac{N}{\theta_2} + \frac{N}{\theta_k} & \cdots & \frac{N}{\theta_k} \\ \vdots & & & \\ \frac{N}{\theta_k} & \frac{N}{\theta_k} & \cdots & \frac{N}{\theta_{k-1}} + \frac{N}{\theta_k} \end{pmatrix}$$

Its determinant is $\frac{N^{k-1}}{\theta_1. \ldots .\theta_k}$, and $\frac{1}{2}\log(|F(\theta)|) = \frac{1}{2}((k-1)\log N - \sum_{i=1..k} \log \theta_i)$.

Recall the MML87 approximation (Sect. 1.6), $msg \approx \frac{1}{2}\log(|F(\theta)|) - \sum_{i=1..k} \#v_i . \log \theta_i + const$, where $const$ does not depend on θ.

So, $\frac{\partial}{\partial \theta_i} msg = \frac{1}{2}(-\frac{1}{\theta_i} + \frac{1}{\theta_k}) - \frac{\#v_i}{\theta_i} + \frac{\#v_k}{\theta_k}$ $= \frac{\#v_k + 1/2}{\theta_k} - \frac{\#v_i + 1/2}{\theta_i}$, $i = 1..k-1$.

Setting these to zero minimises the message length, and gives $\theta_i \propto \#v_i + \frac{1}{2}$, $i = 1..k$, that is $\theta_i = \frac{\#v_i + 1/2}{N + k/2}$, $i = 1..k$.

The MML estimate is therefore $\hat{\theta}_i = \frac{\#v_i + 1/2}{N + k/2}$ [12]. Note that $\hat{\theta}_i > 0$ even if v_i does not appear in the data-set, although it will tend to zero if $N \to \infty$ and v_i still does not appear.

MML87 assumes that there is a "reasonable" amount of data compared to the number of parameters to be estimated, here $k-1$. The MultiState's parameter vector lies in a k-Simplex (Sect. 9.2) and if there are "very few" data the uncertainty region about the estimate may pass outside the boundary of the Simplex and the prior probability of the estimate may even exceed one which is obviously impossible, and wrecks the message length calculations. In other words, MML87's assumptions may not hold in this situation. An implementation, `MultiState`, can include code to carry out checks and either halt, or do something reasonable in such circumstances but there is an alternative that uses the Adaptive code discussed in the next section, and that is robust against such misadventure.

2.4 Adaptive

A two-part message that is based on the MultiState model is not the most efficient way to transmit MultiState data! The first part transmits an opinion about the source of the data and the second part transmits the data assuming the opinion is true. As such strictly more than the data alone is transmitted and there is a price to pay—a small price—for stating the opinion and there is indeed a slightly shorter one-part message that can be used, provided that we are not interested in an answer to the question, "what are the probabilities of the various values for the source?" This was explored by Boulton and Wallace [12].

In the 1960s at least three methods were being used to calculate the information content of a data-set from a MultiState distribution and they did not all give the same result which was plainly unsatisfactory.

data:	[v_2,	v_1,	v_2,		...,	v_3]
c_1:	1	1	2	2	...	#v1+1
c_2:	1	2	2	3	...	#v2+1
c_3:	1	1	1	1	...	#v3
...	...				...	...
c_k:	1	1	1	1	...	#vk+1
sum:	k	k+1	k+2	k+3	...	N+k-1
pr:	$\frac{1}{k}$	$\frac{1}{k+1}$	$\frac{2}{k+2}$		...	$\frac{\#v3}{N+k-1}$

Fig. 2.3 $\mathrm{pr}(v_{i_1}, v_{i_2}, \ldots, v_{i_N}) = \prod_j \mathrm{pr}(v_{i_j}) = \frac{\#v_1!.\#v_2!. \ldots .\#v_k!}{\left(\frac{(N+k-1)!}{(k-1)!}\right)}$

A data-set consists of N trials from a k-state source over V.

$V = \{v_1, v_2, \ldots, v_k\}$, k-state values
N, number of trials of the k-state source
$\#v_i$, number of instances of v_i in a data-set, $\sum_i \#v_i = N$
e.g., $[v_2, v_1, v_2, \ldots, v_3]$, an example data-set
$I(E) = -\log(\mathrm{pr}(E))$, information

The *Adaptive code* uses k counters, $\{c_i\}$, to keep running totals of the number of instances of each value v_i that have been transmitted as the data-set is worked through sequentially. The counters are used to calculate running estimates $\mathrm{pr}(v_i) = \frac{c_i}{\sum_j c_j}$. Counter c_i is incremented *after* an instance of value v_i has been encoded—a transmitter and receiver can both do this and remain in agreement. To effect a uniform prior on the probabilities, the counters are initialised to one so that at any stage c_i holds one more than the number of v_i already seen. The probability of the data-set is simply the product of the running estimates of the elements (Fig. 2.3). (This kind of technique is widely used in data compression.)

The second method is the *Combinatorial code*. Its calculation of information content recognises that one can start by encoding $\#v_1, \#v_2, \ldots$, and $\#v_{k-1}$, that all the $\frac{(N+k-1)!}{N!\,(k-1)!}$ such possible values are equally likely, and that one can then finish by encoding which one of the $\frac{N!}{\prod_j \#v_j!}$ combinations of those numbers of values actually occurred. This gives exactly the same result as the Adaptive code, which is good.

The third method identified [12] as sometimes being used to calculate information content can be called the *maximum likelihood code* after the maximum likelihood estimate of $\mathrm{pr}_{ML}(v_i)$.

$\mathrm{pr}_{ML}(v_i) = \frac{\#v_i}{N}$

$\mathrm{pr}_{ML}(v_{i_1}, v_{i_2}, \ldots, v_{i_N}) = \prod_j \mathrm{pr}_{ML}(v_j)^{\#v_j} = \prod_j \left\{\frac{\#v_j}{N}\right\}^{\#v_j}$

Being based on actual frequencies this gives a message length that is strictly less than for the Adaptive and Combinatorial codes. *If* the $\mathrm{pr}_{ML}(v_i)$ were common knowledge the method would indeed lead to the shortest possible encoding of the data, being based on probabilities that correspond exactly to the frequencies of the values in the data-set. But they are *not* common knowledge and indeed there would be nothing to infer if they were. In particular, due to not knowing them the receiver is incapable of decoding a message that has been encoded by the transmitter using them, so such a code is invalid, useless.

The way to mend this third approach is to transmit an estimate of the $\mathrm{pr}(v_i)$, as the first part of a two-part message, providing the decoder with what was previously missing. When this is done, and the estimate is stated to optimum precision, the result is unsurprisingly the MML code for the MultiState model of the previous Sect. 2.3. It gives a message length that is a fraction of a bit longer, per parameter, than does the Adaptive code and this is cheap at the price because the former transmits strictly more than the latter.

An Adaptive encoding of a MultiState data-set does not include an answer to the question of the bias of the source. It does however assume one property of the source: the data are independent and identically distributed (IID). That is, for each data-set the source uses some fixed $\mathrm{pr}(v_i)$ and any permutation of the data-set would have the same message length. A second data-set may have different $\mathrm{pr}(v_i)$ but they will apply to all of the second data-set. If the probabilities change part way through a data-set, the Adaptive code will be suboptimal for it, and this is testable by comparison against a model that allows for them changing. It is therefore arguable that there is a valid Adaptive model of MultiState data and it can be implemented as `Adaptive` to be a competitor to `MultiState`.

```
Adaptive
 { ...
   pr(d)        -- not allowed,
   pr_n(n)      --    --"--, and
   random_n()   --    --"--   (see text)
   nlLH(ss)     -- -ve log likelihood of dataset ds
                -- where ss=stats(ds)
   random(k)    -- random data-set of k samples
 }
```

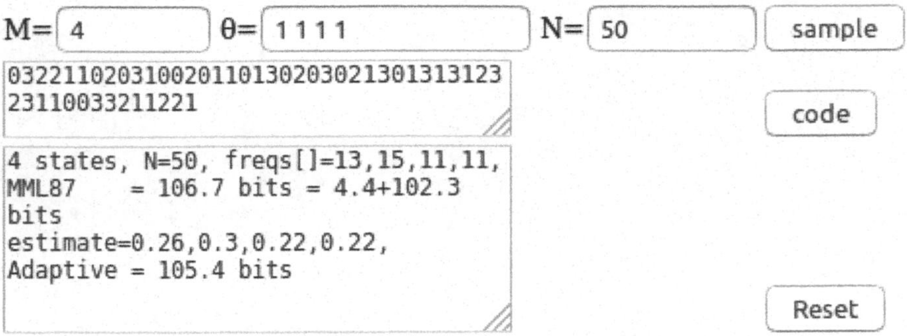

Fig. 2.4 MultiState (click)

A case can be made that `Adaptive` is more properly a model of *sequences* of MultiState data rather than a model of MultiState data. In particular, while `nlLH(ss)` and `Adaptive.random(k)` are valid, `nlPr(d)` and `Adaptive.random()` are not because the homogeneity assumption applies to an entire data-set not to a single datum removed from the context of a data-set. Nevertheless there are applications where it is useful to be able to use `Adaptive` as a direct substitute for `MultiState` (for example, Graphs Chap. 11) which is more convenient if `Adaptive` and `MultiState` are siblings in the model hierarchy.

The unparameterised `Adaptive` model takes the bounds of the data-space and a vector `alpha` (α) as problem defining parameters where α_i is used to initialise the running counter for value v_i (and need not equal 1). Making all the α_i equal is expressing a prior belief that the data values are all equally likely. The fully parameterised model, `Adaptive.M`, has no non-trivial statistical parameters so `Adaptive` provides an instance, `Adaptive.Mdl`.

Finally, recall from the previous section that the MML87 calculation of the first part of the two-part message for a MultiState model may break down if there are only "few" training data compared to the number of parameters to be estimated. Because the message length for the MultiState model exceeds that of the Adaptive model by a known amount, a robust way for an implementation to calculate the former is to calculate the latter and add on the known excess.

The Javascript demonstration (Fig. 2.4) can be used to experiment with discrete models. Its requirements are that $1 \leq M \leq 10$, $|\theta_{[0,k-1]}| > 0$ (the values will be normalised), $N \geq 0$, and $sample \in [0, k)^N$. Notice that, as discussed, MML87's message length is slightly longer than that of the adaptive code. Incidentally, N is common knowledge; the next chapter describes ways of encoding it if it were not.

Chapter 3
Integers

This chapter concerns models of integers, $\mathbb{Z} = \{\ldots, -1, 0, 1, 2, \ldots\}$, most often of non-negative ($\mathbb{Z}_{\geq 0}$) or positive ($\mathbb{Z}_{>0}$) integers. As an example, a simple parameter-less model for positive integers is

$pr(n) = \frac{1}{n(n+1)}$, for $n > 0$.

This is a proper probability distribution that sums to one because

$$\sum_{n>0} pr(n) = \sum_{n>0} \frac{1}{n(n+1)}$$

$$= \sum_{n>0} \left\{ \frac{1}{n} - \frac{1}{n+1} \right\}$$

$$= 1 - \frac{1}{2} + \frac{1}{2} - \frac{1}{3} + \frac{1}{3} \cdots = 1$$

Therefore a non-redundant code can be based on the distribution, and in this code

$$msg(n) = \log(n) + \log(n+1), \text{ for } n > 0,$$

which is approximately $2 \log n$ for large n.

The expectation, the mean, of this distribution is infinite:

$$\sum_{n>0} n pr(n) = \sum_{n>0} \frac{n}{n(n+1)} = \sum_{n>0} \frac{1}{n+1} = \infty$$

Important integer models discussed below include the log* (Sect. 3.1) and WallaceInt (Sect. 3.2) universal models, and the Geometric (Sect. 3.4) and Poisson (Sect. 3.5) models.

L. Allison, *Coding Ockham's Razor*, https://doi.org/10.1007/978-3-319-76433-7_3

3.1 Universal Codes

A model of positive integers that we would often like to have is $\text{pr}(n) \propto \frac{1}{n}$ for $n > 0$ which would give $msg(n) = \log n + const$. This is because in many situations the "order of magnitude" of a number is important: 10 is to 1 as 100 is to 10 and so on. Unfortunately $\text{pr}(n) \propto \frac{1}{n}$ is impossible because $\sum_{n>0} \frac{1}{n} = \infty$. In a certain sense however universal codes nearly achieve that aim.

If an integer n is known to lie in the interval $[1, N]$, or in $[0, N-1]$, it can be encoded in $\lceil \log_2 N \rceil$ bits. However, if no such upper bound is known a receiver does not know how many bits of a bit-stream are devoted to n, does not know n's encoded length, and so cannot decode it. A solution is to send the length of the encoded n first. But hang on, that length is also an integer so the receiver needs to know the length's length before that, and so on. A code can in fact be based on this idea, as shown by Elias [26] who also showed that the code is universal. A code for integers is *universal* if for *any* source with true distribution $\text{pr}_t(n)$ such that $\text{pr}_t(n) \geq \text{pr}_t(n+1)$, the size of the code-word for n is less than some constant c times the optimum, that is less than $-c. \log \text{pr}_t(n)$.

Note that the length of the length of the ... length of an integer n, that is the length^k of n, decreases very rapidly with k, as $\log^k(n)$. The code for n consists of one or more components. *Last* of all comes the component for n itself, using just enough bits. Before that comes $\text{length}(n)$, using just enough bits. And so on, until the first component of all, the one for $\text{length}^k(n)$ that is just two, in binary, 10. Since each component uses just enough bits and no more, a component's leading bit must be a 1, so there would seem to be no need to send that bit except that it can instead be used as a flag to distinguish the final component (1...) from the preceding components (0...) if any.

The code described so far is valid but can be made slightly more efficient: The length of a component only need be encoded if the component itself is at least two bits. So lengths minus one can be encoded rather than lengths of components (Table 3.1).

The probability distribution $\text{pr}(n)$ has an infinite expectation: The probability of large n is greater than under the $\frac{1}{n.(n+1)}$ distribution which as we saw itself has an infinite expectation.

A Javascript demonstration of the code (Fig. 3.1) uses machine `ints` and thus is limited in the values of n that it can handle. In principle the code is not so limited.

n	Components	Code-word	pr(n)
1	1	**1**	1/2
2	1,2	0 **10**	1/8
3	1,3	0 **11**	1/8
4	1,2,4	0 00 **100** , i.e., code'(2)++100	1/64
5	1,2,5	0 00 **101**	1/64
6	1,2,6	0 00 **110**	1/64
7	1,2,7	0 00 **111**	1/64
8	1,3,8	0 01 **1000** , i.e., code'(3)++1000	1/128
9	1,3,9	0 01 **1001**	1/128
10	1,3,10	0 01 **1010**	1/128
...	...	...	...
15	1,3,15	0 01 **1111**	1/128
16	1,2,4,16	0 00 000 **10000** , i.e., code'(4)++100000	1/2048
...	...	...	...
100	1,2,6,100	0 00 010 **1100100**	1/8192
...	...	...	...
1000	1,3,9,1000	0 01 0001 **1111101000**	1/(1024 × 128)
...	...	...	...

$msg(n) = 1 + \lfloor \log_2 n \rfloor + msg(\lfloor \log_2 n \rfloor), \text{ if } n > 1,$

$= 1, \text{ if } n = 1,$

$\mathrm{pr}(n) = 2^{-msg(n)}$

Bold: emphasize added

Table 3.1 Integer code

As an approximation to the code above Rissanen [71] gives

$$r(n) = \log_2^*(n) + \log_2(2.865),\ n > 0,$$

$$\text{where } \log_2^*(n) = \log_2(n) + \log_2^2(n) + \ldots, \text{ positive terms only,}$$

$$\mathrm{pr}(n) = 2^{-r(n)}$$

An implementation has no non-trivial statistical parameters and need only provide one fully parameterised model instance, `logStar0`, the zero to remind us that in this case the lower bound of its range is adjusted to 0. A trivial

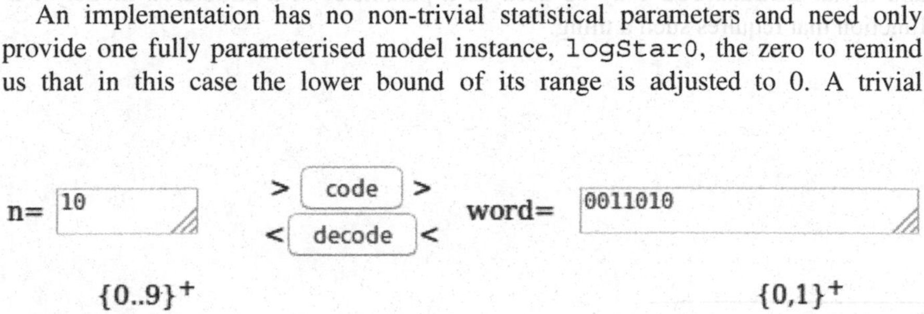

Fig. 3.1 Elias code (click)

unparameterised model `LogStar0UPM`, and trivial `estimator`, may be used as parameters of a structured model or a function that requires such a thing.

3.2 Wallace Tree Code

The Elias and log* codes are not convex and they have code-word lengths increasing in jumps of varying sizes at certain values of n but there is a code where the jumps in length are all of size two. Wallace and Patrick [98] used a code for the structure of Decision Trees (Sect. 8.4) that can be adapted to integers. The starting point is to consider full binary trees. A full binary tree consists of internal *fork* nodes (F) and external *leaf* nodes (L). A fork has exactly two subtrees—the "two" makes the tree binary and the "exactly" makes it full. A leaf has no subtrees. A fork node is encoded as a 0 and a leaf node is encoded as a 1. A full binary tree is encoded by performing a prefix traversal of the tree and outputting the codes of the nodes as they are encountered. When decoding a code-word to recover the tree, the end of the code-word for the tree can be recognised as soon as one more 1 than 0s is met.

This code for trees can be used to encode integers by ordering code-words on increasing length and, for a given length, on lexicographical order (Fig. 3.2). Integer n is given the nth code-word. Counting can start from 0 for non-negative integers or from 1 for positive integers as desired.

It can be shown that $\sum_{i\geq 0} \mathrm{pr}(i) = 1$ for this model: Consider an infinite string of bits, of 0s and 1s, generated independently and each with probability 0.5. Think of a 0 as a step to the *left* and a 1 as a step to the *right*[1] in a one-dimensional random walk on the integers, $\mathbb{Z}$, starting at the origin, 0. Such a random walk is known to visit every point of $\mathbb{Z}$ infinitely often. Break the infinite string up into *words*, into finite substrings, immediately after the first time that the walk visits each of $+1, +2, +3, \ldots$ in turn. Each such word is the code-word for a non-negative integer, the values being sampled at random according to the model.

An implementation need only provide one fully parameterised model instance, `WallaceInt0`, for integers $n \geq 0$. The nth Catalan number is the number of non-isomorphic ordered trees with n nodes and these numbers $(1, 1, 2, 5, 14, \ldots)$ are involved in the algorithms. A trivial unparameterised model `WallaceInt0UPM`, and trivial `Estimator` may be used as a parameter of a structured model or a function that requires such a thing.

[1] Not the Rocky Horror Picture Show.

n	tree	code-word	pr(n)
0	□	1	1/2
1	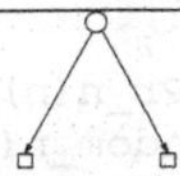	011	1/8
2	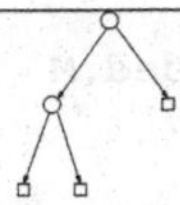	00111	1/32
3	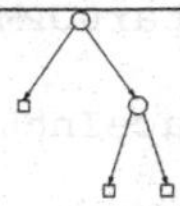	01011	1/32
4	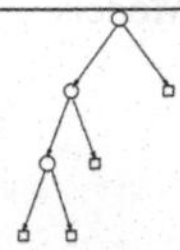	0001111	1/128
5	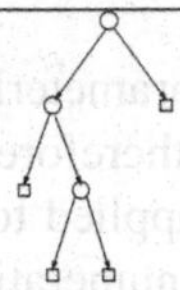	0010111	1/128
6	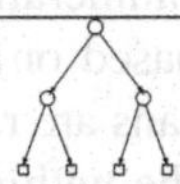	0011011	1/128
7	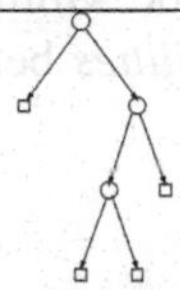	0100111	1/128
8	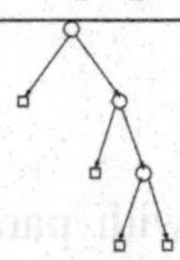	0101011	1/128
9	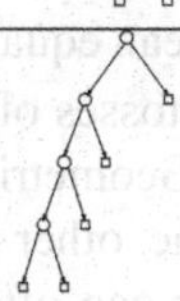	000011111	1/512
…			

Fig. 3.2 Trees

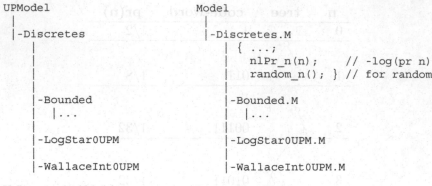

```
UPModel                           Model
 |                                  |
 |-Discretes                        |-Discretes.M
    |                                  | { ...;
    |                                  |   nlPr_n(n);     // -log(pr n)
    |                                  |   random_n(); } // for random
    |                                  |
    |-Bounded                          |-Bounded.M
    |   |...                           |   |...
    |                                  |
    |-LogStar0UPM                      |-LogStar0UPM.M
    |                                  |
    |-WallaceInt0UPM                   |-WallaceInt0UPM.M
```

UnParameterised Models Parameterised Models

3.3 A Warning

There are apparent attractions in the use of a parameterless, universal code for integers: There are no parameters to estimate and therefore no prior on parameters to worry about. In principle, such a code can be applied to any enumerable set of values by mapping a value to its position, i, in an enumeration and then encoding i. On the other hand a universal code is still just (based on) a model and therefore probably wrong [13], distributions with infinite means are rarely encountered in the real world, and, while the code-word length may be within a constant multiple of the optimum, the difference of opinion in *probabilities* between the universal and true distributions is likely much more dramatic.

3.4 Geometric

The Geometric probability distribution (model) with parameter p is sometimes defined as $\mathrm{pr}(n|p) = (1-p)^{n-1}p$ for $n \geq 1$, has mean equal to $\sum_{n>0} n(1-p)^{n-1}p = \frac{1}{p} \geq 1$ and, for example, models the number of tosses of a coin with pr(head) $= p$ up to and *including* the first head. Here, the Geometric is instead defined on non-negative $n \geq 0$ for compatibility with some other integer models, and is parameterised by its mean $\mu > 0$ because a user can often readily relate to and think of a reasonable value for the mean:

$$\mathrm{pr}(n|p) = (1-p)^n p, \text{ for } n \geq 0,$$

$$\mu = \frac{1}{p} - 1,\ p = \frac{1}{\mu+1},\ 1-p = \frac{\mu}{\mu+1}, \text{ so}$$

$$\mathrm{pr}(n|\mu) = \left(\frac{\mu}{\mu+1}\right)^n / (\mu+1), \text{ for } n \geq 0.$$

In this form it models the number of tails thrown *before* the first head, Fig. 3.3. Given N non-negative, integer data $d_1, \ldots, d_N$, the likelihood is

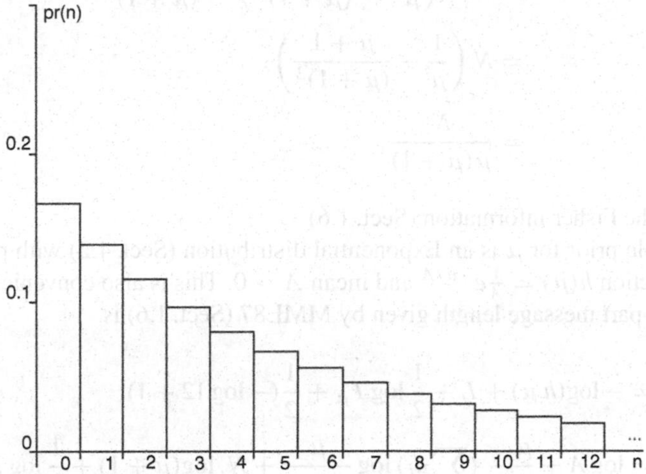

Fig. 3.3 Geometric $\mu = 5$

$$L = \left(\frac{\mu}{\mu+1}\right)^{\sum_i d_i} / (\mu+1)^N$$

The negative log likelihood is

$$-\log L = (\sum_i d_i)(\log(\mu+1) - \log \mu) + N.\log(\mu+1).$$

The first derivative is

$$\frac{d}{d\mu}(-\log L) = (\sum_i d_i)\left(\frac{1}{\mu+1} - \frac{1}{\mu}\right) + \frac{N}{\mu+1}.$$

(So equating this to zero, the maximum likelihood estimate is $\hat{\mu}_{ML} = (\sum_i d_i)/N$.)

The second derivative is

$$\frac{d^2}{d\mu^2}(-\log L) = (\sum_i d_i)\left(\frac{1}{\mu^2} - \frac{1}{(\mu+1)^2}\right) - \frac{N}{(\mu+1)^2}$$

which has expectation

$$F_\mu = N\,\mu\left(\frac{1}{\mu^2} - \frac{1}{(\mu+1)^2}\right) - \frac{N}{(\mu+1)^2}$$
$$= N\left(\frac{1}{\mu} - \frac{\mu+1}{(\mu+1)^2}\right)$$
$$= \frac{N}{\mu(\mu+1)}$$

and this is the Fisher information (Sect. 1.6)

A possible prior for μ is an Exponential distribution (Sect. 4.2) with probability density function $h(\mu) = \frac{1}{A}e^{-\mu/A}$ and mean $A > 0$. This is also convenient to use.

The two-part message length given by MML87 (Sect. 1.6) is

$$m = -\log(h\,\mu) + L + \frac{1}{2}\log F_\mu + \frac{1}{2}(-\log 12 + 1)$$
$$= \log A + \frac{\mu}{A} - (\sum_i d_i)\log\frac{\mu}{\mu+1} + N.\log(\mu+1) + \frac{1}{2}\log N$$
$$-\frac{1}{2}\log\mu - \frac{1}{2}\log(\mu+1).$$

To estimate μ, differentiate m with respect to μ

$$\frac{d}{d\mu}m = \frac{1}{A} + (\sum_i d_i)(\frac{1}{\mu+1} - \frac{1}{\mu}) + \frac{N}{\mu+1} - \frac{1}{2\mu} - \frac{1}{2(\mu+1)}$$
$$= \frac{1}{A} + \frac{1}{\mu+1}(\sum_i d_i + N - \frac{1}{2}) - \frac{1}{\mu}(\sum_i d_i + \frac{1}{2}).$$

Equate this to zero and multiply by $\mu(\mu+1)$,

$$0 = \frac{\mu(\mu+1)}{A} + \mu(\sum_i d_i + N - \frac{1}{2}) - (\mu+1)(\sum_i d_i + \frac{1}{2})$$
$$= \frac{\mu^2}{A} + \mu(\frac{1}{A} + N - 1) - \frac{1}{2} - \sum_i d_i.$$

(Note that if A is large, $\hat{\mu}_{MML} \approx (\sum_i d_i + \frac{1}{2})/(N-1)$.)

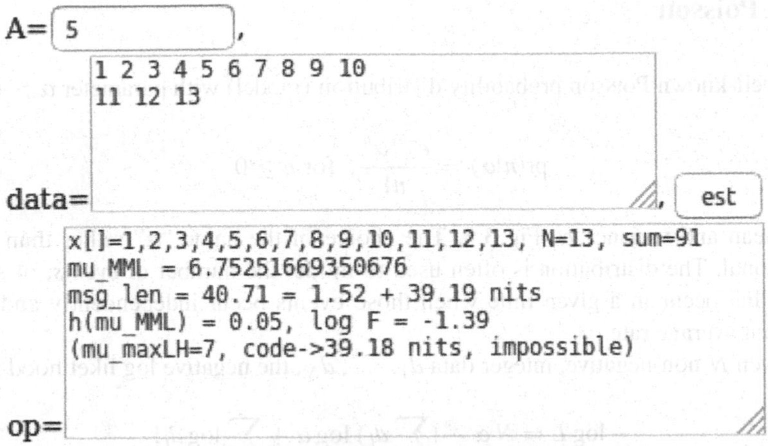

A= 5 ,
1 2 3 4 5 6 7 8 9 10
11 12 13
data= , est
x[]=1,2,3,4,5,6,7,8,9,10,11,12,13, N=13, sum=91
mu_MML = 6.7525169350676
msg_len = 40.71 = 1.52 + 39.19 nits
h(mu_MML) = 0.05, log F = -1.39
(mu_maxLH=7, code->39.18 nits, impossible)
op=

Fig. 3.4 Geometric (click)

The quadratic has solutions

$$\begin{aligned}\hat{\mu}_{MML} &= 1 - N - \frac{1}{A} \\ &\pm\sqrt{\{N^2 + \frac{1}{A^2} + 1 + \frac{2N}{A} - \frac{2}{A} - 2N + \frac{2}{A} + 4\frac{\sum_i d_i}{A}\}}/(2/A) \\ &= 1 - N - \frac{1}{A} \pm \sqrt{\{N^2 + \frac{1}{A^2} + 1 + \frac{2N}{A} - 2N + 4\frac{\sum_i d_i}{A}\}}/(2/A)\end{aligned}$$

but only the "plus" solution is admissible.

The implementation of a Geometric unparameterised model, `Geometric0UPM`, the zero to remind us of the lower bound of the range, has the trivial problem defining parameter, "`()`", so an implementation can provide a single instance `Geometric0`. The `Estimator` has the prior's mean as its parameter. The fully parameterised model, `Geometric0UPM.M`, has one statistical parameter, the mean (Fig. 3.4).

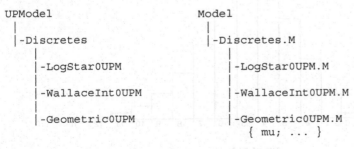

```
UPModel                          Model
 |                                |
 |-Discretes                      |-Discretes.M
    |                                |
    |-LogStar0UPM                    |-LogStar0UPM.M
    |                                |
    |-WallaceInt0UPM                 |-WallaceInt0UPM.M
    |                                |
    |-Geometric0UPM                  |-Geometric0UPM.M
                                        { mu; ... }
```

UnParameterised Models Parameterised Models

3.5 Poisson

The well-known Poisson probability distribution (model) with parameter $\alpha > 0$

$$\mathrm{pr}(n|\alpha) = \frac{e^{-\alpha}\alpha^n}{n!}, \text{ for } n \geq 0$$

has mean and variance α, Fig. 3.5. The choice of the name "α" rather than μ is traditional. The distribution is often used to model the number of *events*, of some kind, that occur in a given time when those events occur independently and at a constant average rate.

Given N non-negative, integer data $d_1, \ldots, d_N$, the negative log likelihood is

$$-\log L = N\,\alpha - (\sum_i d_i)\log\alpha + \sum_i \log d_i!$$

The first derivative is

$$\frac{d}{d\alpha}(-\log L) = N - (\sum_i d_i)/\alpha.$$

Equating this to zero, the maximum likelihood estimate is $\hat{\alpha}_{ML} = (\sum_i d_i)/N$. The second derivative is

$$\frac{d^2}{d\alpha^2}(-\log L) = (\sum_i d_i)/\alpha^2$$

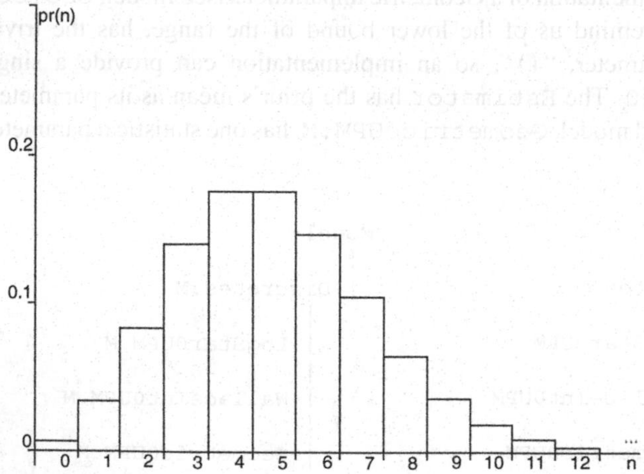

Fig. 3.5 Poisson $\alpha = 5$

which has expectation,

$$F_\alpha = N\,\alpha/\alpha^2 = N/\alpha$$

and this is the Fisher information. Note that $+\log F_\alpha = \log N - \log \alpha$.

As for the Geometric, an Exponential distribution (Sect. 4.2) with probability density function $h(\alpha) = \frac{1}{A}e^{-\alpha/A}$ and mean $A > 0$ is convenient. Note that $-\log(h\,\alpha) = \log A + \frac{\alpha}{A}$.

The two-part message length given by MML87 (Sect. 1.6) is

$$m = -\log(h\,\alpha) + L + \frac{1}{2}\log F_\alpha + \frac{1}{2}(-\log 12 + 1).$$

To estimate α, differentiate m with respect to α

$$\frac{d}{d\alpha}m = \frac{1}{A} + N - (\sum_i d_i)/\alpha - \frac{1}{2\alpha}$$

and equate to zero [73]

$$\hat{\alpha}_{MML} = (\sum_i d_i + \frac{1}{2})/(N + \frac{1}{A}).$$

Note that $\hat{\alpha}_{MML} \to \hat{\alpha}_{ML} = (\sum_i d_i)/N$ as $N \to \infty$.

The implementation of a Poisson unparameterised model, `Poisson0UPM`, the zero to remind us of the lower bound of the range, has the trivial problem defining parameter, "`()`", so an implementation can provide a single instance `Poisson0`. The `Estimator` takes the prior's mean as its parameter. The fully parameterised model, `Poisson0UPM.M`, has one statistical parameter, the mean (Fig. 3.6).

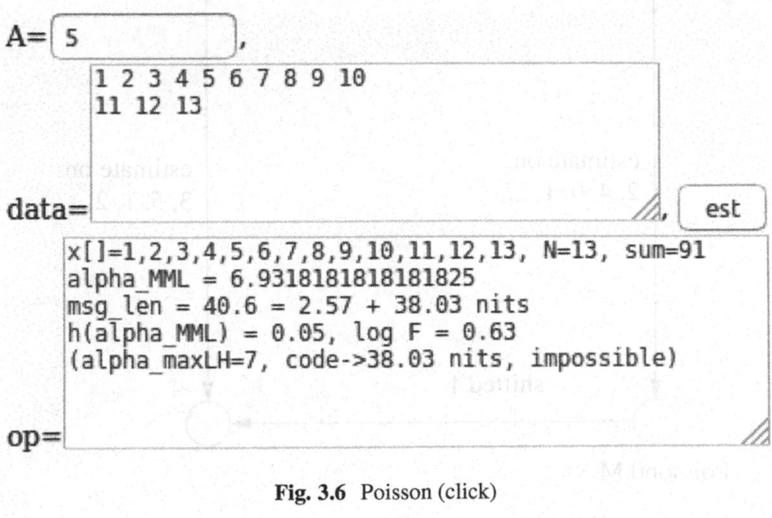

Fig. 3.6 Poisson (click)

Note that the sufficient statistics of a data-set include not only the sum of the data but also the sum of the logs of the data for the benefit of the negative log likelihood function, `nlLH(ss)`.

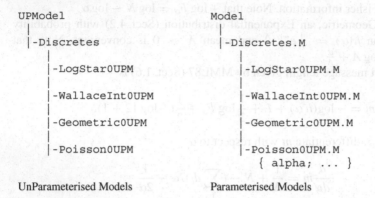

```
UPModel                        Model
 |                              |
 |-Discretes                    |-Discretes.M
     |                              |
     |-LogStar0UPM                  |-LogStar0UPM.M
     |                              |
     |-WallaceInt0UPM               |-WallaceInt0UPM.M
     |                              |
     |-Geometric0UPM                |-Geometric0UPM.M
     |                              |
     |-Poisson0UPM                  |-Poisson0UPM.M
                                       { alpha; ... }

UnParameterised Models         Parameterised Models
```

3.6 Shifting

The integer models above were mostly defined on non-negative integers, $n \geq 0$. Sometimes we do need them to be defined on positive integers, $n > 0$, or even with other origins. A useful operation on the implementation of integer models, in fact on all `Discretes` is `shifted(k)` which moves the origin of a model by `k`.

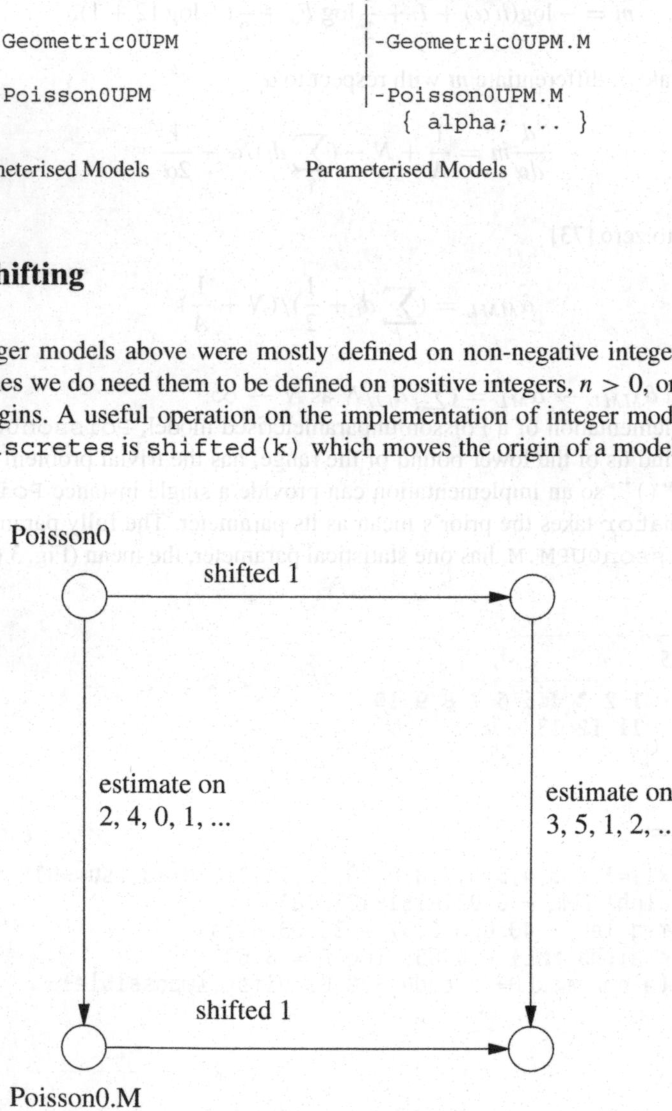

Fig. 3.7 Shifting a model

For example, the Poisson distribution on non-negative integers $n > 0$ can be defined as `Poisson0.shifted(1)`. This is still an unparameterised model complete with an estimator. And 0 is not a legal datum for the shifted model.

Both unparameterised and fully parameterised models can be `shifted` and, if the estimator's prior of the mean is also adjusted appropriately, the diagram in Fig. 3.7 commutes.

Chapter 4
Continuous

The important thing about continuous data—ℝ, real, floating point, double—is that each datum has an accuracy of measurement (AoM), ϵ, and hence a negative log AoM (nlAoM), $-\log \epsilon$. A datum d is of the form $x \pm \frac{\epsilon}{2}$. Models of such data are generally defined in terms of a probability density function pdf(x). If ϵ is small and the probability density function varies slowly near x, the probability of a continuous datum is $\mathrm{pr}(x \pm \frac{\epsilon}{2}) \approx \mathrm{pdf}(x)\,\epsilon$ (Fig. 4.1), and its negative log probability is $-\log(\mathrm{pr}(x \pm \frac{\epsilon}{2})) \approx -\log(\mathrm{pdf}\ x) - \log \epsilon$.

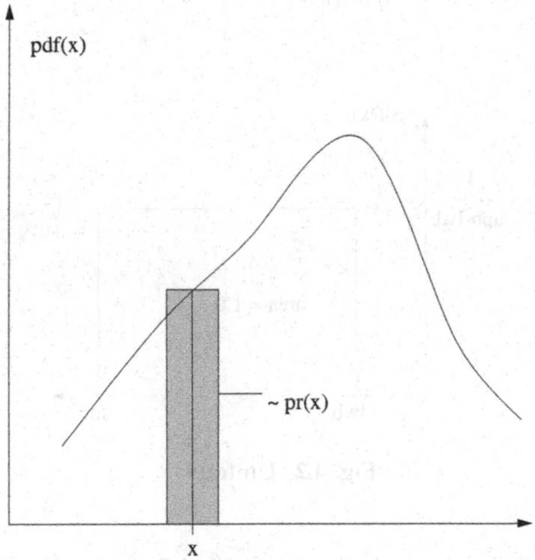

Fig. 4.1 $x \pm \epsilon/2$

As will be seen later (Chap. 9) models of more than just scalar continuous data can be defined in terms of pdf(.) so in an implementation it is convenient to define `Continuous` models and the more general `ByPdf` for all models defined by a pdf(·).

L. Allison, *Coding Ockham's Razor*, https://doi.org/10.1007/978-3-319-76433-7_4

```
UPModel                       UPModel.M
  |                             |
  |-ByPdf                       |-ByPdf.M
      |                             | { pdf(x); nlPdf(x); // -ve log
      |                             |   nlPr(nlAoM,x); ... }
      |                             |
      |-Continuous                  |-Continuous.M
                                        {...
                                         random(AoM);   // given AoM
                                         random_x(); } // a double
```

UnParameterised Models Parameterised Models

Useful continuous models include the Uniform (Sect. 4.1), Exponential (Sect. 4.2), Normal (Gaussian) (Sect. 4.3) and Laplace (Sect. 4.5) distributions.

4.1 Uniform

The bounds of a bounded continuous data-space are given so they are problem defining parameters of models of that data-space. The simplest possible fully parameterised model of such a data-space is the Uniform distribution where each datum has probability density $\frac{1}{upb-lwb}$. The model has no *statistical* parameters (Fig. 4.2).

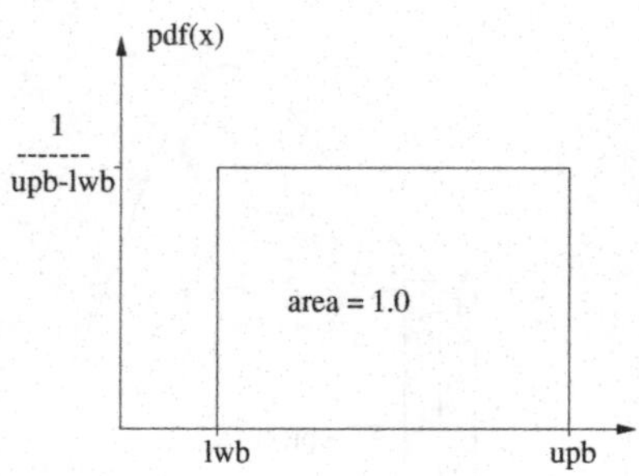

Fig. 4.2 Uniform

Note that in an implementation of `Uniform`, the sufficient statistics `ss=stats(ds)` of a data-set `ds` consist of the number of data and the sum of the negative log AoMs of the data so that the negative log likelihood, `nlLH(ss)`, can be calculated. The fully parameterised Uniform model has no non-trivial statistical parameters so a single instance `Uniform.Mdl` can be provided. This is always returned by the `Estimator`. While this `Estimator` is trivial it can be useful as in the case of the implementation of the discrete `Uniform` model (Sect. 2.1).

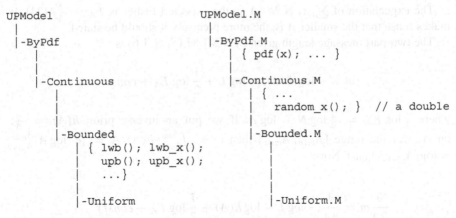

```
UPModel                       UPModel.M
 |                             |
 |-ByPdf                       |-ByPdf.M
    |                             | { pdf(x); ... }
    |                             |
    |-Continuous                  |-Continuous.M
       |                             | { ...
       |                             |   random_x(); }  // a double
       |                             |
       |-Bounded                     |-Bounded.M
          | { lwb(); lwb_x();           |
          |   upb(); upb_x();           |
          |   ...}                      |
          |                             |
          |-Uniform                     |-Uniform.M
```

UnParameterised Models Parameterised Models

4.2 Exponential

The Exponential distribution is a model of non-negative real values, $\mathbb{R}_{\geq 0}$.

$$\mathrm{pdf}(x) = \frac{1}{A} e^{-x/A}, \ x \geq 0,$$
$$-\log \mathrm{pdf}(x) = \log A + x/A.$$

The mean is A and the variance is A^2. The distribution is sometimes parameterised by $\lambda = 1/A$ instead of A

Given a data-set $ds = d_1, \ldots, d_N$ where d_i is of the form $x_i \pm \frac{\epsilon_i}{2}$, the negative log likelihood is

$$-\log L = N.\log A + \frac{1}{A} \sum_i x_i + \sum_i \epsilon_i$$

so

$$\frac{\partial}{\partial A}(-\log L) = \frac{N}{A} - \frac{1}{A^2} \sum_i x_i$$

and the maximum likelihood estimate of A is $\hat{A}_{ML} = (\sum_i x_i)/N$, the sample mean.

$$\frac{\partial^2}{\partial A^2}(-\log L) = -\frac{N}{A^2} + \frac{2}{A^3} \sum_i x_i$$

The expectation of $\sum_i x_i$ is $N \cdot A$ so the expected Fisher is $F_A = \frac{N}{A^2}$ [74]. It makes sense that the smaller A is, the more precisely it should be stated.

The two-part message length given by MML87 (Sect. 1.6) is

$$m = -\log(h(A)) - \log L + \frac{1}{2}\log F_A + const$$

where $\frac{1}{2}\log F_A = \frac{1}{2}\log N - \log A$. If we put an inverse prior, $h(A) = \frac{c}{A}$, on A over the range $[A_{min}, A_{max}]$ then $c = \int_{A_{min}}^{A_{max}} h(A)\ A = [c\ \log A]_{A_{min}}^{A_{max}}$ $= \log(A_{max}/A_{min})$. Now,

$$\begin{aligned}
\frac{\partial}{\partial A}m &= \frac{\partial}{\partial A}(-\log L - \log h(A) + \frac{1}{2}\log F_A + const) \\
&= \frac{\partial}{\partial A}(-\log L + \log A + \frac{1}{2}\log N - \log A + const') \\
&= \frac{N}{A} - \frac{1}{A^2}\sum_i x_i + \frac{1}{A} - \frac{1}{A},
\end{aligned}$$

and, with that prior, $\hat{A}_{MML} = (\sum_i x_i)/N$, the sample mean.

The unparameterised `ExponentialUPM` has no problem defining parameters so an implementation can provide a single instance `Exponential`. The fully parameterised `ExponentialUPM.M` model takes the mean as its statistical parameter.

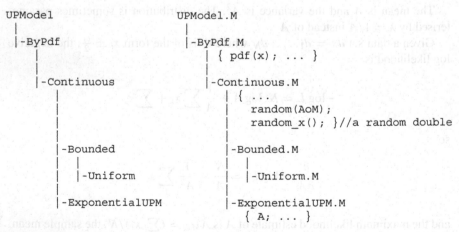

```
UPModel                        UPModel.M
 |                              |
 |-ByPdf                        |-ByPdf.M
    |                              | { pdf(x); ... }
    |                              |
    |-Continuous                   |-Continuous.M
       |                              |{ ...
       |                              |    random(AoM);
       |                              |    random_x(); }//a random double
       |                              |
       |-Bounded                      |-Bounded.M
       |   |                          |   |
       |   |-Uniform                  |   |-Uniform.M
       |                              |
       |-ExponentialUPM               |-ExponentialUPM.M
                                         { A; ... }
UnParameterised Models         Parameterised Models
```

4.3 Normal

The Normal distribution (Fig. 4.3), also known as the Gaussian distribution, has probability density and negative log probability density

$$\mathrm{pdf}(x) = \frac{1}{\sigma\sqrt{2\pi}} e^{-\frac{(x-\mu)^2}{2\sigma^2}},$$

$$-\log \mathrm{pdf}(x) = \log\sigma + \frac{1}{2}\log 2\pi + \frac{(x-\mu)^2}{2\sigma^2},$$

where μ is the mean and σ is the standard deviation. Also frequently used is the variance, $\nu = \sigma^2$.

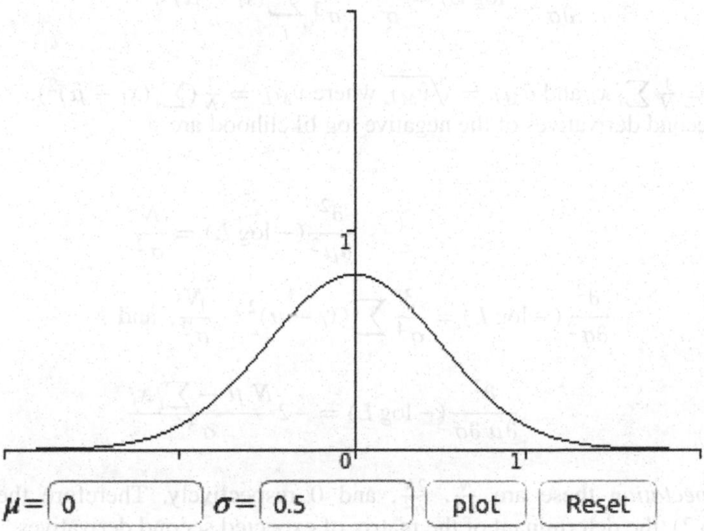

Fig. 4.3 Normal (click) pdf

Given a data set $ds = d_1, \ldots, d_N$ where d_i has AoM ϵ, that is d_i is of the form $x_i \pm \frac{\epsilon_i}{2}$, the negative log likelihood is

$$-\log L = N.\log\sigma + \frac{N}{2}\log 2\pi + \frac{1}{2\sigma^2}\sum_i (x_i - \mu)^2 + \sum_i \log\epsilon_i.$$

Incidentally, it is well known that the sum in the third term can be recast using

$$\sum_i (x_i - \mu)^2 = \sum_i x_i^2 - 2\mu \sum_i x_i + N\mu^2$$
$$= (\sum_i x_i^2) - N\mu^2,$$

where $\mu = \frac{1}{N}\sum_i x_i$, the sample mean.

The first derivatives of the negative log likelihood are

$$\frac{\partial}{\partial \mu}(-\log L) = \frac{N.\mu - \sum_i x_i}{\sigma^2} \text{ and}$$
$$\frac{\partial}{\partial \sigma}(-\log L) = \frac{N}{\sigma} - \frac{1}{\sigma^3}\sum_i (x_i - \mu)^2.$$

$\hat{\mu}_{ML} = \frac{1}{N}\sum_i x_i$ and $\hat{\sigma}_{ML} = \sqrt{\hat{v}_{ML}}$ where $\hat{v}_{ML} = \frac{1}{N}(\sum_i (x_i - \hat{\mu})^2)$.

The second derivatives of the negative log likelihood are

$$\frac{\partial^2}{\partial \mu^2}(-\log L) = \frac{N}{\sigma^2},$$
$$\frac{\partial^2}{\partial \sigma^2}(-\log L) = \frac{3}{\sigma^4}\sum_i (x_i - \mu)^2 - \frac{N}{\sigma^2}, \text{ and}$$
$$\frac{\partial^2}{\partial \mu\, \partial \sigma}(-\log L) = -2\frac{N.\mu - \sum_i x_i}{\sigma^3}.$$

In *expectation* these are $\frac{N}{\sigma^2}$, $\frac{2N}{\sigma^2}$, and 0 respectively. Therefore the Fisher (Sect. 1.6.2), the determinant of the matrix of expected second derivatives

$$\begin{pmatrix} \frac{N}{\sigma^2} & 0 \\ 0 & \frac{2N}{\sigma^2} \end{pmatrix}$$

is $F = \frac{2N^2}{\sigma^4}$.

The simplest prior on $\langle \mu, \sigma \rangle$ is a uniform distribution over a range of values $[\mu_{min}, \mu_{max}]$ for μ and $\frac{1}{\sigma}$ over a range of values $[\sigma_{min}, \sigma_{max}]$ for σ. That is $h(\mu, \sigma) \propto \frac{1}{\sigma}$.

The two-part message length given by MML87 (Sect. 1.6) is

$$m = -\log(h(\mu, \sigma)) - \log L + \frac{1}{2}\log F_{\mu,\sigma} + const$$

So

$$\frac{\partial}{\partial \mu} m = \frac{\partial}{\partial \mu} \{-\log L\},$$

$$\frac{\partial}{\partial \sigma} m = \frac{1}{\sigma} + \frac{\partial}{\partial \sigma} \{-\log L\} - \frac{2}{\sigma}.$$

Setting these to zero, the MML estimator [93] for μ is therefore the same as the maximum likelihood estimator, but the MML estimator for σ uses a divisor of $N-1$, not N, that is $\hat{\mu}_{MML} = \frac{1}{N}\sum_i x_i$, and $\hat{\sigma}_{MML} = \sqrt{\hat{v}_{MML}}$ where $\hat{v}_{MML} = \frac{1}{N-1}\sum (x_i - \hat{\mu})^2$.

Note the difference between the maximum likelihood and MML estimators for σ. It is well known that the use of the factor $\frac{1}{N}$ gives a biased estimate of v and that $\frac{1}{N-1}$ gives an unbiased estimate of v (but not of σ). If N is large the choice matters little. But consider the case of $N = 2$, say, when the use of $\frac{1}{N}$ amounts to assuming that μ lies between x_1 and x_2 which clearly it need not. In any case, using $\frac{1}{N-1}$ minimises the message length.

The Javascript demonstration (Fig. 4.4) shows the MML message length and, for comparison, the hypothetical length of encoding only the data using a code based on the maximum likelihood estimate. The latter is impossible, unless the receiver is psychic, because it omits the cost of stating any parameter values and the receiver cannot decode such a message.

The unparameterised Normal distribution `NormalUPM` has no problem defining parameters so an implementation need only provide a single instance, `Normal`. The fully parameterised `NormalUPM.M` model takes the mean and standard deviation as its statistical parameters. The `Estimator` takes the ranges of μ and of σ as its statistical parameters. The sufficient statistics of a data-set include, `N`, the sum of the data, the sum of the squares of the data, and the sum of the negative log of the

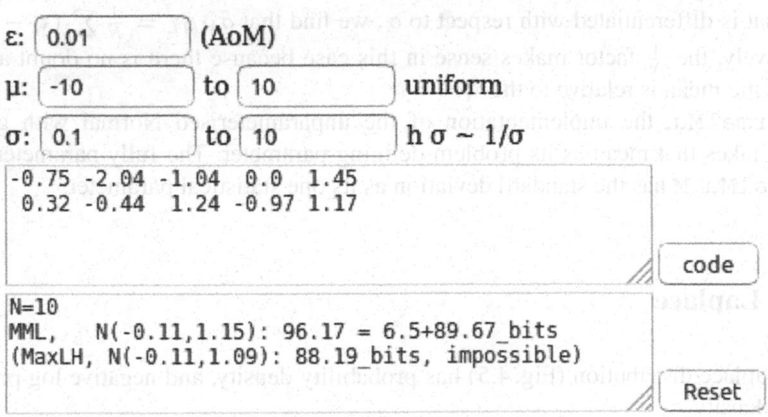

Fig. 4.4 Normal (click)

accuracy (nlAoM) of the data. It is often, although not necessarily, the case that all items in a data-set have the same AoM and, if so, the data-set's total nlAoM can be calculated in constant time.

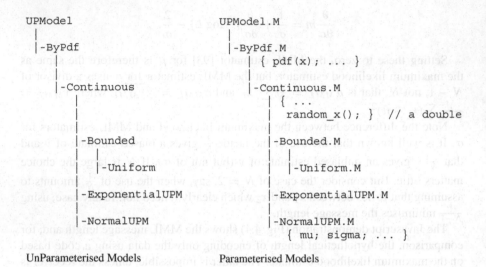

```
UPModel                          UPModel.M
  |                                |
  |-ByPdf                          |-ByPdf.M
     |                               |{ pdf(x); ... }
     |                               |
     |-Continuous                    |-Continuous.M
        |                              |{ ...
        |                              |  random_x(); }  // a double
        |                              |
        |-Bounded                      |-Bounded.M
        |  |                           |  |
        |  |-Uniform                   |  |-Uniform.M
        |                              |
        |-ExponentialUPM               |-ExponentialUPM.M
        |                              |
        |-NormalUPM                    |-NormalUPM.M
                                         { mu; sigma; ... }
```

UnParameterised Models Parameterised Models

4.4 Normal Given μ

Sometimes the mean of a Normal distribution is given, leaving only σ to be estimated. The mean is then a problem defining parameter, not a statistical parameter to be estimated. And the Fisher is the expectation of $\frac{\partial^2}{\partial\sigma^2}(-\log L)$ which is $\frac{2N}{\sigma^2}$, so $\frac{1}{2}\log F = \frac{1}{2}\log(2N) - \log\sigma$. When this is put into the message length formula and that is differentiated with respect to σ, we find that $\hat{\sigma}_{MML} = \frac{1}{N}\sum_i (x_i - \mu)^2$. Intuitively, the $\frac{1}{N}$ factor makes sense in this case because there is no doubt about where the mean is relative to the x_i.

NormalMu, the implementation of the unparameterised Normal with given mean, takes that mean as its problem defining parameter. The fully parameterised NormalMu.M has the standard deviation as its one statistical parameter.

4.5 Laplace

The Laplace distribution (Fig. 4.5) has probability density, and negative log probability density

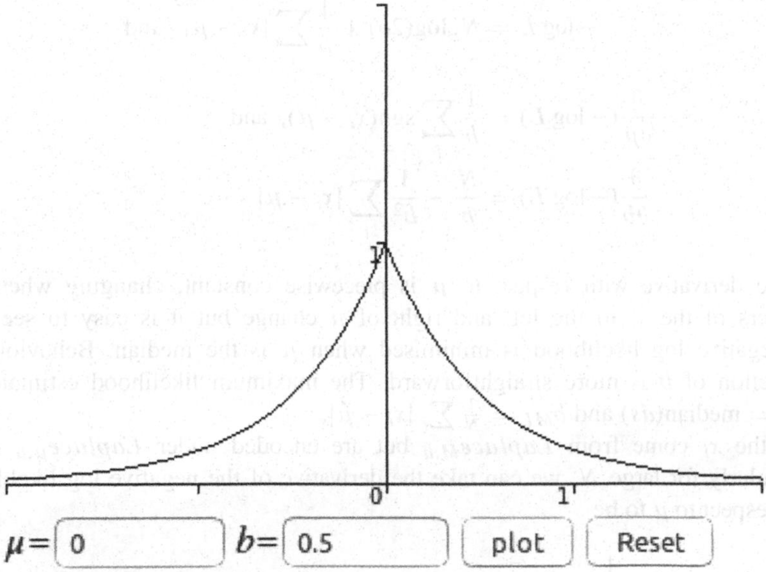

Fig. 4.5 Laplace (click) pdf

$$\mathrm{pdf}(x) = \frac{1}{2b} e^{\frac{-|x-\mu|}{b}}$$

$$-\log \mathrm{pdf}(x) = \log(2b) + \frac{|x-\mu|}{b}$$

where μ is the mean; the variance is $2b^2$.

The Laplace deals in the absolute distance, $|x - \mu|$, of a value from the mean where the Normal deals in the squared distance of a value from the mean. The Laplace distribution is in effect two Exponential distributions (Sect. 4.2) "back to back" and normalised, one for $x \geq \mu$ and one, reflected, for $x \leq \mu$. Its cumulative distribution function is

$$\begin{aligned} \mathrm{cdf}(x) &= \frac{1}{2} e^{(x-\mu)/b} & &= \frac{1}{2} e^{-|x-\mu|/b} & &\text{if } x < \mu, \\ &= 1 - \frac{1}{2} e^{-(x-\mu)/b} & &= 1 - \frac{1}{2} e^{-|x-\mu|/b} & &\text{if } x \geq \mu \end{aligned}$$

(Note that the mean of an Exponential distribution over $y \geq 0$ with $\mathrm{pdf}(y) = \frac{1}{b} e^{\frac{-y}{b}}$ is b so the mean absolute distance from the mean for a Laplace distribution is also b.)

Given a data-set $ds = d_1, \ldots, d_N$ where d_i is $x_i \pm \frac{\epsilon_i}{2}$, the negative log likelihood is

$$-\log L = N.\log(2b) + \frac{1}{b}\sum_i |x_i - \mu|, \text{ and}$$

$$\frac{\partial}{\partial\mu}(-\log L) = \frac{1}{b}\sum_i \text{sgn}(x_i - \mu), \text{ and}$$

$$\frac{\partial}{\partial b}(-\log L) = \frac{N}{b} - \frac{1}{b^2}\sum_i |x_i - \mu|$$

The derivative with respect to μ is piecewise constant, changing when the numbers of the x_i to the left and right of μ change but it is easy to see that the negative log likelihood is minimised when μ is the median. Behaviour as a function of b is more straightforward. The maximum likelihood estimator is $\hat{\mu}_{ML} = \text{median}(ds)$ and $\hat{b}_{ML} = \frac{1}{N}\sum_i |x_i - \hat{\mu}|$.

If the x_i come from $Laplace_{M,b}$ but are encoded under $Laplace_{\mu,b}$ then, particularly for large N, we can take the derivative of the negative log likelihood with respect to μ to be

$$\begin{aligned}\frac{\partial}{\partial\mu}(-\log L) &= \frac{1}{b}\{(\text{count of } x_i \text{ that are } > \mu) - (\text{count of } x_i \text{ that are } < \mu)\}\\ &= \frac{N}{b}((1 - \text{cdf}(\mu)) - \text{cdf}(\mu))\\ &= \frac{N}{b}(1 - 2.\text{cdf}(\mu))\\ &= \frac{N}{b}\text{sgn}(\mu - M)(1 - e^{-\frac{|\mu - M|}{b}})\end{aligned}$$

so

$$\frac{\partial^2}{\partial\mu^2}(-\log L) = \frac{N}{b^2}e^{-\frac{|\mu-M|}{b}},$$

$$\frac{\partial^2}{\partial b^2}(-\log L) = -\frac{N}{b^2} + \frac{2}{b^3}\sum_i |x_i - \hat{\mu}|, \text{ and}$$

$$\frac{\partial^2}{\partial\mu\,\partial b}(-\log L) = -\frac{N}{b^2}\text{sgn}(\mu - M)(1 - e^{-\frac{|\mu-M|}{b}}) + \frac{N}{b}\frac{|\mu - M|}{b^2}e^{-\frac{|\mu-M|}{b}}$$

In expectation these are $\frac{N}{b^2}$, $\frac{N}{b^2}$, and 0 respectively. The Fisher is therefore $F = \frac{N^2}{b^4}$ (Kasarapu and Allison, 2015b, Minimum message length estimation of the Laplace distribution, Private communication).

The simplest prior on $\langle\mu, b\rangle$ is a uniform distribution over a range of values $[\mu_{min}, \mu_{max}]$ for μ, and $\frac{1}{b}$ over a range of values $[b_{min}, b_{max}]$ for b. That is $h(\mu, b) \propto \frac{1}{b}$.

It is easy to see that the MML estimate of the mean is the median. It can also been seen that the inverse fourth power of b in the Fisher for the Laplace has the same effect of giving a divisor of $N-1$ as it did for $\hat{\sigma}$ in the Normal (Sect. 4.3). The MML estimator is $\hat{\mu}_{MML} = \text{median}(ds)$, and $\hat{b}_{MML} = \frac{1}{N-1}\sum_i |x_i - \hat{\mu}|$ (Fig. 4.6).

The unparameterised Laplace distribution `LaplaceUPM` has no problem defining parameters so an implementation need only provide a single instance `Laplace`. The fully parameterised `Laplace.M` takes μ and b as its statistical parameters.

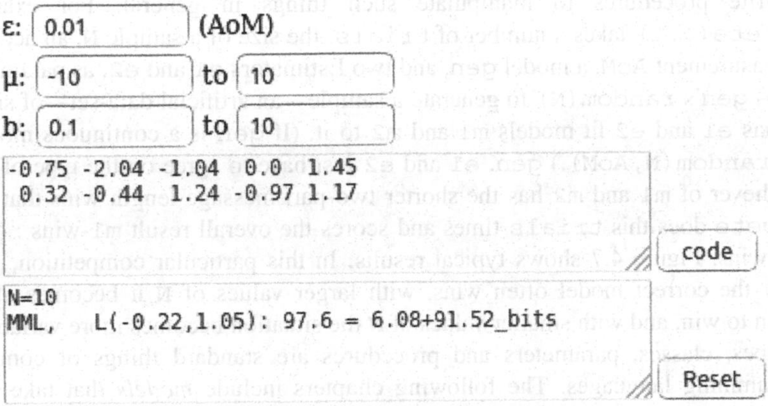

Fig. 4.6 Laplace (click)

```
UPModel                          UPModel.M
 |                                 |
 |-ByPdf                           |-ByPdf.M
    |                                 |{pdf(x); nlPdf(x); // -log pdf
    |                                 | nlPr(nlAoM,x); ... }
    |-Continuous                      |-Continuous.M
       |                                 |{ ...
       |                                 |  random_x(); } // a double
       |                                 |
       |-Bounded                         |-Bounded.M
       |  |                              |  |
       |  |-Uniform                      |  |-Uniform.M
       |                                 |
       |-ExponentialUPM                  |-ExponentialUPM.M
       |                                 |
       |-NormalUPM                       |-NormalUPM.M
       |                                 |
       |-NormalMu                        |-NormalMu.M
       |                                 |
       |-LaplaceUP                       |-LaplaceUPM.M
                                             { mu; b; ... }
```

UnParameterised Models   Parameterised Models

The `Estimator` takes the ranges of μ and of b as its parameters. The sufficient statistics of a data-set are the sorted data-set itself—if one is to be able to combine and split data-sets as the `Estimators` of some structured models require.

4.6 Comparing Models

Because Model, UPModel and Estimator define standard classes, it is possible to write procedures to manipulate such things in general. For example, `compete(...)` takes a number of `trials`, the size of a sample `N`, an accuracy of measurement `AoM`, a model `gen`, and two Estimators `e1` and `e2`, as parameters. It uses `gen`'s `random(N)` to generate a sample—an artificial data-set—of size `N`, and has `e1` and `e2` fit models `m1` and `m2` to it. (If `gen` is a continuous model it uses `random(N,AoM)`.) `gen`, `e1` and `e2` just have to agree on the type of data. Whichever of `m1` and `m2` has the shorter two-part message length wins that trial. `compete` does this `trials` times and scores the overall result `m1`-wins : draws : `m2`-wins. Figure 4.7 shows typical results. In this particular competition, when `N=20` the correct model often wins, with larger values of `N` it becomes almost certain to win, and with smaller values of `N` the situation becomes more variable.

Types, classes, parameters and procedures are standard things of computer programming languages. The following chapters include *models* that take other models as parameters.

```
compete(10x, N=20, AoM=0.1, gen=(Normal (0.0, 1.0)),
  e1=Normal.estimator((-10.0, 10.0, 0.1, 10.0)),
  e2=Laplace.estimator((-10.0, 10.0, 0.1, 10.0)))
0 : *112.2 bits (Normal(-0.2, 0.9)) v.  116   bits (Laplace( 0.0, 0.8))
1 :  111.5 bits (Normal(-0.2, 0.9)) v. *111.4 bits (Laplace(-0.0, 0.7))
2 : *113.8 bits (Normal( 0.4, 0.9)) v.  116.1 bits (Laplace( 0.4, 0.8))
 ... etc.
m1:draw:m2 = 7:0:3
```

(a)

```
compete(10x, N=20, AoM=0.1, gen=(Laplace (0.0, 1.0)),
  e1=Normal.estimator((-10.0, 10.0, 0.1, 10.0)),
  e2=Laplace.estimator((-10.0, 10.0, 0.1, 10.0)))
0 :  125.5 bits (Normal(-0.3, 1.4)) v. *121.6 bits (Laplace(-0.2, 1.0))
1 :  128.7 bits (Normal( 0.6, 1.6)) v. *122.1 bits (Laplace( 0.3, 1.0))
2 : *111.6 bits (Normal( 0.6, 0.9)) v.  112.4 bits (Laplace( 0.2, 0.7))
 ... etc.
m1:draw:m2 = 3:0:7
```

(b)

Fig. 4.7 Normal v. Laplace. **(a)** Normal v. Laplace on $\mathcal{N}_{0,1}$ data. **(b)** Normal v. Laplace on $\mathcal{L}_{0,1}$ data

Chapter 5
Function-Models

It is quite common for one data variable to depend statistically upon another variable. This is similar to the input-output relationship of a function such as $y = \sin(x)$ except that the relationship between x and y is statistical rather than exact. Because of this similarity we call a model of such a relationship a *function-model* with an input datum id and an output datum od. od is also called the dependent variable and id the independent variable. A datum is now bivariate, $d = \langle id, od\rangle$, but note that id and od can themselves be multivariate. For example, if od is conditional on id_1 and on id_2 we can say that it is dependent on the pair $\langle id_1, id_2\rangle$. Just as we talk of data from a data-space, we also have input-data from an input-(data-)space and output-data from an output-(data-)space.

The term *regression* is sometimes used for function-model in the statistical literature, especially when the variables are continuous. The word comes from Galton's "regression to the mean" in his writings about heredity [37, 38].

The main duty of a fully parameterised function-model is to provide the conditional probability of output od given input id, that is $\mathrm{pr}(od|id)$. As far as the function-model is concerned, it only explains the way in which the output variable depends on the input variable; the input data are common knowledge so a transmitter need not encode them in any message to a receiver and we can take it that $\mathrm{pr}(id) = 1$. Therefore, since a function-model is also a model (Sect. 1.2), $\mathrm{pr}(\langle id, od\rangle) = \mathrm{pr}(od|id)$. If in some wider setting the input data are not common knowledge and must themselves be modelled, a function-model can be used as part of a Dependent model as seen later in (Sect. 6.2).

L. Allison, *Coding Ockham's Razor*, https://doi.org/10.1007/978-3-319-76433-7_5

In an implementation of function-models we have,

```
UPModel                              Model
 |                                    |
 |                                    |-FunctionModel
 |                                    |  { condModel(id);
 |                                    |    condPr(id, od);
 |                                    |    random(id);
 |                                    |    ... }
 |                                    |
 |-UPFunctionModel                    |-UPFunctionModel.M
    { Est; M; ... }
```

UnParameterised FunctionModels — Parameterised FunctionModels

For a given `FunctionModel` we are interested in the conditional probability of output *od* given input *id* and require that `condModel(id).pr(od)` = `condPr(id,od)` = pr(*od*|*id*).[1] A random output value, `random(id)`, depends on an input value, `id`, in general, and `random()` is an error.

The constant (Sect. 5.1), Multinomial (Sect. 5.2), Intervals (Sect. 5.3) and conditional probability table (CPT) (Sect. 5.4) function-models are discussed next. More function-models are seen later in Chaps. 8 and 10.

5.1 Konstant Function-Model, K

The simplest possible function-model is *K*, named because of its similarity to the Konstant combinator of combinatory logic [21] (in which $\mathrm{K}\,x\,y = x$). The unparameterised function-model *K* has an unparameterised *model U* as its single problem defining parameter—*K* is a *function*-model and *U* is an ordinary model. The corresponding fully parameterised function-model has statistical parameters θ for $M = U(\theta)$ and always returns *M* as its conditional model regardless of the value of input datum *id*. The estimator uses *U* and the output-data to estimate θ.

The implementation of `K` is simple and is based around

`K(upm)(sp).condModel(id) = mdl,` $\forall$ `id,`

where `upm(sp) = mdl`

[1]The packaging of a parameterised `M` and an estimator `Est` inside an unparameterised `UPFunctionModel` is simply often convenient and, as for `UPModel.M` and `UPModel.Est` in `UPModel` (Sect. 1.3), is not compulsory.

Note that `K(upm)` is an unparameterised model, and `K(upm)(sp)` is the corresponding fully parameterised model `K.M` where `sp` are statistical parameters passed on to `upm`. `K`'s `Estimator` ignores the input field of the data and estimates a fully-parameterised model `mdl` of the output data. For all values of `id`, the `condModel(id)` of `K(upm)(sp)` always returns `mdl = upm(sp)`.

```
UPModel                                Model
 |                                       |
 |                                       |-FunctionModel
 |                                       |  { condModel(id);
 |                                       |    condPr(id, od);
 |                                       |    ... }
 |                                       |
 |-UPFunctionModel                       |-UPFunctionModel.M
    |                                       |
    |-K                                     |-K.M
      { upm;  // UPmodel                      { mdl;  // & Model of od
        ... }                                   ... }

UnParameterised                        Parameterised
FunctionModels                         FunctionModels
```

K is occasionally needed, for example, to be passed to some function or model that requires a function-model as parameter. It is itself an example, albeit a trivial one, of a function-model that takes another model as a parameter. More interesting examples of models parameterised by models are given in following sections and in Chap. 6.

5.2 Multinomial

Given k categories and conditional on n trials, a Multinomial distribution gives the probabilities of categories c_i, $i = 1 \ldots k$, occurring with frequencies f_i where $\sum_i f_i = n$. For example, with $k = 4$ it can model the numbers of times the four DNA bases occur in sequences of length n. A Multinomial is a function-model and corresponds to, but is a different kind of thing from, a MultiState model (Sect. 2.3) which is a simple model. The former takes a number of trials n as input datum and gives the probability of a vector of frequencies conditional on n. The latter gives the probability of the next trial being a c_i.

```
UPFunctionModel                UPFunctionModel.M
|                              |
|-K                            |-K.M
|                              |
|-Multinomial                  |-Multinomial.M
   { k; // #categories            { nlPrs;  //-ve log probs
     ... }                          ...
                                    condModel(n);
                                    ... }
```

UnParameterised FunctionModels   Parameterised FunctionModels

In the implementation, the unparameterised `Multinomial` takes the number of categories k as a problem defining parameter. The fully parameterised `Multinomial.M` takes a vector of k probabilities as its statistical parameter. It uses (the negative logs of) these probabilities to create a conditional model `condModel(n)` of vectors of frequencies. There is the question of what should happen if the frequencies f_i do not add up to n—should a probability of zero be returned, or should an error be raised? The latter choice was made.

5.3 Intervals

There is sometimes a need to *discretise* (partition) continuous data into a number of intervals, for example, to be used by some model that can only handle discrete data. At the problem's most general, the variable need not be continuous—the minimum condition is that its type (data-space) be totally ordered. For example, strings, integers, and direct-products with their natural orders are all candidates. A discretisation into $k \geq 1$ intervals can be specified by stating first the value of $k-1 \geq 0$ and then $k-1$ *cut-points* $cp_1, \ldots, cp_{k-1}$ where $cp_j < cp_{j+1}$, which correspond to the interval ranges $(-\infty, cp_1), [cp_1, cp_2), \ldots, [cp_{k-2}, cp_{k-1}), [cp_{k-1}, \infty)$.

One criterion for discretising input-data is based on how much information the discretisation gives about output-data. Assume that the data, the input-output pairs, are sorted on the input-data, if not sort them. The unparameterised function-model *Intervals* takes an unparameterised model M of the output space as its problem defining parameter. Given a data-set $[d_0, \ldots, d_{N-1}]$, where $d_i = \langle id_i, od_i \rangle$, Intervals seeks a discretisation of the input-space specified by zero or more cut-points $id_{i_1}, \ldots, id_{i_{k-1}}$ where $i_j < i_{j+1}$. For each interval $[id_{i_j}, id_{i_{j+1}})$, it infers a fully parameterised instance of M, for the corresponding $od_{i_j}, \ldots, od_{i_{j+1}}$. The objective is to minimise the message length of encoding the output data, that is encoding $k-1$, the $k-1$ cut-points, the k statistical parameters of the fully parameterised M models, and the output data given those models.

The length of the first part of the message is the length of encoding $k-1$, the $k-1$ cut-points, and the k statistical parameters. The integer $k-1 \geq 0$ can be encoded using any model of non-negative integers such as the tree code for integers (Sect. 3.2), say. (In theory, a small saving is possible by taking account of the upper limit on $k-1$ and renormalising the truncated model, but it is small.) Recall that the input data are common knowledge. There are $\binom{N}{k-1}$ possible sets of $k-1$ cut-points and the simplest assumption is that all sets are equally likely leading to a cost of $\log\binom{N}{k-1}$ (an alternative is discussed in the context of classification trees (Sect. 8.4)). The model M knows how to estimate its statistical parameters and to what precision and at what message length.

The length of the second part of the message is the length of encoding the output data given the k fully parameterised models of the output space. This is the sum over the k fully parameterised instances of encoding those members of the output-data for which each one is responsible, and M knows how to do this.

The implementation of `Intervals` is straightforward and its `Estimator` uses a one-dimensional dynamic programming algorithm to choose the number and the values of the cut-points. The `Estimator` has a parameter, possibly trivial, which it passes on to `M`'s `Estimator`. The parameter might, for example, control the prior on `M`'s parameter(s).

```
UPFunctionModel                UPFunctionModel.M
 |                              |
 |-K                            |-K.M
 |                              |
 |-Multinomial                  |-Multinomial.M
 |                              |
 |-Intervals                    |-Intervals.M
    { upm; // UPmodel, od         { mdls;    // Models of od
      ... }                         cutPts; // discretise input
                                    ... }
UnParameterised                Parameterised
FunctionModels                 FunctionModels
```

`Intervals` is a non-trivial example of a model, here an unparameterised function-model, that takes another model, here an unparameterised model, as its parameter. Creating such high-order models is made much easier by models being first-class values, and by the complexity of a model and of data being measured in the same units, that is as message lengths in nits (Sect. 1.3).

5.4 Conditional Probability Table (CPT)

A conditional probability table (CPT) is, conventionally, a function-model having a discrete, univariate or multivariate input-space, and a discrete output-space. For each possible value of the input datum it conditionally provides a different MultiState (Sect. 2.3) model of the output datum. For example, in Melbourne the probability of a day being clear in various seasons is shown in Table 5.1 where the input variable

Season	pr(clear day)
Spring	0.114
Summer	0.184
Autumn	0.148
Winter	0.087

Table 5.1 CPT *season* → *clear_day* for Melbourne, from 'Climate statistics for Australian locations', 1955–2010, Bureau of Meteorology (2016)

takes one of the values spring, summer, autumn or winter, and the output variable takes one of the values clear or some-cloud.

The CPT concept can be generalized to allow any suitable model of any output-space; it need not be restricted to MultiState models of a discrete output-space: An unparameterised CPT takes an unparameterised model M of the output-space as its problem-defining parameter. M can be any model at all provided it is a model of the output-space. For each possible value of the input datum, CPT uses M's estimator to infer a fully parameterised M-model from those data that have the value in their input fields.

The first part of the message states the statistical parameters of the various fully parameterised M-Models. There is no need to state how many of these exist because the type of the input-space is common knowledge. M knows how to estimate its statistical parameters and to what precision and at what message length.

The second part of the message encodes the output data given the fully parameterised CPT model. The input data are common knowledge so the receiver knows which one of the component M-models is being used for each output datum.

In an implementation of CPT we have,

```
UPFunctionModel                  UPFunctionModel.M
  |                                |
  |-K                              |-K.M
  |                                |
  |-Multinomial                    |-Multinomial.M
  |                                |
  |-Intervals                      |-Intervals.M
  |                                |
  |-CPT                            |-CPT.M
     { upm; // for od                { condMdls;       // od Models
       ... }                           condModel(id); // given id
                                       ... }

UnParameterised                  Parameterised
FunctionModels                   FunctionModels
```

Nothing in the description of the CPT function-model anywhere requires the output data to be discrete data modelled by a MultiState model so `CPT` accepts any model at all as its problem defining parameter, only provided that it is a model of the output data, for example, say the `Normal` for continuous data.

The fully parameterised `CPT.M` takes a vector of parameter values as its statistical parameter, one element per model of the output data.

More `FunctionModels` are described in Chap. 8.

Chapter 6
Multivariate

Multivariate data is where each datum d is a k-tuple of $k > 1$ components (fields), $d = \langle d_1, d_2, \ldots, d_k \rangle$, and hence a data-set has more than one column. We have already encountered a special case of bivariate data where the relationship between an input datum (independent variable) and an output datum (dependent variable) is modelled by a function-model (Chap. 5). Note that a component need not be atomic (univariate), for example, field d_2 could have sub-fields $d_{2.1}$ and $d_{2.2}$, say. Two components need not have the same type, for example, the data on a person in a certain data-set might consist of name (String), gender (Discrete, $\{m, f\}$), age ($\mathbb{N}_{\geq 0}$), height ($\mathbb{R}_{\geq 0}$), and weight ($\mathbb{R}_{\geq 0}$).

```
UPModel                              Model
 |                                    |
 |-Multivariate                       |-Multivariate.M
    { width(); // #columns            { width();
      .. }                              functionModel(c,t);
                                        .. }
```

UnParameterised models — Parameterised models

Note that a Multivariate model can easily produce a function-model (Chap. 5) from id to od where the output, od, is one of the Multivariate's input columns (variables) of bounded discrete type t and the input, id, is the data-space of all the other columns. This function-model's conditional model, given id, is implemented by running through all possible values for od, calculating the negative log probabilities of the corresponding full tuples with od inserted into the appropriate position in id, and converting them to probabilities for a fully parameterised MultiState (Sect. 2.3), for example, Table 6.1.

L. Allison, *Coding Ockham's Razor*, https://doi.org/10.1007/978-3-319-76433-7_6

	$b_2 = F$	$b_2 = T$	$b_1 \to b_2$
$b_1 = F$	0.2	0.4	$\frac{1}{3} : \frac{2}{3}$
$b_1 = T$	0.1	0.3	$\frac{1}{4} : \frac{3}{4}$
$b_2 \to b_1$	$\frac{2}{3} : \frac{1}{3}$	$\frac{4}{7} : \frac{3}{7}$	

Table 6.1 Multivariate *Bool* × *Bool* can produce two function-models (→)

Also note that the components of a multivariate datum need not be of the same type (data-space) but they can be, and an important special case of this is continuous D-dimensional Vectors in $\mathbb{R}^D$. Vectors in $\mathbb{R}^D$ are discussed in Chap. 9.

6.1 Independent

Independent is the simplest model of multivariate data. Each component (field, variable) is modelled independently of the others; an alternative is the Dependent model (Sect. 6.2). The unparameterised Independent model requires a k-tuple of component unparameterised models, one per component of the data.

$$d = \langle d_1, d_2, \ldots \rangle \qquad \text{– a datum,}$$

$$(\mathrm{pr}\langle d_1, d_2, \ldots \rangle = \prod_i \mathrm{pr}(d_i)$$

In an implementation, the unparameterised `Independent` model takes a tuple of unparameterised `UPmodels`, one per data component, as its problem defining parameters—a tuple of models makes a model of tuples. The `Estimator` projects the multivariate data onto each component data-space and invokes the `Estimator` of the corresponding component `UPModel`. The fully parameterised `Independent.M` model takes a tuple of statistical parameters, one for each parameterised component model.

```
UPModel                         Model
 |                               |
 |-Multivariate                  |-Multivariate.M
   | { width();                    |
   |   ... }                       |
   |                               |
   |-Independent                   |-Independent.M
      { upms;                         { ms; // upms parameterised
        ... }                           ... }
```

UnParameterised models   Parameterised models

For an inference of Independent, the first part of the message encodes the statistical parameter of the fully parameterised Independent model, that is a k-tuple of statistical parameters, one per component model, and its length is the sum of the first parts of the messages for each component model. The second part of the message encodes the data, using the appropriate component model for each column.

6.2 Dependent

A *Dependent* model is a model of bivariate data where the second (output, dependent) component of the data is dependent on the first (input, independent) component in some way,

$$d = \langle id, od \rangle \qquad \text{– a datum,}$$

$$\mathrm{pr}\langle id, od \rangle = \mathrm{pr}(id) \cdot \mathrm{pr}(od|id).$$

Note that id, or od, or both can be multivariate.

The unparameterised Dependent model takes a pair, an unparameterised model of the first data component and an unparameterised function-model (Chap. 5) relating the first and second data components, as its problem defining parameter.

In an implementation of `Dependent`, the `Estimator` fits the unparameterised `UPModel` to the first column of the data and fits the unparameterised `UPFunctionModel` to both columns. The statistical parameter of a fully parameterised `Dependent.M` model is a pair, the statistical parameters of the fully parameterised `Model` together with the statistical parameters of the fully parameterised `FunctionModel`. To generate a sample, `random()` invokes the `Model`'s `random()` to generate an input datum, `id`, and the `FunctionModel`'s `random(id)` to generate a dependent output datum.

```
UPModel                                Model
 |                                      |
 |-Multivariate                         |-Multivariate.M
    | { width();                           |
    |   ... }                              |
    |                                      |
    |-Independent                          |-Independent.M
    |                                      |
    |-Dependent                            |-Dependent.M
       { upm;  // of id                       { im; // parameterised
         upfm; // id->od                        fm; // parameterised
         ... }                                  ... }
```

UnParameterised models   Parameterised models

6.3 Data Operations

Functional programming [9] has rich set of operations on collections of data that can be adopted for use on data-sets, some being relevant to multivariate data, including

columns, select certain columns of a multivariate Vector,

map, apply a function f to each element (row),

slice, select rows (elements) $[i, j)$, i inclusive to j exclusive,

unzip, given a multivariate data-set (of tuples), return a tuple of data-sets (columns), inverse of zip,

zip, given a tuple of data-sets, return a multi-variate data-set of tuples, inverse of unzip.

These can be used to rearrange a multivariate data-set, `ds`, so that particular columns become the input and output for a Dependent model, for example,

```
let rearrange ds =                ---ds: [<x,y,z>]
  let (xs, ys, zs) = unzip ds
  in zip (zip xs zs) ys           ---    [<<x,z>,y>]
```

A number of operations of this kind are implemented in class `Vector`, data-sets being `Vector`s of values.

Chapter 7
Mixture Models

> What evidence is there that classification – the core of learning – is agreeable to men and to animals also? [44, p.434].

If $M_1, \ldots, M_k$ are fully parameterised models over the same data-space, D, and if *weights* $w_1, \ldots, w_k \geq 0$ obey $\sum_i w_k = 1$, then M defined by the probability function $\mathrm{pr}(d) = \sum_i w_i \cdot \mathrm{pr}_i(d)$ is also a model over the data-space. In particular, $\sum_{d \in D} \mathrm{pr}(d) = 1$ for discrete data. M is a *Mixture model* , being a mixture of the *component* submodels, M_i. Similarly, if the M_i are models of continuous data defined by probability density functions $\mathrm{pdf}_i(d)$ then M defined by $\mathrm{pdf}(d) = \sum_i w_i \cdot \mathrm{pdf}_i(d)$ is a Mixture model of the continuous data, and $\int_D \mathrm{pdf}(d) = 1$. Figure 7.1 gives an example of a mixture of two normal distributions. Note that the M_i are often parameterised instances of the same unparameterised model although this need not be the case. Mixture models are useful where it is believed that a data-set is a mixture of two or more *classes* (clusters, kinds, types, species, families, subpopulations), C_i, of data. Component submodel M_i is a model of hypothetical class C_i of data, and we sometimes use "class C_i," or just "class i," to refer to either the class, or the model M_i of that class, as determined by the context.

Sometimes the data-set is known to be a mixture of k classes yet the class of each datum is unknown, and the problem is to find a Mixture model with one component submodel per class to describe the data. For example, someone presents the heights of a set of basketball players but the record of which players are female and which are male was not made or was lost somehow. One could fit a mixture of two Normal distributions (Sect. 4.3) to the data.

L. Allison, *Coding Ockham's Razor*, https://doi.org/10.1007/978-3-319-76433-7_7

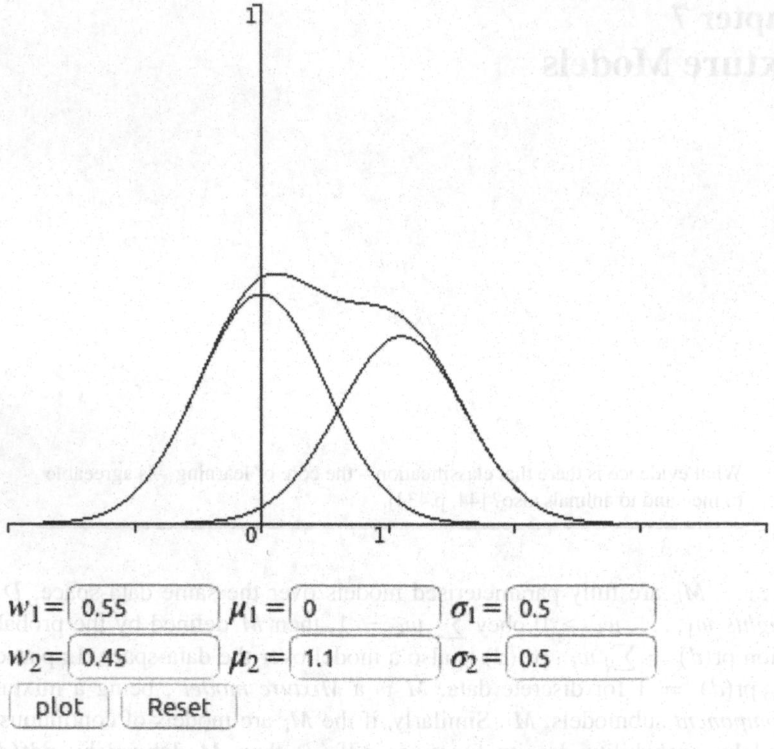

Fig. 7.1 $w_1 : w_2$ mixture (click) of $\mathcal{N}_{\mu_1,\sigma_1}$ and $\mathcal{N}_{\mu_2,\sigma_2}$

More often the data-set is *suspected* to be a mixture of $k \geq 1$ classes but k and the class of each datum are all unknown. The problem is to find a Mixture model of an unknown number of components to describe the data: Find the best value for k, weights w_i and statistical parameters for k component submodels. This is a difficult problem.

7.1 The Message

Given a data-set, the exact form of a two-part message encoding the data depends subtly on the question for which we want the message to be an answer.

Q1: How many classes, k, are present in the data?

Q2: How many classes are there, and what are the relative proportion and statistical parameters of each class?

Q3: How many classes are there, what are the proportion and statistical parameters of each class, and to which class does each datum belong?

The fact that there are at least these three reasonable questions that can be asked about the data-set is sometimes overlooked in the literature on clustering. Note for example that Q1 can lead to a different value of k from Q2, say: Suppose there are really only three plausible models of the data-set, two for $k = 2$ and one for $k = 3$, having odds $0.3 : 0.3 : 0.4$ respectively. The most likely value for k is $k = 2$ (answering Q1), but the most likely model is the third one (answering Q2) which has $k = 3$. However Q1 itself is rarely asked—and would be hard to answer in practice—and it is not considered further. Both Q2 and Q3 are frequently asked but not necessarily with the distinction being made explicit.

The first part of the message, for Q2 and for Q3, contains the statistical parameters of the Mixture model: (1) the number of component submodels k, (2) the weights, $w_1, \ldots, w_k$, of the components, (3) the statistical parameters of each component model. k is encoded according to some model of positive Integers (Chap. 3). The weights amount to the statistical parameters of a MultiState model (Sect. 2.3) over the classes. The class parameters are encoded according to the method of the unparameterised class model.

The second part of the message, for question Q2, encodes the data according to the probability function of the Mixture model, $\text{pr}(d) = \sum_{i=1}^{k} w_i \cdot pr_i(d)$. This method embodies no opinion as to which class a particular datum belongs. After getting the data, the receiver can work out the posterior probabilities of the class memberships but cannot tell if these match the transmitter's opinions because the transmitter did not send any such opinions. This method is sometimes called *fractional* or *soft* assignment of membership, although one might better say that it does not "assign" membership at all.

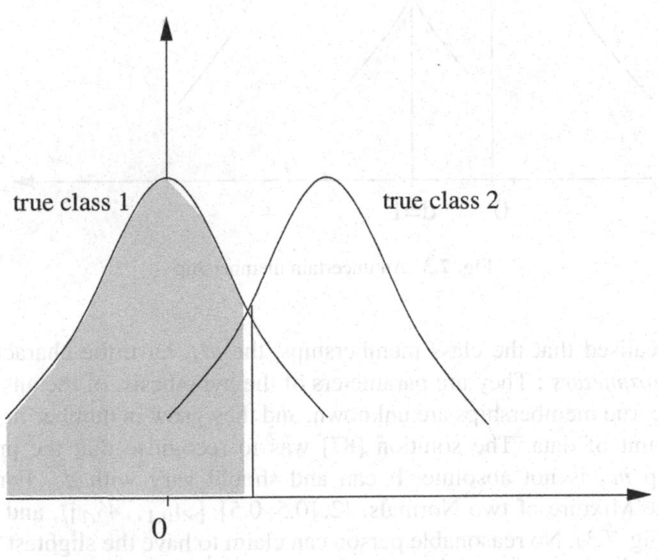

Fig. 7.2 Total assignment and bias

The message corresponding to question Q3 includes the class to which each datum d_j belongs. The most obvious way to do this is to encode m_j, $1 \leq m_j \leq k$, where d_j is thought to be a member of class C_{m_j}, according to the MultiState model based on the class weights. This is sometimes called *total* or *hard* assignment of membership, and the obvious choice for m_j is the class that has the greatest likelihood of containing d_j, even if this is much less than 1.0.

A serious problem with total assignment is that if, for example, the data-set truly comes from a two-component Mixture, when the components are close enough together a one-component model will give a message length that is shorter than that of any two-component model, regardless of the number of data. Total assignment can also lead to biased estimates of a class's parameters because they miss out on data that *probably*, but not certainly, belongs to a different class, for example, class one in Fig. 7.2 is estimated only from data in the shaded area. The previous fractional assignment method does not have these problems.

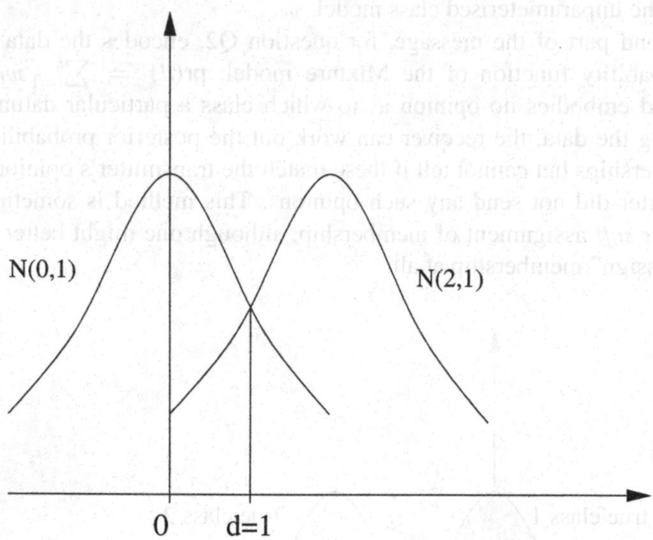

Fig. 7.3 An uncertain membership

It was realised that the class memberships, the m_j, have the characteristics of *nuisance parameters* : They are parameters of the hypothesis, of the answer to Q3, because the true memberships are unknown, and they grow in number in proportion to the amount of data. The solution [87] was to recognise that the precision of membership m_j is not absolute. It can and should vary with d_j. For example, consider the Mixture of two Normals, $\langle 2, [0.5, 0.5], [\mathcal{N}_{0,1}, \mathcal{N}_{2,1}] \rangle$, and the datum $d_j = 1.0$ (Fig. 7.3). No reasonable person can claim to have the slightest idea of the class to which d_j belongs; a choice of class 1, or of class 2, would be quite arbitrary and one bit would be wasted. The difficulty is to encode membership m_j to optimal precision. The coding technique is, in this case of d_j, to choose a value for m_j so as to send (just once) the first bit of the *remainder* of the message, that is whatever follows d_j, encoding d_{j+1} and so on. (The transmitter and receiver previously agreed that the code would have this feature.) On decoding d_j, the receiver can see what the transmitter has done and knows that m_j already tells the first bit of the message for d_{j+1}; that bit will not be sent a second time.

This strategy reclaims or reuses the bit that would otherwise be wasted. In effect m_j has no precision at all in this case. The technique was extended to two or more classes and to less finely balanced memberships than above [87, 92]. It was rediscovered by others and is sometimes called "bit borrowing" or "bits back." Interestingly, when this encoding of memberships is adopted, the message length per datum is the same as in the fractional assignment method adopted for question Q2, except for the last datum which has no message tail from which to scavenge a bit or bits [92].

MML shows how to assess a proposed mixture model of data and how to compare two models and choose the better one. However, finding the globally best mixture model is a hard problem. The next section on the search problem is framed in terms of answering question Q2 with the corresponding data encoding.

7.2 Search

Given a data-set ds, the search problem is to find the best answer to question Q2, that is to find the Mixture model that gives the shortest two-part message length. No fast algorithm is known to find the optimal solution in all cases. There are however heuristics that usually find a good solution that is at least a local optimum.

Note that given a Mixture model, that is given k, weights w_i, and component parameters θ_i, the posterior membership probability $p_{i,j} = \text{pr}(m_i = j)$ of each datum d_j can be evaluated. And, given these membership probabilities, which we can think of as fractional memberships, the weights of the classes and the component parameters can be reestimated. This classic chicken and egg situation where the current Mixture model gives memberships, and memberships give a new Mixture model, leads to an expectation maximization (EM) algorithm, to a message length minimization algorithm: At each step the new memberships reflect the previous model's parameters at least as well as the previous memberships, and the reestimated Mixture model reflects the new memberships at least as well as the previous model. Hence for a given k this greedy algorithm must converge although possibly to a local optimum rather than a global one. Iterate until there is "little" improvement.

The value of k remains to be chosen. A number of operations are available to *perturb* the current working Mixture model:

Split, divide one of the component classes into two.

Join, merge two classes, provided that $k > 1$.

Kill, delete a class and redistribute its members, provided that $k > 1$.

Each of these operations directly affects one or two classes. It can also affect all of the other classes indirectly via classes gaining or losing members thus causing the parameters of other classes to change. Consequently a few EM steps are run to settle the situation after a perturbation. Only then, the total message length of the new candidate Mixture model is compared with that of the previous working model to see if the new candidate should become the new working model. To begin, the initial Mixture model is set to be the one-class "Mixture" model. The process is stopped when no perturbation leads to an improved Mixture model. The perturbations described above, together with expectation maximization, form the core of various versions of the *Snob* Mixture modelling program, at first with total assignment [11, 12, 93], later with fractional assignment [87], and even extended to hierarchical Mixture models [92].

There are many possible variations in the details of exactly how and when perturbations can be applied to the current working Mixture model. The simplest choices for a *split* operation on class i are to remove the class and allocate its members (recalling that these are fractional memberships as corresponding to question Q2) to new classes $i.1$ and $i.2$ uniformly at random. EM steps may then cause readjustment of the remaining older classes and these two new classes. In principle, all possible splits should be tried. Initially it is likely that classes $i.1$ and $i.2$ closely resemble each other and their late parent; this may cause the EM steps to be slow to improve. If class i's members can be redistributed so as to make $i.1$ and $i.2$ less similar to each other [45] the subsequent EM steps *may* work faster although (1) doing this requires extra knowledge of the component unparameterised model, thus constraining the search algorithm, and (2) there is no firm guarantee that it will lead to a better solution any more quickly.

In principle all possible *join* perturbations should be tried. This is time consuming, particularly if the current Mixture model has many classes. It is plausible that two "close" classes are better candidates for merging than two classes that are far apart; Kullback-Leibler divergence (KLD) [51] is a possible measure of class distance. If class distance can be calculated quickly and only the closest pair, or a few close pairs, are considered for merging, a join step is certainly speeded up [45]. But the ability to calculate KLD, say, does constrain the algorithm and, as before, there is no guarantee that it will lead to a better solution.

With this kind of greedy search, and also with related stochastic searches where an increase in message length may be accepted probabilistically, there is always the risk that attempts to make the method faster by being more selective in the perturbations it explores, may in fact reduce the chance of it finding a solution as good as one that a simpler, more thorough strategy perhaps can.

7.3 Implementation

An implementation of Mixture modelling, `Mixture`, is an unparameterised `UPModel` that takes an unparameterised `UPModel`, `upm`, as its problem defining parameter. A fully parameterised instance of `upm` is estimated for each component submodel, for each inferred class, of the Mixture model. `Mixture`'s `Estimator` runs the `EM` algorithm and the perturbations—`split`, `join` and `kill`—described previously (Sect. 7.2), and invoking upm's `Estimator` when necessary. Any parameters passed to `Mixture`'s `Estimator` are passed on the upm's `Estimator`. `Mixture` uses a model of positive integers, currently `WallaceInt0` (Sect. 3.2), to encode $k-1$, and `MultiState` (Sect. 2.3) to estimate and encode the weights w_i. The current working Mixture model is initialised to the one-class Mixture model.

The statistical parameters of a fully parameterised Mixture model, `Mixture.M`, are $k \geq 1$, the weights, and the statistical parameters of each component model. To generate a random sample, `Mixture.M`'s `random()` selects a class according to the `random()` of the weights' `MultiState`-model and then generates a value using that class's `random()`.

```
UPModel                          Model
  |                                |
  |-Mixture                        |-Mixture.M
     { ump;   // unparam'd            { mixer(); // weights multistate
       ... } // component               ms();    // param'd components
                                        ... }
```

UnParameterised models UnParameterised models

`Mixture` can be used to analyse univariate data but it is more often applied to multivariate data. In the latter case upm must of course be some kind of `Multivariate` model (Chap. 6) of the multivariate data-space.

A `Mixture` is not naturally a `Multivariate` but we might like a Mixture of Multivariate models to behave like a Multivariate model, in particular so that it is able to produce a `functionModel(c,t)` (Chap. 6) if necessary. For this reason, `asMultivariateM()` returns a `Mixture.M` in the form of a `Multivariate.M`, *provided that* the Mixture's component model, upm, is itself a `Multivariate`.

7.4 An Example Mixture Model

The well known Anderson-Fisher Iris data-set is a five-variate data-set of measurements of fifty Iris flowers of each of three species, Iris-setosa, Iris-verginica, and Iris-versicolor. The data-set was collected by Anderson [4, 5] and used by Fisher [30] to illustrate statistical techniques. For each of the 150 flowers the length and width of the sepal, the length and width of the petal, and the species were recorded: $\mathbb{R}_{>0} \times \mathbb{R}_{>0} \times \mathbb{R}_{>0} \times \mathbb{R}_{>0} \times \mathit{Species}$. The first four attributes, the dimensions without the species, form a four-variate data-set suitable for Mixture modelling.

```
Vector ds4 = ds.cols(new int[]{0,1,2,3}); // drop
    Species
```

Making the gross simplifying assumption that the dimensions are independent, a four-variate `Independent` (Sect. 6.1) `Normal` (Sect. 4.3) model is a possible model of one class (species) of Iris. Reasonable bounds on the means and standard deviations are [0, 10] and [0.1, 10], say. The estimator returns the following model:

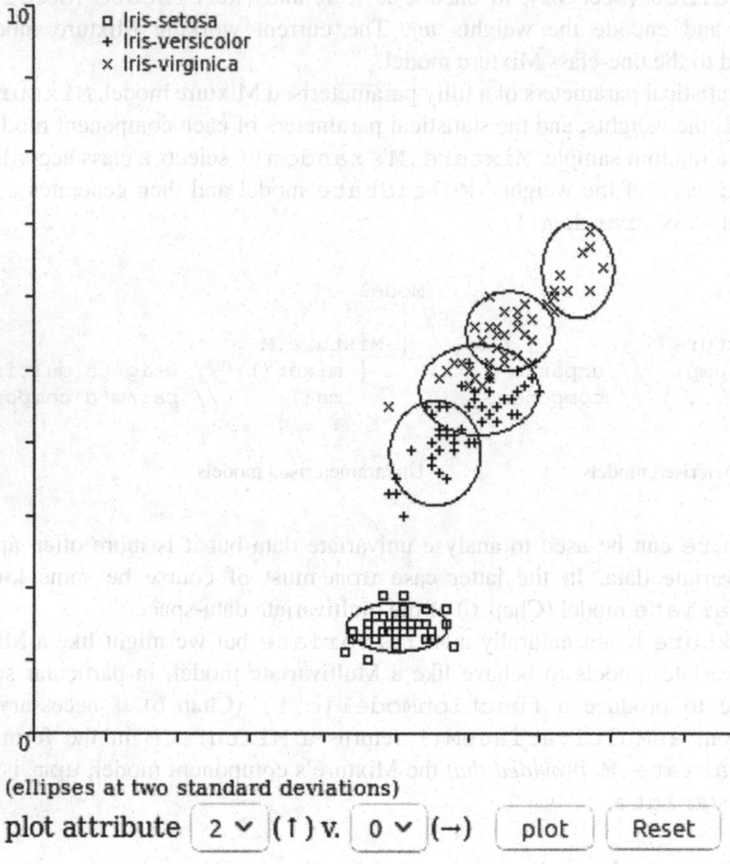

Fig. 7.4 Iris mixture model

```
((mml.Independent (Normal, Normal, Normal, Normal))
    (5.84, 0.83), (3.05, 0.43), (3.76, 1.76),
    (1.20, 0.76))
)
)
msg = 2153. = 27.38 + 2126. (nits)
    = 3107. = 39.5  + 3067. (bits)
```

The One-Class Model

`Mixture` is *not* given the true number of species, nor the species of any flower, and it finds a five class mixture:

```
((mml.Mixture (mml.Independent (Normal, Normal, Normal,
                                     Normal)))
  ([0.331, 0.276, 0.152, 0.069, 0.171],
    ---weights &
   [((5.01, 0.35), (3.42, 0.38), (1.46, 0.17),
     (0.24, 0.11)), --c1
    ((6.15, 0.42), (2.85, 0.27), (4.73, 0.31),
      (1.57, 0.22)), --c2
    ((5.54, 0.32), (2.58, 0.26), (3.86, 0.36),
      (1.17, 0.14)), --c3
    ((7.54, 0.25), (3.14, 0.43), (6.38, 0.33),
      (2.09, 0.24)), --c4
    ((6.58, 0.31), (3.06, 0.22), (5.54, 0.27),
      (2.14, 0.24))] --c5
  )
)
msg = 1760. = 137.2 + 1623.  (nits)
    = 2540. = 198   + 2342.  (bits)
```

The Mixture Model

This mixture beats the one-class model by 2540 = 198 + 2342 to 3107 = 39.5 + 3067 bits, despite the former having to encode considerably more parameters than the latter. We however know more than `Mixture` and can also cross-tabulate the inferred classes and their posterior memberships against the true species:

```
              Classes
  1      2      3      4      5
50.0,   0.0,   0.0,   0.0,   0.0,---Iris-setosa
 0.0,  22.7,  27.2,   0.0,   0.1,---Iris-versicolor
 0.0,   0.0,  14.5,  10.0,  25.5,---Iris-virginica
```

Classes v. Species

Class 1 corresponds to Iris-setosa. Classes 2 and 3 correspond to Iris-versicolor but there is some overlap with Iris-virginica. The remainder of Iris-virginica is split between class 4 and 5. Attributes 0 and 2 (Fig. 7.4) give the clearest picture. Note Fisher's remark, "I.setosa is a 'diploid' species with 38 chromosomes, I.virginica is a 'tetraploid' with 70, and I.versicolor … is a hexaploid. [Randolph suggested that possibly I.versicolor] is a polyploid hybrid of the two other species" [30, §VI, p. 185].

Because we do know that there are three species in equal proportions and also to which class each flower belongs, it is possible to "cheat" by building a mixture of three equally weighted classes, one per species:

```
msg = 1772. =  80. + 1692. (nits)
    = 2557. = 116. + 2441. (bits)
```

Results for the "Cheating" Mixture

This is a worse model than the five-class model above. Note that the cheat's first-part message length is for the parameters of the three classes; it does not include the cost of stating their weights which are known to be $[\frac{1}{3}, \frac{1}{3}, \frac{1}{3}]$.

The Irises are revisited in Sect. 8.8 which examines the problem of predicting species given a flower's dimensions, and in Sect. 10.2 which examines the inter-dependence of a flower's dimensions.

7.5 The 27 Club

The so-called *27 Club* is a hypothesis in pop-music culture that the age of 27 carries a high risk of death for musicians, particularly for rock stars—think Kurt Cobain, Jimi Hendrix, Brian Jones, Janis Joplin, Jim Morrison and Amy Winehouse. However, Wolkewitz et al concluded that "There was no peak in risk around age 27, but the risk of death for famous musicians throughout their 20s and 30s was two to three times higher than the general UK population" [100].

Recently Kenny carried out a *large* "population study of performing pop musicians … who died between 1950 and June 2014" [46, 48]. During the study, the number of musicians examined varied from eleven thousand to over thirteen thousand [48]. Among other conclusions was, as before, that "The 27 Club is a

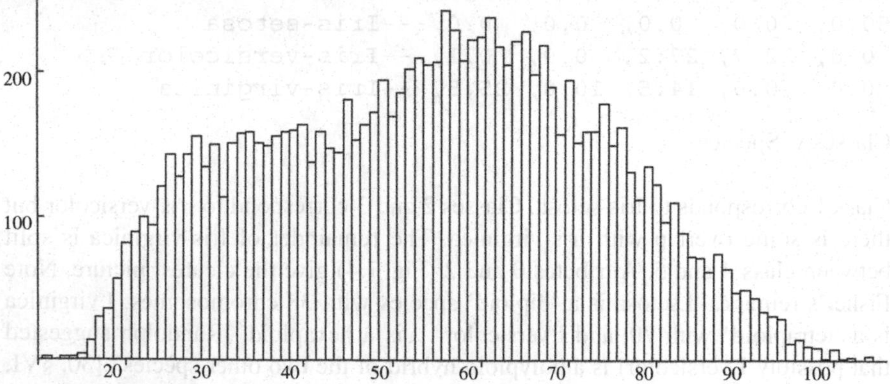

Fig. 7.5 Frequency v. Age (Kenny, November 2017, Age data on 11,221 musicians, Private communication)

myth" [47]. This has been widely reported, for example, "144 of them died at the age of 27 ... [but] a much larger 239 died at the [mode] age of 56" [79]. Nevertheless, gazing at one of the histograms (Fig. 7.5) of age versus frequency (Kenny, November 2017, Age data on 11,221 musicians, Private communication), $N = 11{,}221$, even though the data are very noisy it is hard to resist thinking that there could well be a good mixture model of the data with a component class having a mean of approximately 27.

Note that the data-set does not need to be represented by a sequence of more than 11,000 ages. Instead, fewer than 100 pairs—$\langle age_i, frequency_i\rangle$ where the frequency is taken as the `weight` of the age—can do the trick.

Attempting to fit a mixture of Normal distributions (Sect. 4.3) to the age data (Kenny, November 2017, Age data on 11,221 musicians, Private communication), `Mixture`, with its standard search (Sect. 7.2), fails to find an acceptable model with more than one component.

```
((mml.Mixture Normal) ([1.0],
                       [(54.3, 18.7)]))   // mean, std d.

msg = 48802. = 10.8 + 48791. nits
    = 70407. = 15.6 + 70391. bits
```

The One-Class "Mixture"

Well, it is a very noisy data-set and a non-trivial mixture might be wishful thinking. However, the estimator, `Mixture.Est`, provides programming access to its various tactics. For example, it is possible to start with a given mixture model and run expectation maximization (EM) steps to improve on it.

Starting with a mixture of $0.1 \times \mathcal{N}_{27,4}$ plus $0.9 \times \mathcal{N}_{55,19}$ in this way leads to the following mixture that includes a 15% component of $\mathcal{N}_{28,5.7}$

```
((mml.Mixture Normal) ([0.15, 0.85],
                       [(28.1, 5.7), (59.0, 16.2)]))

msg = 48401. = 26.3 + 48374. nits
    = 69827. = 38.  + 69789. bits
```

Two-Component Mixture

Note that this model's first-part costs 26.3 nits, more than twice that of the previous model because it includes parameters of two Normals and a 2-state distribution. Since 48,401 nits beats 48,802, this suggests that there might actually be a 28 Club, 28 being the mean of the first class. However going a little further, the improvement is less but there is a slightly better three-component mixture

```
((mml.Mixture Normal) ([0.13, 0.09, 0.78],
                       [(25.9, 4.8), (36.8, 5.3),
                        (61. , 15.2)]))

msg = 48355. = 41.1 + 48313. nits
    = 69761. = 59.3 + 69702. bits
```

Three-Component Mixture

So maybe there is a 26 Club *and* a 37 Club? Or maybe there is just a group of musicians that die young? Or maybe a mixture of Normals is simply the wrong kind of model to be fitting to data about age at death?

Chapter 8
Function-Models 2

Function-models were introduced in Chap. 5. They are used when one data component (variable) depends statistically upon another. In this situation a datum is bivariate, $d = \langle id, od \rangle$, although note that the input id and the output od can themselves be multivariate. Recall that the input data are common knowledge so a transmitter need not encode them in any message to a receiver and we can take it that $\mathrm{pr}(id) = 1$. For a given function-model we are interested in the conditional probability of od given id, $\mathrm{pr}(od|id)$ which is `condPr(id,od)` in the implementation and which must equal `condModel(id).pr(od)`.

The `K` (constant) (Sect. 5.1), `Intervals` (Sect. 5.3) and `CPT` (conditional probability table) (Sect. 5.4) function-models are discussed in Chap. 5. The NaiveBayes (Sect. 8.1) and Tree (Sect. 8.4) function-models are discussed below.

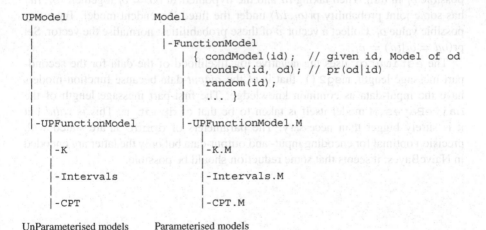

```
UPModel                  Model
 |                         |
 |                         |-FunctionModel
 |                            | { condModel(id);   // given id, Model of od
 |                            |   condPr(id, od); // pr(od|id)
 |                            |   random(id);
 |                            |   ... }
 |                            |
 |-UPFunctionModel            |-UPFunctionModel.M
    |                            |
    |-K                          |-K.M
    |                            |
    |-Intervals                  |-Intervals.M
    |                            |
    |-CPT                        |-CPT.M

UnParameterised models   Parameterised models
```


L. Allison, *Coding Ockham's Razor*, https://doi.org/10.1007/978-3-319-76433-7_8

8.1 Naive Bayes

For a discrete bounded output data-space, O, and an arbitrary input data-space, I, *NaiveBayes* is a function-model, $I \to O$, based on a Dependent model (Sect. 6.2) acting in the opposite direction, backwards, $\langle O, O \to I\rangle$, and on the (naive) assumption, when I is multivariate, that I's components are independent. From Bayes's theorem (Eq. (1.1) in Chap. 1) we have

$$\begin{aligned} \mathrm{pr}\langle id, od\rangle &= \mathrm{pr}(id)\cdot\mathrm{pr}(od|id) = \mathrm{pr}(od)\cdot\mathrm{pr}(id|od) \quad \text{Bayes} \\ \mathrm{pr}(od|id) &= \frac{\mathrm{pr}(od)\cdot\mathrm{pr}(id|od)}{\mathrm{pr}(id)} \\ \mathrm{pr}(od|id) &\propto \mathrm{pr}(od)\cdot\mathrm{pr}(id|od) \end{aligned}$$

In the last line above, pr(od) is given by a model of O, and pr($id|od$) is given by a function-model of $O \to I$.

An unparameterised Dependent model (Sect. 6.2) of $O \times I$ consists of two parts, an unparameterised model of O and an unparameterised function-model of $O \to I$. A given data-set $ds : (I \times O)^*$ can easily be flipped around to make $ds_{flip} : (O \times I)^*$. The Dependent model's estimator can be fitted to ds_{flip}, giving a fully parameterised Dependent model of $O \times I$. The latter consists of a fully parameterised model of O and a fully parameterised function-model of $O \to I$. These can be turned into a function-model $I \to O$ as follows. For a given input datum $id : I$, the unknown od could equal any value o_i in the output data-space, $o_i : O$. We know that O is discrete and bounded so simply try each possible o_i in turn. Then taking id and the hypothetical $od = o_i$ together, $\langle o_i, id\rangle$ has some joint probability $\mathrm{pr}\langle o_i, id\rangle$ under the fitted Dependent model. Try every possible value o_i. Collect a vector $\vec{p}$ of these probabilities; normalise the vector. Set $\mathrm{pr}(od = o_i|id) = p_i$.

The `estimator` uses the negative log likelihood of the data for the second-part message length, `msg2()`, that is of the *output*-data because function-models have the input-data as common knowledge. The first-part message length of the `NaiveBayes.M` model itself is taken to be that of `dpndt_m`. This is *valid* but it is surely bigger than necessary: The parameters of `dpndt_m` are stated with precision optimal for encoding input- and output-data but only the latter are encoded in NaiveBayes; it seems that some reduction should be possible.

In the implementation of `NaiveBayes` we have,

```
UPFunctionModel               UPFunctionModel.M
 |                             |
 |-NaiveBayes                  |-NaiveBayes.M // FM for I->O
    { dpndt; // unparam'd        { dpndt_m;   // Dependent for OxI
      ... }                        Omdl;      // dpndt_m's model of O
                                   O2I;       // dpndt_m's f.m. O->I
                                   ... }
```

UnParameterised models   Parameterised models

What `NaiveBayes` is doing is using `O2I` : $O \to I$ to construct a function-model in the opposite, desired direction $I \to O$. The words *invert* and *inverse* spring to mind for this process, and indeed posterior probability was known as inverse probability until the mid-twentieth century [29].

```
-- run Ducks --
If X walks like a duck and talks like a duck,
pr(X is a duck) = .9135
using function-model
 ((mml.NaiveBayes (mml.Dependent
    ((mml.MultiState (coot, swan)),
     (mml.CPT (coot, swan, (mml.Independent
        ((mml.MultiState (false, true)),
         (mml.MultiState (false, true)))))))))
 ([0.5, 0.3, 0.2],
  [([0.9, 0.1], [0.9, 0.1]),
   ([0.1, 0.9], [0.1, 0.9]),
   ([0.1, 0.9], [0.9, 0.1])]))
...
-- done with Ducks --
```

Fig. 8.1 Running(?) Ducks

8.2 An Example

From observation, about half of the birds at the local lake are coots, 30% are ducks, and 20% are swans. Most ducks and swans, say 90%, have been seen to waddle.

$$\mathrm{pr}(B \text{ waddles} \mid B \text{ is a duck}) = 0.9,$$

$$\mathrm{pr}(B \text{ waddles} \mid B \text{ is a swan}) = 0.9$$

but no coot has been seen to waddle (although maybe one could),

$$\mathrm{pr}(B \text{ waddles} \mid B \text{ is a coot}) = 0.1, \text{ say.}$$

Most ducks, say 90%, have been heard to quack. No coot has been heard quacking,

$$\mathrm{pr}(B \text{ quacks} \mid B \text{ is a coot}) = 0.1, \text{ say.}$$

Similarly for swans.

Someone reports that a certain bird, X, was observed to waddle and to quack. What kind of bird, S, is X?

$$\begin{aligned}\mathrm{pr}(B \text{ is a } S \mid B \text{ waddles and quacks}) \propto\ & \mathrm{pr}(B \text{ is a } S)\\ & \cdot\ \mathrm{pr}(B \text{ waddles} \mid B \text{ is a } S)\\ & \cdot\ \mathrm{pr}(B \text{ quacks} \mid B \text{ is a } S) \text{ by Bayes,}\end{aligned}$$

There are three possibilities,

$$\begin{aligned}\mathrm{pr}(X \text{ is a coot} \mid \text{evidence}) &\propto 0.5 \times 0.1 \times 0.1 = 0.005,\\ \mathrm{pr}(X \text{ is a duck} \mid \text{evidence}) &\propto 0.3 \times 0.9 \times 0.9 = 0.243,\\ \mathrm{pr}(X \text{ is a swan} \mid \text{evidence}) &\propto 0.2 \times 0.9 \times 0.1 = 0.018,\\ \mathit{total} &= 0.005 + 0.243 + 0.018 = 0.266.\end{aligned}$$

So, $\mathrm{pr}(X \text{ is a duck} \mid X \text{ waddles and } X \text{ quacks}) = 0.243/0.266 = 0.91$; also see Fig. 8.1. In other words, if it walks like a duck and talks like a duck it is (probably) a duck, according to NaiveBayes, "Bayes" because of the use of Bayes's theorem, and "naive" because waddling and quacking are assumed to be independent.

8.3 Note: Not So Naive

The NaiveBayes function-model $I \to O$ was described (Sect. 8.1) as being based on a `Dependent` model $\langle O, O \to I \rangle$ (Sect. 6.2). The `Dependent` model contains a model of O and a backwards function-model fm of $O \to I$. Given a datum $\langle id, od \rangle$ the implementation of the function-model fm returns `condModel(od)`, a model of I. It was tacitly assumed that when I is multivariate then the components of an I-datum are independent of each other—hence *naive*—that `condModel(od)` returns an `Independent` model (Sect. 6.1) but no actual use was made of this. In principle there is nothing to stop `condModel(od)` from returning a `Dependent` model of I or absolutely any other model of I that may or may not assume independence of the components of I from each other. The method is only completely naive if the model of I is `Independent`.

The function-model `NaiveBayes` would perhaps better be called plain "Bayes" in the light of the above. However, other dedicated "naive Bayes" software hides, or at least wraps-up, the details of workings so the name stands.

8.4 Classification Trees

A *Classification-Tree* is a particular kind of function-model from an input data-space I to a discrete bounded output data-space O of "classes". I is frequently multivariate although it need not be. The function-model works by repeatedly splitting the data at *Fork*-nodes into two or more subsets based on the result of a test on a component (attribute, variable) of I until eventually a *Leaf*-node of the Tree is reached and a model of O is delivered up. The Leaf model can be taken as a probabilistic prediction, or its mode can be taken as a value prediction of the output value $od = o_i$ that best corresponds to `id`. Subtrees deeper within the Classification-Tree process more restricted subsets of data and so can potentially develop more precise models of those subsets. Classification-Trees are also known as *Decision-Trees* or as *Expert Systems*. The archetypal programs are Quinlan's ID3 [68] and the later C4.5 [69]. Decision-Trees have also been generalized to Decision Graphs [62, 63] which are able to express disjunctive relationships more economically than Trees.

There is no particular reason for the output data-space O to be limited to being discrete and bounded. The only thing that is required is that the Leaf models are models of the output data-space whatever that is, discrete or continuous, atomic or multivariate, and so on. A Tree having a continuous output data-space is sometimes called a *Regression-Tree*.

A Tree is not only a means of predicting an O-value from a I-value. It is also an *explanation* of the relationship between input I and output O variables. It can be examined to learn what are the most important components of I, what has the most influence on O, and what value of a component of I in some test is critical in changing the prediction.

If you have been to a doctor recently you might have noticed the doctor informally applying a Tree-like process—"How are you feeling? Do you have a temperature? How is your appetite? Do you have any stomach pain? Does this hurt?" Each question tries to narrow down the possible causes of the visit. Perhaps you have appendicitis, or maybe it is just indigestion.

8.5 The Message

A two-part message to encode a given data-set first encodes the inferred Classification- or Regression-Tree and then encodes the data assuming that the Tree is true. The encoding of the Tree contains the structure of the Tree, the test applied in each Fork node, and the statistical parameters of the model in each Leaf node.

First consider a *binary* (Classification- or Regression-) Tree in which every Fork node has exactly two subtrees. In this case its *structure* is that of a *complete* binary Tree. There is a simple, efficient encoding for the structure of complete binary Trees (Sect. 3.2): Perform a pre-order traversal of the Tree, encoding each Fork node as a 0 and each Leaf node as a 1 (Fig. 8.2). The end of the encoding can be detected when the number of 1s read is one more than the number of 0s read: a complete binary Tree has one more Leaf node than it has Fork nodes.

This 0|1-encoding of Forks and Leaves corresponds to a probability of $\frac{1}{2}$ for a Fork and the same for a Leaf. A complete *ternary* Tree with f Fork nodes has $2f+1$

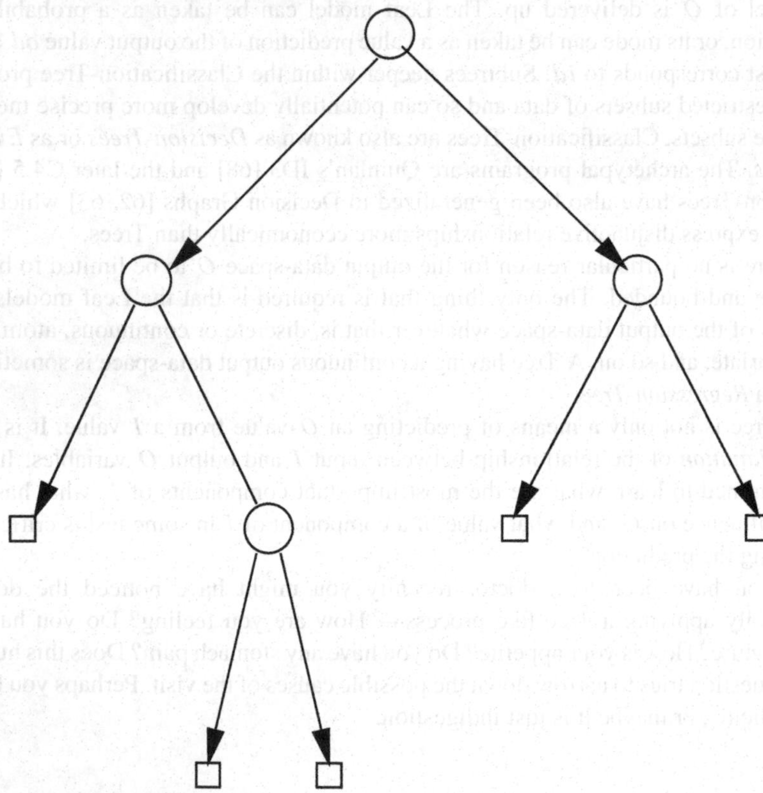

Fig. 8.2 A complete binary tree, preorder gives FFLFLLFLL, encoding=001011011

Leaf nodes so a Fork has a probability of $\frac{1}{3}$, a Leaf $\frac{2}{3}$. In general, a complete *k-ary* Tree with f Fork nodes has $(k-1)f+1$ Leaf nodes so the asymptotic odds of an arbitrary node being a Fork versus a Leaf are 1 to $k-1$. However in a Classification- or Regression-Tree, the *arity* of one Fork node may differ from that of another and Wallace and Patrick [98] adopted a scheme where the arity of a Fork—which is known as soon as the attribute that it tests is specified (see below)—adjusts the assumed probability of Forks and Leaves in its subtrees accordingly, so that the length of the code-word for a node depends on the arity of its parent node.

To specify the test in a Fork node, first state the input attribute (component, column, variable) that the Fork tests. If the attribute is discrete and bounded with $k \geq 2$ values the Fork node has k subtrees, one for each of the k values, Fig. 8.3. Otherwise if the attribute is ordered the Fork node has two subtrees, one for data having attribute values $\leq v$ and one for values $> v$ where v is a splitting value, Fig. 8.4. It is sufficient to nominate one of the given input-data as v; recall that the input-data of a function-model are common knowledge, known to both transmitter and receiver. If there are N data, one *might* do this in $\log_2(N-1)$ bits but Wallace and Patrick [98] introduced a more cunning scheme: Encode the median in one bit, a quartile in three bits, an octile in five bits, and so on. Note that $\sum_{i \geq 0} 2^i/2^{2i+1} = \sum_{i \geq 0} 1/2^{i+1} = 1$. The virtue of this scheme is that if, for example, the 259th largest value out of 1024 happens to be the best value according to the likelihood but only by a tiny margin, the first quartile can be seen as a close approximation to it and one that is cheap to state at three bits against ten bits in the uniform scheme. In effect it achieves variable precision for splitting value parameters.

Each Leaf node contains its own fully parameterised model of the output data-space. The unparameterised model of output data-space, which is a problem defining parameter to the Tree Function-model, knows how to estimate parameters for such models and to what precision.

The second part of the message encodes the output data components of the given data-set. To do this, the input component(s) of a datum are tested as specified by the

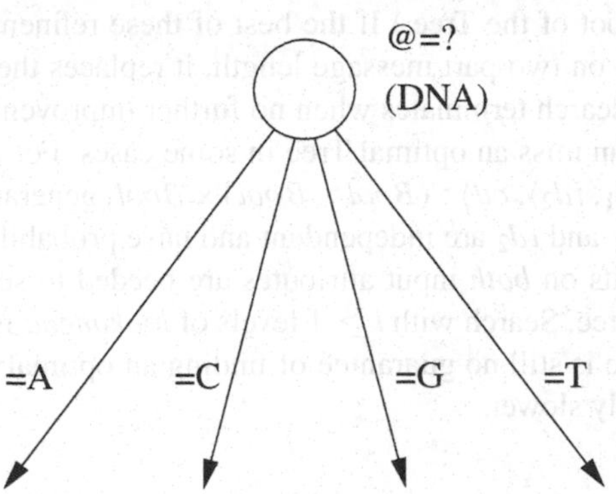

Fig. 8.3 Fork for a Discrete (DNA) attribute

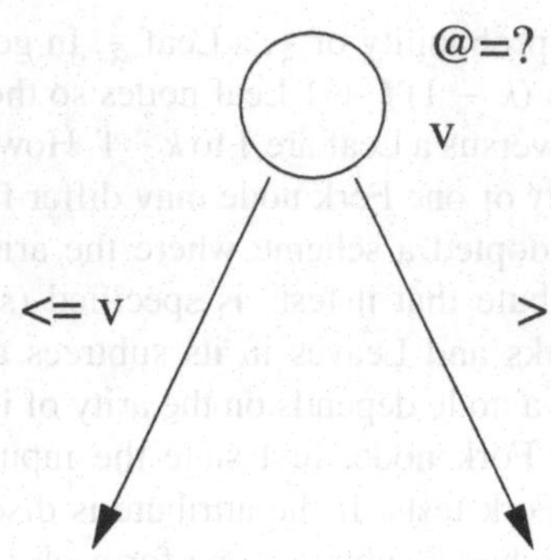

Fig. 8.4 Fork for an ordered attribute

appropriate Fork nodes of the Tree, beginning at its root. This leads to one of the Leaf nodes where the output component of the datum is encoded using the model in the Leaf.

8.6 Search

The search for an optimal Tree function-model is hard: If the input data-space has several components, or if some of the components are ordered non-Discrete, there are a great many possible Trees. The simplest strategy is a *greedy* search. The current working Tree is initialised to be the simplest possible Tree, the one-Leaf Tree, and its two-part message length is calculated. At each step the search examines each Leaf of the current working Tree to see of it pays to replace the Leaf with a Fork and subtrees. For each such Leaf, the search considers splitting on each available attribute in turn to form a new one-Fork subtree. (Note, there is no point in reconsidering a discrete bounded attribute that has already been used to split closer to the root of the Tree.) If the best of these refinements beats the Leaf under consideration on two-part message length, it replaces the Leaf in the current working Tree. The search terminates when no further improvement is found.

Greedy search can miss an optimal Tree in some cases. For example, if a datum d is of the form $\langle\langle id_1, id_2\rangle, od\rangle : (Bool \times Bool) \times Bool$, generated by the rule $od = (id_1 \neq id_2)$, and id_1 and id_2 are independent and have probability 0.5 of taking the value true, then splits on *both* input attributes are needed to see any improvement over the one-Leaf Tree. Search with $l \geq 1$ levels of *lookahead* is more likely to find good Trees but there is still no guarantee of finding an optimal Tree in general and the search is certainly slower.

8.7 Implementation

`Tree`, the implementation of the unparameterised Tree function-model takes the Type of the input-space and an unparameterised `UPModel` of the output-space, `leafUPM`, as its problem defining parameters. Its Estimator, `Tree.Est`, passes any parameters on to `leafUPM`'s `Estimator` whenever that is invoked. It calls the search routine, presently with a hard-coded `lookahead` value, generally 0 or 1. The search is recursive and determines whether or not to expand a `Leaf` into a `Fork` with sub-trees. To generate a random output value, `random(id)` (which is inherited from `UPFunctionModel.M`) uses input datum `id` to select a `Leaf` and then invokes the `random()` of the `Leaf`'s fully parameterised `leafUPM`-model, `mdl`.

```
UPFunctionModel                UPFunctionModel.M
  |                              |
  |-NaiveBayes                   |-NaiveBayes.M
  |                              |
  |-Tree                         |-Tree.M
     { leafUPM; // unparam'd        |
       ... }                        |-Leaf
                                    | { mdl; // leafUPM param'd
                                    |   ... }
                                    |
                                    |-Fork
                                       |
                                       |-DFork  // Discrete Fork
                                       |   { col;  // relevant column
                                       |     subTrees;
                                       |     ... }
                                       |
                                       |-OFork  // Ordered Fork
                                           { col;    // test column
                                             split; // test value
                                             subTrees;
                                             ... }

UnParameterised models         Parameterised models
```

If `leafUPM` is for a discrete bounded output data-space we get a Classification-Tree, if it is for a Continuous output data-space we get a Regression-Tree. But `leafUPM` can in fact be a `Model` for any output data-space at all, discrete or continuous, atomic or multivariate, even a function-model—truly a Regression-Tree.

8.8 An Example

The Anderson-Fisher Iris data-set [4, 5, 30] was used in Sect. 7.4 to illustrate mixture modelling. There, no use was made of the known species of the sampled flowers. Here however the Species—Iris-setosa, Iris-verginica, and Iris-versicolor—makes an excellent output data-space for a function-model, the input data-space of course being the length and width of the sepal, and the length and width of the petal, collectively $\mathbb{R}^4_{>0}$.

As a *null* hypothesis, a single `MultiState` model (Sect. 2.3) was fitted to the Species attribute alone. Recalling that there are fifty examples of each Species (Sect. 7.4) the cost of the data, the second part of the message, is approximately $150 \log_2 3 \approx 238$ bits.

```
Estimator:
 (mml.MultiState (Iris-setosa,          --lower bound
                  Iris-virginica))      --upper bound
                 .estimator(())


Model:
 ((mml.MultiState (Iris-setosa, Iris-virginica))
                   [0.33, 0.33, 0.33]) --stat params
msg = 169.2 = 4.143 + 165.1 (nits)
    = 244.2 = 5.977 + 238.2 (bits)
```

Single MultiState Model of Species

If you are concerned by the message length above being much less than that of the one-class "mixture" (Sect. 7.4) in Chap. 7, recall that the latter had to model four continuous dimensions. The dimensions are not used above and they are "free" in what follows.

The minimum message length `Tree` function-model found with `lookahead=1` contains two Ordered `Fork` nodes both, as it happens, testing the third attribute (@2), and three `Leaf` nodes with between 90 and 98% purity. The Tree comprehensively beats the single `MultiState` in terms of two-part message length despite the`Tree` itself, the first part of the message, being much more expensive than the single `MultiState`'s statistical parameters.

Textual representation of the Estimator and Tree:

```
Estimator:
 (mml.Tree ((R4 CTS CTS CTS CTS),
           (mml.MultiState (Iris-setosa,
            Iris-virginica)))
          .estimator(())
```

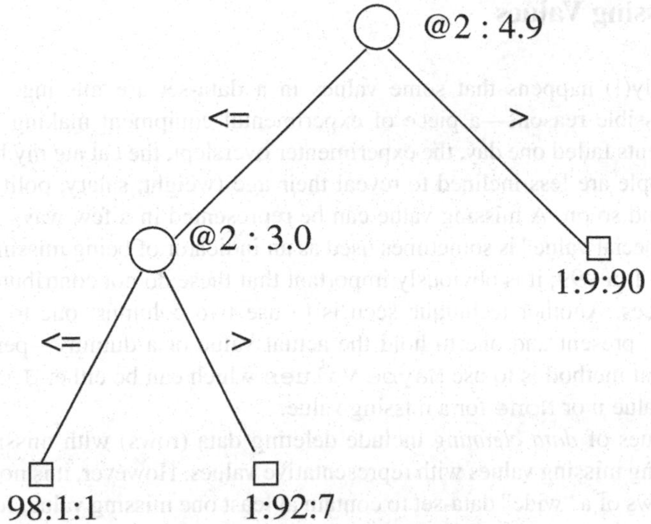

Fig. 8.5 The Tree function-model

```
Model:
 ((mml.Tree ((R4 CTS CTS CTS CTS),
            (mml.MultiState (Iris-setosa,
             Iris-virginica)))
    (OFork 2 4.9
       [(OFork 2 3.0
            [(Leaf [0.98, 0.01, 0.01]),
             (Leaf [0.01, 0.92, 0.07])]),
          (Leaf [0.01, 0.09, 0.90])
       ]
 )  )

msg = 68.31 = 40.06 + 28.26 (nits)
    = 98.56 = 57.79 + 40.77 (bits)
```

Tree FunctionModel of $\mathbb{R}^4_{>0} \rightarrow Species$

Figure 8.5 gives a graphical representation of the Tree function-model. Examining scatter plots for the Iris data (Sect. 7.4), Fig. 7.4, supports the conclusion that the third attribute (@2) is indeed the most informative about species.

8.9 Missing Values

It frequently(!) happens that some values in a data-set are missing. There is a host of possible reasons—a piece of experimental equipment making one of the measurements failed one day, the experimenter overslept, the cat ate my homework, certain people are less inclined to reveal their age (weight, salary, politics, ...) in a survey, and so on. A missing value can be represented in a few ways. In spreadsheets a "special value" is sometimes used as an indicator of being missing, perhaps an age of -1 or 999; it is obviously important that these do not contribute to means and variances. Another technique seen is to use two columns, one to indicate if the value is present and one to hold the actual value or a dummy—perhaps 0. A more elegant method is to use `Maybe Values` which can be either `Just(v)` for a present value v or `None` for a missing value.

Techniques of *data cleaning* include deleting data (rows) with missing values, and replacing missing values with representative values. However, it is not unknown for most rows of a "wide" data-set to contain at least one missing value, for example [72], and the notion of representative value rather presupposes no function-model relationship with other variables. So let us deal with missing data rather than remove them.

Representing missing values is straightforward; modelling them has a bit more to consider. If the fact of one value being missing is independent of any other value then it is possible to use a dummy value and set its weight in the data-set to zero. If the data are multivariate, set only the weight of the missing field to zero. This is in fact valid *if* both the transmitter and receiver know in advance which values are missing. However if they, particularly the receiver, do not know in advance it underestimates the message length, but *every* competing model underestimates by the *same* amount so it does not affect estimates of parameters—other than of absence and presence.

If one value's absence or presence might not be independent of other variables (columns) the best thing to do is to model it. 'Missing' is a simple model of missing values which uses a 2-state model of $\{false, true\}$ to model whether or not a value is *present*, together with a suitable model of those values that are present.

The implementation, `Missing`, takes an unparameterised model of (present) values as its problem defining parameter and sets `valueUpm`. The `estimator` takes a pair containing the parameters for the estimators of `presentUpm` and `valueUpm`. The value model is estimated from those values that are present. `pr(None)` is the probability of absence and `pr(Just(v))` is the probability if presence times the probability of `v`. Most internal operations are done in two parts—for presence and for value.

When `Missing` is used as part of a structured model, say as the leaf model of `Tree` (Sect. 8.4), it is invoked several times, once per leaf. Each of these instances may well be parameterised differently, both for the proportion of missing values and for those values that are present. Both may influence the structure of the tree. In this way absence and presence can become informative.

Chapter 9
Vectors

A D-dimensional *Vector*, $\vec{x} = [x_1, \ldots, x_D]$ in $\mathbb{R}^D$ has D components, x_i, where each x_i is a real number, a member of $\mathbb{R}$. Vectors are an important kind of data and everyone is familiar with points or positions in the plane or two-dimensional space $\mathbb{R}^2$, and in three-dimensional space $\mathbb{R}^3$.

There are many different notions of the *size* (length, magnitude) of a Vector or more formally its *norm* $\|\vec{x}\|_p$. For a real $p \geq 1$ the $\mathbb{L}_p$-norm or p-norm is defined by

$$\|\vec{x}\|_p = (|x_1|^p + \ldots + |x_D|^p)^{\frac{1}{p}}.$$

If a collection of Vectors all have the same ($\mathbb{L}_p$–) norm of 1.0 they are said to be $\mathbb{L}_p$-*normalised*, or just normalised, and they vary only in *direction*, in the ratios of their components. In this case, necessarily $-1 \leq x_i \leq 1$. The most widely seen values for p are two and one, and indeed the $\mathbb{L}_2$-norm is sometimes just called the norm and written $\|\vec{x}\|$. A Vector of probabilities, such as those in a MultiState distribution (Sect. 2.3) say, is $\mathbb{L}_1$-normalised. A normalised Vector has $K = D - 1$ degrees of freedom because of the constraint of being normalised.

Models of Directions are used for the obvious compass bearings in two-dimensional (2-D) and three-dimensional (3-D) space, and also for periodic—hourly, daily, weekly, yearly—events, and even for documents in *topic space* in text processing. The following sections cover models of $\mathbb{R}^D$ (Sect. 9.1), the K-Simplex (Sect. 9.2), directions in $\mathbb{R}^D$ (Sect. 9.3), and the von Mises-Fisher model of directions (Sect. 9.3.2). Note that a function-model (Chap. 5) that returns a model of continuous values, or of Vectors, conditional upon an input datum is sometimes called a regression; some examples are given in Chap. 10.

L. Allison, *Coding Ockham's Razor*, https://doi.org/10.1007/978-3-319-76433-7_9

9.1 *D*-Dimensions, $\mathbb{R}^D$

A D-dimensional Vector, $\vec{x} = [x_1, \ldots, x_D]$, in $\mathbb{R}^D$ has D components. Addition and subtraction of two such Vectors are performed component by component. Some Vector operations including the *dot product* ($\cdot$) of two Vectors and the *cross product* ($\times$) of two three-dimensional Vectors are given below:

$$
\begin{aligned}
(\vec{x} + \vec{y})_i &= x_i + y_i,\\
(\vec{x} - \vec{y})_i &= x_i - y_i,\\
(-\vec{x})_i &= -x_i,\\
(r\,\vec{x})_i &= r\,x_i,\ \forall r : \mathbb{R},\\
\vec{x} \cdot \vec{y} &= \sum_{i=1}^{D} x_i\, y_i : \mathbb{R}, \quad \text{dot product},\\
\|\vec{x}\|_2 &= \sqrt{\vec{x}\,.\vec{x}},\\
\vec{x} \times \vec{y} &= [x_2y_3 - x_3y_2,\ x_3y_1 - x_1y_3,\ x_1y_2 - x_2y_1], \quad \text{for } D = 3 \text{ only},\\
\vec{y} \times \vec{x} &= -(\vec{x} \times \vec{y}).
\end{aligned}
$$

9.1.1 Implementation

In an implementation of a model over $\mathbb{R}^D$, the unparameterised `UPModel`, `R_D`, generally takes the dimension `D` as a problem defining parameter. *D* is a given, a constant in some problem.

```
UPModel                     UPModel.M
|                           |
|-ByPdf                     |-ByPdf.M
    |                           |
    |-R_D                       |-R_D.M           // abstract
      { D();
        ... }
```

UnParameterised models — Parameterised models

A function-model (Chap. 5) can return a model of Vectors if appropriate.

9.1.2 Norm and Direction

One way to define a model of Vectors in $\mathbb{R}^D$ is by means of a model of Vector Norms together with a model of Vector Directions. Examples of the latter are given in Sect. 9.3.

The implementation, `NrmDir`, is an unparameterised `UPModel` of Vectors. It takes `normUPM` an unparameterised `UPModel` of Norms, of $\mathbb{R}_{\geq 0}$, and `dirnUPM` one of Directions (Sect. 9.3), as problem defining parameters. The latter knows the dimension, D, so there is no need to include it separately.

```
UPModel                        UPModel.M
 |                              |
 |-ByPdf                        |-ByPdf.M
    |                              |
    |-R_D                          |-R_D.M
       |                              |
       |-NrmDir                       |-NrmDir.M
          { normUPM;                     { normMdl;
            dirnUPM;                       dirnMdl;
            ... }                          ... }
```

UnParameterised models Parameterised models

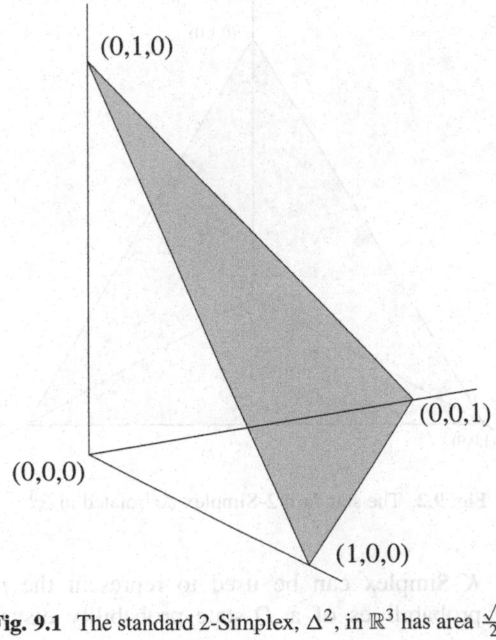

Fig. 9.1 The standard 2-Simplex, Δ^2, in $\mathbb{R}^3$ has area $\frac{\sqrt{3}}{2}$

The fully parameterised `NrmDir.M` takes a 2-tuple—the statistical parameters of the two sub-models—as its statistical parameter.

9.2 Simplex and $\|\vec{x}\|_1 = 1$

The *standard K-Simplex* Δ^K is the set of $\mathbb{L}_1$-normalised, D-dimensional Vectors, $D = K + 1$,

$$\Delta^K = \left\{ [x_1, \ldots, x_D] | 0 \le x_i \le 1,\ \sum_{i=1}^{D} x_i = 1 \right\}, \text{ where } D = K + 1,$$

for example, $K = 2$ (Figs. 9.1 and 9.2). Note that $0 \le x_i \le 1$.

A second, equivalent definition is

$$\left\{ [x_1, \ldots, x_K] | 0 \le x_i \le 1,\ \sum_{i=1}^{K} x_i \le 1 \right\},$$

for example Fig. 9.3; the first definition is preferred as it has the advantage of greater symmetry and everything that follows is in terms of it.

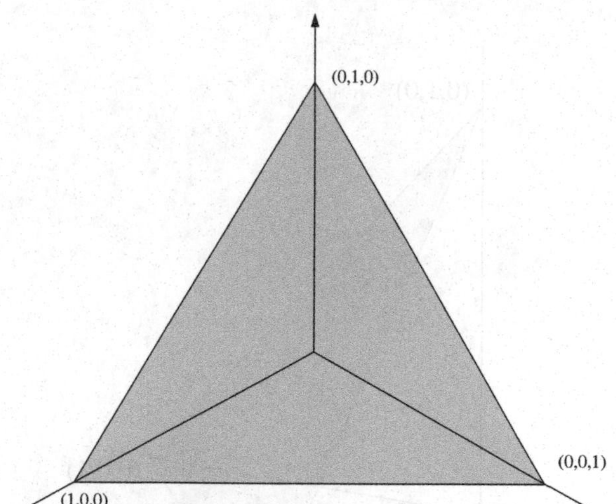

Fig. 9.2 The standard 2-Simplex Δ^2 rotated in $\mathbb{R}^3$

A value in the K-Simplex can be used to represent the *proportions* of D categories. The D probabilities of a D-state probability distribution (Sect. 2.3) model and of a D-nomial probability distribution (Sect. 5.2) model form a point in the K-Simplex.

9.2.1 Uniform

The simplest model over a K-Simplex is the Uniform distribution. The size (length, area, volume, ...) of the standard K-Simplex in $\mathbb{R}^D$ is $\frac{\sqrt{K+1}}{K!}$. The uniform probability density is the inverse of the size.

9.2.2 Implementation

In an implementation of a model over the K-`Simplex`, the unparameterised `UPModel`, such as `Simplex.Uniform`, generally takes `K` as a problem defining parameter. There is a choice to be made over whether the fully parameterised `Model`'s negative log probability function, `nlPdf(d)`, should accept $\mathbb{L}_1$-normalised $D = K + 1$-element, or bounded, unnormalised K-element Vectors. The first option is taken here as arguably it has advantages of symmetry but it is important to remember that a datum nevertheless has K degrees of freedom, not D, which has implications when considering its negative log accuracy of measurement, `nlAoM`, for example. A data value can be generated uniformly at `random` [24]

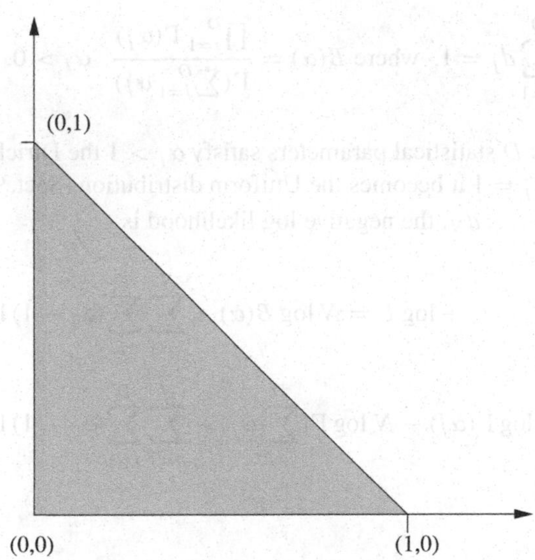

Fig. 9.3 Alternatively, the standard 2-Simplex Δ^2 in $\mathbb{R}^2$

by generating D components from an Exponential distribution (Sect. 4.2) and $\mathbb{L}_1$-normalising the resulting Vector.

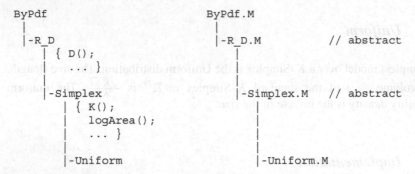

```
ByPdf                          ByPdf.M
 |                               |
 |-R_D                           |-R_D.M             // abstract
    | { D();                        |
    |   ... }                       |
    |                               |
    |-Simplex                       |-Simplex.M      // abstract
       | { K();                        |
       |   logArea();                  |
       |   ... }                       |
       |                               |
       |-Uniform                       |-Uniform.M
```

UnParameterised models Parameterised models

9.2.3 Dirichlet

The Dirichlet distribution is another model over the K-Simplex, $K = D - 1$,

$$\text{pdf}(\vec{d}|\vec{\alpha}) = \frac{1}{B(\alpha)} \prod_{j=1}^{D} d_j^{\alpha_j - 1}, \quad 0 \le d_j \le 1,$$

$$\sum_{j=1}^{D} d_j = 1, \text{ where } B(\alpha) = \frac{\prod_{j=1}^{D} \Gamma(\alpha_j)}{\Gamma(\sum_{j=1}^{D} \alpha_j)}, \ \alpha_j > 0.$$

When all of its D statistical parameters satisfy $\alpha_j > 1$ the Dirichlet is unimodal. When all of the $\alpha_j = 1$ it becomes the Uniform distribution (Sect. 9.2.1).

Given data $\vec{d}_1, \ldots, \vec{d}_N$, the negative log likelihood is

$$-\log L = N \log B(\alpha) - \sum_{n=1}^{N} \sum_{j} (\alpha_j - 1) \log d_{nj}$$

$$= N \sum_{j=1}^{D} \log \Gamma(\alpha_j) - N \log \Gamma(\sum_{j=1}^{D} \alpha_j) - \sum_{n=1}^{N} \sum_{j=1}^{D} (\alpha_j - 1) \log d_{nj}$$

so

$$\frac{\partial}{\partial \alpha_i}(-\log L) = N\psi(\alpha_i) - N\psi(\sum_k \alpha_k) - \sum_n \log d_{ni},$$

where ψ is the first polygamma function $\psi(z) = \frac{\partial}{\partial z} \log \Gamma(z)$ also known as the digamma function.

There is no closed form for the maximum likelihood estimator [59], neither for the MML estimator.

The second derivatives are

$$\frac{\partial^2}{\partial \alpha_i^2}(-\log L) = N\psi_1(\alpha_i) - N\psi_1(\sum_k \alpha_k),$$

$$\frac{\partial^2}{\partial \alpha_i\, \partial \alpha_j}(-\log L)) = -N\psi_1(\sum_k \alpha_k)$$

where ψ_1 is the second polygamma function $\psi_1(z) = \frac{\partial^2}{\partial z^2} \log \Gamma(z)$ also known as the trigamma function.

The Fisher information is

$$F = N^D \left\{ \prod_{k=1}^{D} \psi_1(\alpha_k) \right\} \left\{ 1 - \psi_1(\sum_k \alpha_k) \left(\sum_{k=1}^{D} \frac{1}{\psi_1(\alpha_k)} \right) \right\}$$

this is because

$$\begin{aligned} \begin{pmatrix} a-z & -z \\ -z & b-z \end{pmatrix} &= \begin{pmatrix} a-z & -z \\ -a & b \end{pmatrix} \\ &= ab - zb - za \\ &= ab(1 - z(1/a + 1/b)), \end{aligned}$$

and

$$\begin{aligned} \begin{pmatrix} a-z & -z & -z \\ -z & b-z & -z \\ -z & -z & c-z \end{pmatrix} &= \begin{pmatrix} a-z & -z & -z \\ -a & b & 0 \\ -a & 0 & c \end{pmatrix} \\ &= (a-z)bc - zac - zab \\ &= abc(1 - z(1/a + 1/b + 1/c)), \end{aligned}$$

etc.

The `Dirichlet` is often used as a prior distribution over the parameters of the MultiState (Sect. 2.3) and Multinomial (Sect. 5.2) distributions because it is a *conjugate* prior for them: With this prior, the posterior distribution over the parameters is also a Dirichlet. The α_i minus one can be taken as pseudo-counts prior to seeing any real data and, in the posterior, the frequencies of values in the data-set are added to them. An estimator is unnecessary for this role.

9.3 Directions in $\mathbb{R}^D$

A K-Sphere is the surface of a ball in $D = K + 1$-dimensional space, $\mathbb{R}^D$, for example Fig. 9.4. There are K degrees of freedom (dimensions) in a K-Sphere itself, that is to say in the set of points making up the Sphere. For example, a globe—a model of the earth—is a two-Sphere. The K-Sphere having unit radius is denoted by S^K. A *Direction* in $\mathbb{R}^D$ can be represented by an $\mathbb{L}_2$-normalised Vector, that is by a point in S^K.

$$S^K = \{[x_1, \ldots, x_D] | \sum_{i=1}^{D} x_i^2 = 1\}, \text{ where } D = K + 1 \text{ and } K \geq 0,$$

$$S^0 = \{-1, +1\},$$

S^1 a circle,

S^2 an everyday sphere.

In general the size, the surface area of an K-Sphere, $K > 0$, of radius r is

$$A = ((2\pi)^{(K+1)/2} r^K) / \Gamma((K + 1)/2),$$

$$K = 1, \quad A = 2\pi r,$$

$$K = 2, \quad A = 4\pi r^2.$$

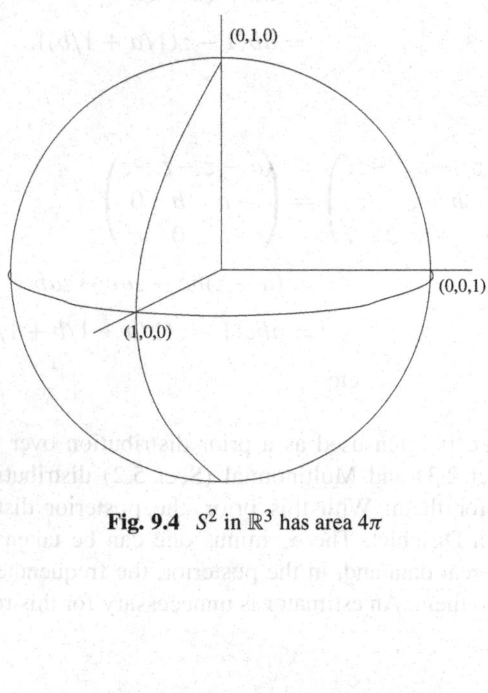

Fig. 9.4 S^2 in $\mathbb{R}^3$ has area 4π

9.3.1 *Uniform*

The simplest model of Directions in $\mathbb{R}^D$, equivalently points on the K-Sphere S^K, is Uniform. The probability density is the inverse of the Sphere's area.

In the implementation the unparameterised model, `Direction.Uniform`, takes the dimension `D` as problem defining parameter. The trivially fully parameterised `Model`, `Direction.Uniform.M`, accepts normalised D-dimensional Vectors as data for `pr(d)`, and `nlPr(d)`. It generates a `random` Direction by generating values for D Vector components from a Normal distribution (Sect. 4.3) and normalising the result [55].

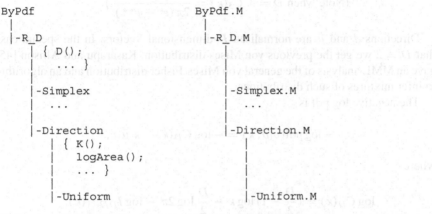

```
ByPdf                               ByPdf.M
 |                                   |
 |-R_D                               |-R_D.M
    | { D();                            |
    |   ... }                           |
    |                                   |
    |-Simplex                           |-Simplex.M
    |   ...                             |   ...
    |                                   |
    |-Direction                         |-Direction.M
       | { K();                            |
       |   logArea();                      |
       |   ... }                           |
       |                                   |
       |-Uniform                           |-Uniform.M
```

UnParameterised models   Parameterised models

9.3.2 *von Mises–Fisher (vMF) Distribution*

The von Mises distribution, which is a special case of the von Mises-Fisher distribution, is a probability distribution for Directions in $\mathbb{R}^2$, for points on the circle S^1. Such a point can be represented as a normalised two-dimensional Vector $d = \langle x, y \rangle$ where $x^2 + y^2 = 1$, or more commonly by an angle $\theta \in [0, 2\pi)$ where $x = \cos\theta$ and $y = \sin\theta$,

$$\text{pdf}(\theta|\mu, \kappa) = \frac{e^{\kappa \cos(\theta-\mu)}}{2\pi I_0(\kappa)}, \text{ where } \kappa \geq 0, \text{ and } \theta, \mu \in [0, 2\pi).$$

$I_0(.)$ is the modified Bessel function of order 0. μ is the mean Direction and κ is the concentration parameter. Wallace and Dowe [95] performed an MML analysis of the von Mises distribution. Note that $\cos(\theta - \mu)$ is the dot product of the datum and mean *Vectors*, $\vec{d} \cdot \vec{\mu}$. When $\kappa = 0$ we get the Uniform distribution

(Sect. 9.3.1). When κ becomes large, and there is little "wrap around" of the circle, the von Mises distribution approaches a Normal distribution (Sect. 4.3) with mean μ and variance $\frac{1}{\kappa}$.

The more general von Mises-Fisher (vMF) distribution [32] for Directions in $\mathbb{R}^D$ of arbitrary dimension D, and equivalently points on S^K where $K = D - 1$, has

$$\mathrm{pdf}(\vec{d}\,|\vec{\mu}, \kappa) = C_D(\kappa) e^{\kappa\, \vec{\mu}.\vec{d}},$$

$$\text{where } C_D(\kappa) = \frac{\kappa^{D/2-1}}{(2\pi)^{D/2} I_{D/2-1}(\kappa)},$$

$$\kappa \geq 0,\ \|\vec{d}\|_2 = \|\vec{\mu}\|_2 = 1.$$

$$(\text{Note when } D = 3,\ C_3(\kappa) = \frac{\kappa}{2\pi(e^{\kappa} - e^{-\kappa})}.)$$

Directions $\vec{d}$ and $\vec{\mu}$ are normalised D-dimensional Vectors. In the special case that $D = 2$ we get the previous von Mises distribution. Kasarapu and Allison [45] gave an MML analysis of the general von Mises-Fisher distribution and an algorithm to infer mixtures of such distributions.

The negative log pdf is

$$-\log \mathrm{pdf}(\vec{v}\,|\vec{\mu}, \kappa) = -\log C_D(\kappa) - \kappa\, \vec{\mu}.\vec{v},$$

where

$$\log C_D(\kappa) = (\frac{D}{2} - 1)\log \kappa - \frac{D}{2}\log 2\pi - \log I_{D/2-1}(\kappa).$$

Given data $[\vec{d}_1, \ldots, \vec{d}_N]$, define their sum, a D-Vector, by

$$\vec{R} = \sum_{i=1}^{N} \vec{d}_i,$$

and the scalar

$$\bar{R} = \|\vec{R}\|/N.$$

The negative log likelihood is

$$-\log L = -N \log C_D(\kappa) - \kappa\, \vec{\mu}.\vec{R}.$$

It is obvious that the maximum likelihood estimate of $\vec{\mu}$ is $\vec{R}$, normalised,

$$\hat{\mu}_{ML} = \vec{R}/\|\vec{R}\|,$$

and that the MML estimate is the same,

$$\hat{\mu}_{MML} = \hat{\mu}_{ML} = \vec{R}/\|\vec{R}\|,$$

the blandest, most general *prior* for $\vec{\mu}$ being the uniform distribution.

For given $\vec{\mu}$ and κ, the *expected* value of $\bar{R}$ [80] is

$$A_D(\kappa) = I_{D/2}(\kappa)/I_{D/2-1}(\kappa),$$

and the (less obvious) maximum likelihood estimate of κ is

$$\hat{\kappa}_{ML} = A_D^{-1}\bar{R}.$$

This is because

$$\frac{\partial}{\partial\kappa}(-\log L) = -N\frac{\partial}{\partial\kappa}\log C_D(\kappa) - \vec{\mu}.\vec{R}$$

which is zero if

$$-\frac{\partial}{\partial\kappa}\log C_D(\kappa) = \vec{\mu}.\vec{R}/N,$$

where

$$\begin{aligned}
\frac{\partial}{\partial\kappa}\log C_D(\kappa) &= \omega/\kappa - I'_\omega(\kappa)/I_\omega(\kappa), \text{ where } \omega = \frac{D}{2} - 1 \\
&= \omega\{I_\omega(\kappa) - \frac{\kappa}{\omega}I'_\omega(\kappa)\}/(\kappa I_\omega(\kappa)) \\
&= \omega\{\frac{\kappa}{2\omega}\{I_{\omega-1}(\kappa) - I_{\omega+1}(\kappa)\} - \frac{\kappa}{2\omega}\{I_{\omega-1}(\kappa) + I_{\omega+1}(\kappa)\}\}/(\kappa I_\omega(\kappa)) \\
&= -I_{D/2}(\kappa)/I_{D/2-1}(\kappa),
\end{aligned}$$

using the "well known" relations,

$$I_\nu(z) = \frac{z}{2\nu}\{I_{\nu-1}(z) - I_{\nu+1}(z)\},$$

and

$$I'_\nu(z) = \frac{1}{2}\{I_{\nu-1}(z) + I_{\nu+1}(z)\},\ I'_0(z) = I_1(z).$$

The MML estimate, $\hat{\kappa}_{MML}$, is the value that minimises the two-part message length; no closed form is known for κ_{MML} so a numerical method (Sect. 13.1) must be used to find it. The message length calculations also require the vMF's Fisher information, F, and a choice of prior for κ.

9.3.2.1 Fisher Information of the vMF Distribution

The vMF has D statistical parameters, that is degrees of freedom, $D-1$ in the mean $\vec{\mu}$ and one in κ. The expected second derivative of $-\log L$ with respect to κ is

$$\frac{\partial^2}{\partial\kappa^2}(-\log L) = N\, A'_D(\kappa).$$

The vMF distribution is symmetric about $\vec{\mu}$ on the $(D-1)$-Sphere; there is no preferred orientation around $\vec{\mu}$. A direction, such as $\vec{\mu}$, has $D-1$ degrees of freedom. The expected second derivative of $-\log L$ with respect to any one of $\vec{\mu}$'s degrees of freedom is

$$N\kappa A_D(\kappa).$$

This is for the following reason: Without loss of generality, let $\vec{\mu} = (1, 0, \ldots)$, and then $\vec{\mu} \to [\cos\delta, \sin\delta, 0, \ldots]$, say, where δ is small,

$$\frac{\partial}{\partial\delta}(-\log L) = N\kappa \|\vec{R}\| \sin\delta,$$

$$\frac{\partial^2}{\partial\delta^2}(-\log L) = N\kappa \|\vec{R}\| \cos\delta \approx N\kappa\|\vec{R}\| \text{as } \delta \text{ is small,}$$

$$\text{which is } N\kappa A_D(\kappa) \text{ in expectation.}$$

Symmetry implies that the off-diagonal elements of F for $\vec{\mu}$ are zero. And, $\vec{\mu}$ is a position parameter and κ a scale parameter, so the off-diagonal elements between $\vec{\mu}$ and κ are also zero. F, the Fisher information of the vMF is therefore,

$$F = N^D(\kappa A_D(\kappa))^{D-1} A'_D(\kappa).$$

The implementation, `vMF`, is an unparameterised `UPModel` that takes D as problem defining parameter. The statistics, `stats(ds)`, of a data-set `ds` of size N are ⟨`N, R, nlAoM`⟩. The `Estimator` for `vMF` has no non-trivial parameters. The prior on κ is $\text{pr}\kappa = \frac{1}{(k+1)^2}$ but this is simple to change if one prefers another. A rough and ready maximum likelihood estimate for κ of $\bar{R}(D-\bar{R}^2)/(1-\bar{R}^2)$ is used as the starting point to minimise the two-part message length and find $\hat{\kappa}_{MML}$. A little care is required to guarantee that $\|R\| < N$, that $\bar{R} < 1$ even if all the data happen to be colinear as given in the data-set, which might appear to suggest an infinite κ. However, the data are measured to an accuracy of measurement that is strictly > 0 so a little "jitter" is implied and $\hat{\kappa}$ must certainly be finite.

```
ByPdf                       ByPdf.M
 |                           |
 |-R_D                       |-R_D.M
    |                           |
    |-Direction                 |-Direction.M
         |                           |
         |-vMF                       |-vMF.M
                                       { mu;    // mean direction
                                         kappa; // concentration
                                         ... }
```

UnParameterised models — Parameterised models

The fully parameterised model `vMF.M` takes $\langle \mu, \kappa \rangle$ as its statistical parameters. A `random()` Direction is generated by Wood's method [101].

Chapter 10
Linear Regression

A linear regression is a form of function-model (Chaps. 5, 8) between continuous variables. An output (dependent) variable y is approximated by a function $f(x)$ of an input (independent) variable x with the error, $y - f(x)$, being modelled by a model of continuous data (Chap. 4), most commonly by the Normal distribution (Sect. 4.3).

10.1 Single Variable

In linear regression with a single input (independent) variable x and a single output (dependent) variable y we have

$$\begin{aligned} y &= f_{a,b}(x) + \mathcal{N}(0, \sigma) \\ &= ax + b + \mathcal{N}(0, \sigma) \\ &= \mathcal{N}(ax + b, \sigma) \end{aligned}$$

y is approximated by a straight line with slope a and intercept b (Fig. 10.1).

The data are of the form

$$\langle x_1, y_1 \pm \frac{\epsilon_1}{2} \rangle, \ldots, \langle x_N, y_N \pm \frac{\epsilon_N}{2} \rangle$$

As for all function-models, the input data, the x_i, are common knowledge (Chap. 5).

Recall the Normal distribution $\mathcal{N}_{\mu,\sigma}$ (Sect. 4.3) which has

$$\text{pdf}(z) = \frac{1}{\sigma\sqrt{2\pi}} e^{-\frac{(z-\mu)^2}{2\sigma^2}}$$

L. Allison, *Coding Ockham's Razor*, https://doi.org/10.1007/978-3-319-76433-7_10

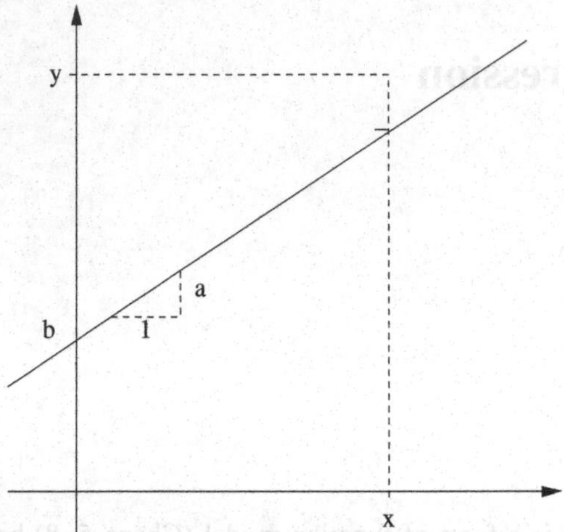

Fig. 10.1 $y = ax + b + N_{0,\sigma}$

The negative log likelihood for the y_i given the x_i is

$$-\log L = N\left(\log\sigma + \frac{1}{2}\log 2\pi\right) + \frac{1}{2\sigma^2}\sum_{i=1}^{N}(y_i - ax_i - b)^2 - \sum_{i=1}^{N}\log\epsilon_i$$

The first derivatives are

$$\frac{\partial}{\partial a}(-\log L) = -\frac{1}{\sigma^2}\sum_{i=1}^{N}x_i(y_i - ax_i - b)$$

$$= \frac{1}{\sigma^2}\left\{a\sum_{i=1}^{N}x_i^2 - \sum_{i=1}^{N}x_i(y_i - b)\right\}$$

$$\frac{\partial}{\partial b}(-\log L) = -\frac{1}{\sigma^2}\sum_{i=1}^{N}(y_i - ax_i - b)$$

$$= -\frac{N}{\sigma^2}(\bar{y} - a\bar{x} - b), \quad \text{where } \bar{y} \text{ is the mean of the } y_i$$

$$\frac{\partial}{\partial \sigma}(-\log L) = \frac{N}{\sigma} - \frac{1}{\sigma^3}\sum_{i=1}^{N}(y_i - ax_i - b)^2$$

Setting the first derivatives to zero, the maximum likelihood estimates satisfy

$$\hat{a}_{ML}\sum_{i=1}^{N}x_i^2 = \sum_{i=1}^{N}x_i(y_i - \hat{b}_{ML})$$

$$\hat{b}_{ML} = \bar{y} - \hat{a}_{ML}\bar{x}$$

showing that the line passes through $\langle \bar{x}, \bar{y} \rangle$, the centre of gravity of the $\langle x_i, y_i \rangle$ (Fig. 10.2). The residual variance is $\hat{\sigma}^2_{ML}$ as per usual (Sect. 4.3).

Substituting, we get

$$\hat{a}_{ML} = \sum_{i=1}^{N} x_i (y_i - \bar{y}) \Big/ \left(\sum_{i=1}^{N} x_i^2 - \bar{x} \sum_{i=1}^{N} x_i \right)$$

The second derivatives are

$$\frac{\partial^2}{\partial a^2}(-\log L) = \frac{1}{\sigma^2} \sum_{i=1}^{N} x_i^2$$

$$\frac{\partial^2}{\partial a\, \partial b}(-\log L) = \frac{1}{\sigma^2} \sum_{i=1}^{N} x_i$$

$$\frac{\partial^2}{\partial a\, \partial \sigma}(-\log L) = \frac{2}{\sigma^3} \sum_{i=1}^{N} x_i (y_i - a x_i - b), \qquad \text{expectation} = 0$$

$$\frac{\partial^2}{\partial b^2}(-\log L) = \frac{N}{\sigma^2}$$

$$\frac{\partial^2}{\partial b\, \partial \sigma}(-\log L) = \frac{2}{\sigma^3} \sum_{i=1}^{N} (y_i - a x_i - b), \qquad \text{expectation} = 0$$

$$\frac{\partial^2}{\partial \sigma^2}(-\log L) = -\frac{N}{\sigma^2} + \frac{3}{\sigma^4} \sum_{i=1}^{N} (y_i - a x_i - b)^2, \quad \text{expectation} = \frac{2N}{\sigma^2}$$

The Fisher information matrix of expected second derivatives is

$$\left(\frac{N}{\sigma^2}\right)^3 \begin{pmatrix} \overline{x^2} & \bar{x} & 0 \\ \bar{x} & 1 & 0 \\ 0 & 0 & 2 \end{pmatrix} = 2 \left(\frac{N}{\sigma^2}\right)^3 (\overline{x^2} - \bar{x}^2)$$

Unsurprisingly this somewhat resembles the case of $\mathcal{N}_{\mu,\sigma}$ (Sect. 4.3)—given that here a and b (and the x_i), are supplying μ.

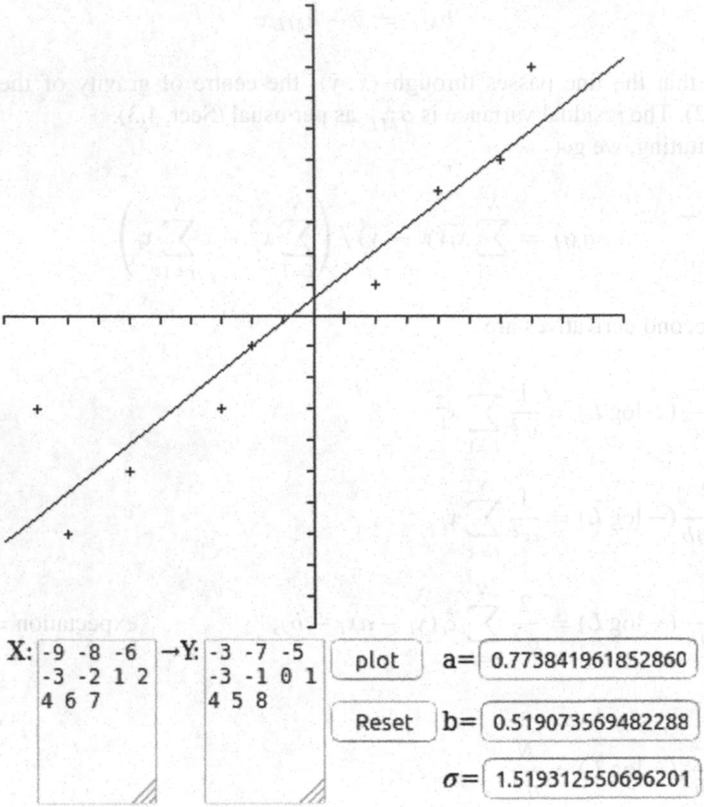

Fig. 10.2 $y = ax + b + \mathcal{N}(0, \sigma)$

A possible prior on the parameters is uniform on the slope angle $\phi = \tan^{-1}(a)$, uniform in b over some range $[b_{min}, b_{max}]$, and $\frac{1}{\sigma}$ on σ over some range $[\sigma_{min}, \sigma_{max}]$.

10.1.1 Implementation

The unparameterised function-model, `Linear1`, has no problem-defining parameters so an implementation need only provide a single instance `MML.Linear1`. It has an estimator, `Linear1.Est`, which can produce a fully parameterised model, `Linear1.M`. The estimator exposes the negative log prior, `nlPrior(, ,)`, which can be overridden if desired.

10.2 Single Dependence

The Mixture model described earlier (Chap. 7) found a mixture of five components (classes) when applied to the Anderson [4, 5]–Fisher [30] Iris data (Sect. 7.4). The data consist of the length and width of the sepal, and the length and width of the petal, of 50 flowers from each of the three species Iris-setosa, Iris-verginica, and Iris-versicolor. The mixture was found under the assumption that the four measurements are independent. This assumption is likely to be false for such *sizes*; it is reasonable to anticipate some correlation between them because changes in size tend to apply to all or most measurements.

Forest is a simple model of $\mathbb{R}^D$ that allows a column (a variable) of the data to depend on at most one other, to have at most one *parent*. The parent-child relationships define a forest, of one or more trees, over the columns.

```
UPModel                              UPModel.M
 |                                    |
 |-ByPdf                              |-ByPdf.M
    |                                    |
    |-R_D                                |-R_D.M
       |                                    |
       |-NrmDir, Simplex,                   |-NrmDir.M, etc
       | Direction, etc                     |
       |                                    |
       |-Forest                             |-Forest.M
          { parents; ... }                     { Nrml; Lin1; ... }

UnParameterised Models               Parameterised Models
```

In the implementation, the unparameterised model, `Forest` takes a vector of parents as its problem defining parameter; a negative number indicates "no parent". The fully parameterised Model, `Forest.M`, contains `Nrml` an array of Normal (Sect. 4.3) models, one for each column that has no parent, and `Lin1` an array of Linear1 (Sect. 10.1) function-models, one for each column that has a parent. (It would be straightforward to generalise `Forest` take sub-models, other than Normal and Linear1, as problem defining parameters.)

It is plausible that the length and breadth of a part of an Iris are dependent and that the dimensions of one part are dependent on another part, see for example Fig. 10.3. In this case the forest is a single tree. The first measurement (`@0`) has no parent (`-1`).

When a single `Forest` model and a `Mixture` of `Forests` model are fitted to the Iris data they beat the single `Normal`×4 and the `Mixture` of `Normals`×4 models (Sect. 7.4) respectively by wide margins.

```
msg = 1873. = 49.34 + 1823.  (nits)
    = 2702. = 71.19 + 2630.  (bits)
```

The One-Class Forest Model

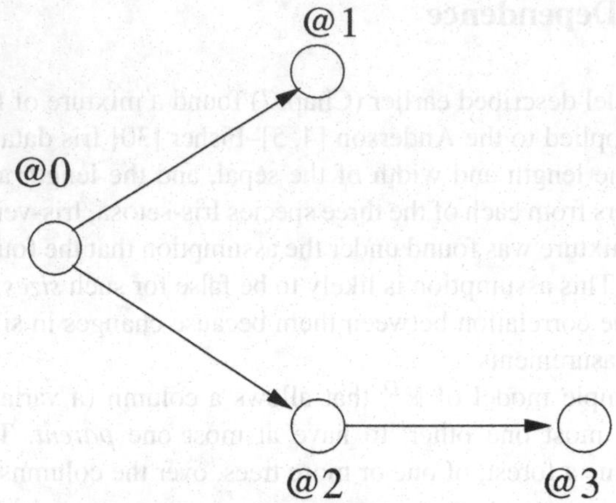

Fig. 10.3 Forest suitable for Iris parents = −1, 0, 0, 2

```
msg = 1711. = 100.2 + 1611. (nits)
    = 2469. = 144.6 + 2325. (bits)
```

The Mixture of Forests Model

This time `Mixture` finds just two classes, one for *Iris-setosa* and one for everything else.

```
  Classes
  0     1
50.0,  0.0, -- Iris-setosa
 0.0, 50.0, -- Iris-versicolor
 0.0, 50.0, -- Iris-virginica
```

Classes v. Species

Just as before (Sect. 7.4), we can "cheat" by using the species information—which was not given to `Mixture`—to build a mixture model of three classes, one class per species:

```
msg = 1718. = 139. + 1579. (nits)
    = 2479. = 200. + 2279. (bits)
```

Results for the "Cheating" 3-Class Mixture

And, as before, this is a worse model than the one found by `Mixture`. (Recall, "[Randolph suggested that possibly I.versicolor] is a polyploid hybrid of the two other species" [30, §VI, p. 185].)

There are many other statistical techniques for modelling correlated variables. Two examples in the MML research literature are single factor analysis [97] and multiple factor analysis [90]. (They are not yet in the Java mml package (Chap. 13).)

10.2.1 Unknown Single Dependence

If we do not know a plausible Forest of dependencies (Sect. 10.2), `ForestSearch` can be used to search for one. The model's *structure*—the parents—is now one of the statistical parameters that must be estimated.

Statistics for the purposes of estimating a model `stats()` must be enough to calculate all *possible* variable to variable dependencies so as to compare them. Once a parameterised model `ForestSearch.M` has been settled upon, only statistics for the particular structure `stats()` are needed for the negative log likelihood, `nlLH(.)`.

10.3 Multiple Input Variables

When there are several input variables $\vec{x} = \langle x_1, \ldots x_D\rangle$, then y is approximated by a *plane*

$$\begin{aligned} y &= f_{\vec{a}b\sigma}(\vec{x}) + \mathcal{N}(0,\sigma) \\ &= \left(\sum_{j=1}^{D} a_j x_j\right) + b + \mathcal{N}(0,\sigma) \\ &= \vec{a}\cdot\vec{x} + b + \mathcal{N}(0,\sigma) \end{aligned}$$

The data takes the form

$$\langle \vec{x_1}, y_1\rangle,\ \ \ldots,\ \langle \vec{x_N}, y_N\rangle$$

equivalently

$$\langle\langle x_{11},\ldots,x_{1D}\rangle, y_1 \pm \frac{\epsilon_1}{2}\rangle,\ \ \ldots,\ \langle\langle x_{N1},\ldots,x_{ND}\rangle, y_N \pm \frac{\epsilon_N}{2}\rangle$$

equivalently

$$X,\ \vec{y} = \begin{pmatrix} x_{11} \ldots x_{1D} \\ . \\ . \\ . \\ x_{N1} \ldots x_{ND} \end{pmatrix}, \begin{pmatrix} y_1 \\ . \\ . \\ . \\ y_N \end{pmatrix}$$

It is customary to consider each $\vec{x_i}$ to be augmented with an extra element that is equal one, $\vec{x_+} = \langle x_1, \ldots, x_D, x_{D+1} = 1\rangle$

$$X_+ = \begin{pmatrix} x_{11} \ldots x_{1D} \; 1 \\ . \\ . \\ . \\ x_{N1} \ldots x_{ND} \; 1 \end{pmatrix}$$

and to turn b into an extra last element of $\vec{a_+} = \langle a_1, \ldots, a_D, a_{D+1} = b\rangle$ which allows the model to be written as $y = f_{\vec{a_+}\sigma}(\vec{x_+}) + \mathcal{N}(0, \sigma) = \vec{a_+} \cdot \vec{x_+} + \mathcal{N}(0, \sigma)$. This is just a convenience that simplifies the working.

The negative log likelihood for $\vec{y}$ is

$$-\log L = N\left(\log\sigma + \frac{1}{2}\log 2\pi\right) + \frac{1}{2\sigma^2}\sum_{i=1}^{N}(y_i - \vec{x_{i+}} \cdot \vec{a_+})^2 - \sum_{i=1}^{N}\log\epsilon_i$$

It can be seen that statistics for calculating the negative log likelihood are $N, X_+^T X_+, Y^T X_+, Y \cdot Y$, and the negative log accuracy of measurement (nlAoM) of Y.

The first derivatives of the negative log likelihood are

$$\begin{aligned} \frac{\partial}{\partial a_k}(-\log L) &= \frac{-1}{\sigma^2}\sum_{i=1}^{N}\left(y_i - \sum_{j=1}^{D+1} x_{ij}\, a_j\right) x_{ik} \\ &= \frac{1}{\sigma^2}\left\{\left(\sum_j a_j\left(\sum_i x_{ij}x_{ik}\right)\right) - \sum_i x_{ik}\, y_i\right\} \\ \frac{\partial}{\partial\sigma}(-\log L) &= \frac{N}{\sigma} - \frac{1}{\sigma^3}\sum_{i=1}^{N}(y_i - x_{i+} \cdot a_+)^2 \end{aligned}$$

L is maximised, $-\log L$ is minimised, when the plane goes through the centre of gravity of the data points and its slope(s) set the first derivatives to zero.

$$\hat{a}_{+ML} = \left(X_+^T X_+\right)^{-1} X_+^T\vec{y}$$

$\hat{\sigma}$ is as for the Normal (Sect. 4.3).

The second derivatives are

$$\frac{\partial^2}{\partial a_k^2}(-\log L) = \frac{1}{\sigma^2}\sum_{i=1}^{N} x_{ik}^2 = (X_+^T X_+)_{kk}$$

$$\frac{\partial^2}{\partial a_k\,\partial a_l}(-\log L) = \frac{1}{\sigma^2}\sum_{i=1}^{N} x_{ik}\,x_{il} = (X_+^T X_+)_{kl}$$

$$\frac{\partial^2}{\partial a_k\,\partial \sigma}(-\log L) = \frac{2}{\sigma^3}\sum_{i=1}^{N}\left(\left(y_i - \sum_{j=1}^{D+1} x_{ij}a_j\right)x_{ik}\right), \qquad \text{expectation} = 0$$

$$\frac{\partial^2}{\partial \sigma^2}(-\log L) = \frac{-N}{\sigma^2} + \frac{3}{\sigma^4}\sum_{i=1}^{N}\left(y_i - \sum_{j=1}^{D+1} x_{ij}a_j\right)^2, \quad \text{expectation} = \frac{2N}{\sigma^2}$$

Remember that the expectations are for y, given $\vec{x}$. The $(D+2)\times(D+2)$ Fisher information matrix is

$$\frac{1}{\sigma^{2(D+2)}}\begin{pmatrix} \begin{pmatrix} X_+^T X_+ \end{pmatrix} & \begin{matrix} 0 \\ \vdots \end{matrix} \\ 0 \ \ldots & 2N \end{pmatrix}$$

10.3.1 Implementation

The Linear model with multiple input variables has been implemented as `LinearD` in the Java `mml package` (Chap. 13). `LinearD` takes `D`, the dimension of the input data space, as its problem defining parameter. The fully parameterised model `LinearD.M` takes ⟨`a,sigma`⟩ ($\langle\vec{a},\sigma\rangle$) as its statistical parameter but note that '`a`' has `D+1` elements, the last one being the constant term (b). The estimator `LinearD.Est` exposes the negative log prior, `nlPrior(.,.)`, so that it can be overridden if necessary.

Chapter 11
Graphs

This chapter is concerned with statistical models of graphs including some models based on motifs (patterns, subgraphs) that may occur frequently in graphs. The properties of families of graphs is a venerable but still current research area and the chapter is an example of applying MML and the accompanying software (Chap. 13) to something challenging. In addition, graphs are quite useful things: They are also known as networks and can represent many kinds of data—finite-state automata [36, 39], electronic circuits, road maps, social networks of "friends", chemical compounds, and protein-protein interactions to name just a few.

A *graph*, G, consists of a non-empty set of *vertices*, $V = \{v_0, \ldots v_{|V|-1}\}$, and a set of *edges*, E. That is $G = \langle V, E\rangle$ where $|V| \geq 1$[1] and $|E| \geq 0$. The term *node* is sometimes used as an alternative to vertex, and *arc* as an alternative to edge.

A graph may be directed or undirected. In a *directed* graph each edge consists of an ordered pair of vertices, $\langle v_i, v_j\rangle$, and it has a direction, from v_i to v_j. $\langle v_j, v_i\rangle$ is quite a different edge to $\langle v_i, v_j\rangle$. In an *undirected* graph each edge consists of an unordered pair of vertices, (v_i, v_j); in this case (v_j, v_i) is considered to be the very same edge as (v_i, v_j), just another way of writing it. If it is allowable for v_i to equal v_j, an Edge such as $\langle v_i, v_i\rangle$ or (v_i, v_i) is called a self-loop or just a *loop*.

The *degree* of a vertex is the number of edges involving the vertex. If loops are allowed, a loop contributes two to the degree of its vertex. In a directed graph, the *in-degree* of a vertex v is the number of edges of the form $\langle ?, v\rangle$, the *out-degree* of v is the number of edges of the form $\langle v, ?\rangle$ and $\text{degree}(v) = \text{inDegree}(v) + \text{outDegree}(v)$, as in Table 11.1.

A graph that has close to the maximum possible number of edges is said to be *dense*. A graph that has far fewer edges than the maximum possible number of edges is said to be *sparse*. The terms "close to" and "far fewer" are imprecise, particularly when considering a single graph, but if a family of graphs of varying sizes is such that $|E|$ grows much more slowly than $|V|^2$, that is $|E|$ is $o(|V|^2)$, then a large

[1] The general consensus is that $|V| \geq 1$ and that $\langle\{\}, \{\}\rangle$ is not a graph.

L. Allison, *Coding Ockham's Razor*, https://doi.org/10.1007/978-3-319-76433-7_11

	Loops allowed	Loops disallowed
Directed	$\|V\|^2$	$\|V\|.(\|V\|-1)$
Undirected	$\|V\|.(\|V\|+1)/2$	$\|V\|.(\|V\|-1)/2$

Table 11.1 The maximum possible number of edges, $maxEdges(|V|)$, in a graph

member of the family will certainly be sparse. This is the case in, for example, a family of graphs of bounded vertex degree. At the risk of being shot down for making a vast generalisation, most graphs derived from real-world data are sparse.

A graph may be unlabelled, vertex-labelled, edge-labelled, or both vertex- and edge-labelled. For example, omitting chirality, a chemical compound can be represented by an undirected graph where each vertex is labelled with a chemical element and each edge is labelled with a bond type [2]. An edge-labelled graph where the edge labels are numerical is commonly called a weighted graph. A graph where each vertex is numbered by a unique integer in $[0, |V|)$ is called an *ordered* graph.

There are many generalisations of graphs, for example, a multigraph may have multiple edges with the same end vertices (normal graphs may not). And a hypergraph contains hyperedges where each hyperedge is a set of vertices. Here however we are concerned with plain ordinary graphs, directed or undirected, mostly unlabelled, mostly sparse.

Models of graphs, some based on the ideas of Gilbert, Erdos and Renyi (Sect. 11.4), a Skewed model (Sect. 11.6), and motif models (Sect. 11.7) are described after some preliminaries. In passing there are some special cases, for example, a tree is a graph and we saw (Sect. 3.2) that a full (rooted) binary tree can be encoded in $|V|+1$ bits, a tree of arbitrary and variable arity can be encoded in $2|V|-1$ bits, and a plane graph—one that can be embedded in the plane without edge crossings—can be encoded in less than 4 bits per edge [84].

11.1 Ordered or Unordered Graphs

A natural starting point to the modelling of graphs is to consider models of graphs that work by encoding the adjacency matrix of a graph. In the case of an *ordered* graph, the numbering of the vertices, which is a permutation of the vertices, specifies a permutation of the rows and columns of the adjacency matrix. And this permutation of the rows and columns matters: A decoding must reproduce the adjacency matrix with that same ordering. In the case of an unordered graph, it is only necessary to produce an equivalent adjacency matrix that equals the original under *some* renumbering (permutation) of the vertices, of rows and columns.

Graphs G_1 and G_2 (undirected) are *isomorphic* if $|V_{G_1}| = |V_{G_2}|$ and if (u, v) is an edge of G if and only if $(\rho\, u, \rho\, v)$ is an edge of G_2 for some one-to-one function $\rho : V_{G_1} \to V_{G_2}$.

$$\forall u, v \in V_{G_1},\ (u, v) \text{ is an edge of } G_1 \iff (\rho\, u, \rho\, v) \text{ is an edge of } G_2.$$

Similarly for directed graphs. When it comes to algorithms [56, 57], graph isomorphism is clearly in the complexity class NP but it is not known if it is in P or if it is in NPC; Babai has claimed a quasipolynomial-time algorithm [7].

An *automorphism* of a graph G, that is an isomorphism of G with itself, is a renumbering (permutation) ρ of the vertices of G that gives the very same ordered graph.

For example, the directed graph

$$G = \langle V = \{u, v, w\},\ E = \{\langle u, v\rangle, \langle v, u\rangle, \langle u, w\rangle, \langle v, w\rangle\}\rangle$$

has three vertices and four edges (Fig. 11.1).

G has two automorphisms: the identity, ι, and swap u with v, $u \leftrightarrow v$.

There are three different versions of its adjacency matrix depending whether vertex w is given the number 0, 1 or 2, Fig. 11.2.

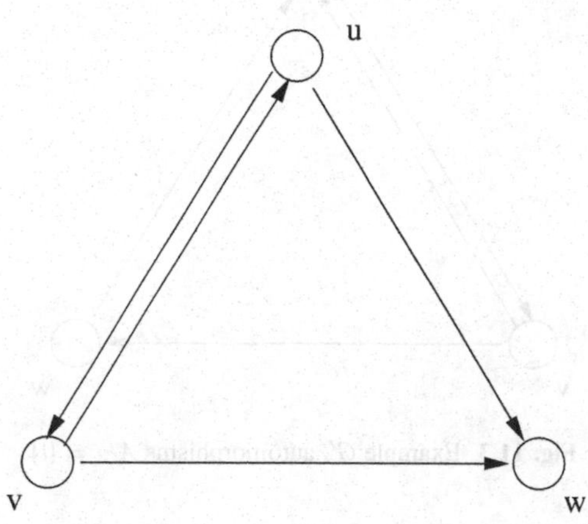

Fig. 11.1 Example graph, G

```
        u v w          u w v          w u v
0   u: 0 1 1      u: 0 1 1      w: 0 0 0
1   v: 1 0 1      w: 0 0 0      u: 1 0 1
2   w: 0 0 0      v: 1 1 0      v: 1 1 0

        v u w          v w u          w v u
0   v: 0 1 1      v: 0 1 1      w: 0 0 0
1   u: 1 0 1      w: 0 0 0      v: 1 0 1
2   w: 0 0 0      u: 1 1 0      u: 1 1 0
```

Fig. 11.2 Top row $\leftrightarrow$ bottom row, $u \leftrightarrow v$

The automorphisms A_G of a graph G form a mathematical *group*: The identity permutation, ι, is obviously an automorphism. The product of two permutations is defined to be their functional composition and the product of two automorphisms can be seen to be an automorphism. And, every automorphism has an inverse permutation which can also be seen to be an automorphism.

If an unordered graph G has some non-trivial automorphisms not all orderings of its vertices are distinguishable: $\frac{|V|!}{|A_G|}$ different adjacency matrices can be obtained by ordering the vertices (by permuting rows and columns of the matrix) in various ways. But renumbering the vertices according to a member of the automorphism group leaves the adjacency matrix unchanged. At one extreme the automorphism group can be as large as the *symmetric group*, S_V, of all permutations of V—for example if $G = K_{|V|}$ the complete graph—in which case every renumbering gives the same adjacency matrix. At the other extreme the automorphism group can be as small as $\{\iota\}$ (Fig. 11.3), when every renumbering gives a different adjacency matrix.

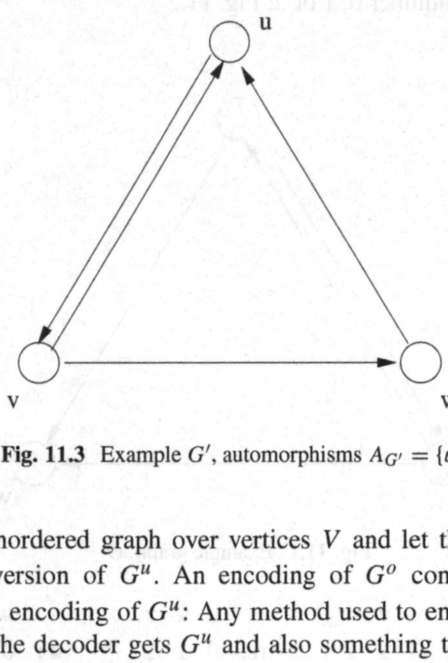

Fig. 11.3 Example G', automorphisms $A_{G'} = \{\iota\}$

Let G^u be an unordered graph over vertices V and let the ordered graph G^o be some ordered version of G^u. An encoding of G^o contains $\log \frac{|V|!}{|A_{G^u}|}$ more information than an encoding of G^u: Any method used to encode G^o can be used to encode G^u, but the decoder gets G^u and also something they do not need, that is one of the $\frac{|V|!}{|A^{G^u}|}$ distinguishable orderings of V. That extra information (message length) can be recovered in various ways. For example, given a data-set of several unordered graphs $G^u_1, G^u_2, \ldots, G^u_n$, the transmitter can choose an ordering G^o_i of G^u_i so that the "excess" information in the encoding of G^o_i represents the first $\log_2 \frac{|V_i|!}{|A_{G^u_i}|}$ bits of the encoding of G^o_{i+1}, and so on (except for the last G^u_n). Conversely, any method used to encode G^u can be used to encode G^o by appending an encoding of which one of the $\frac{|V|!}{|A^{G^u}|}$ orderings of G^u it is that gives G^o. So, every model

M^u of unordered graphs corresponds to a model M^o of ordered graphs such that $msg(G^o|M^o) = msg(G^u|M^u) + \log \frac{|V|!}{|A_{G^u}|}$ and vice versa.

In summary, when comparing models of graphs it does not matter whether we consider ordered graphs and their models or we consider unordered graphs and their models, provided that we are consistent and compare like with like.

11.2 Adjacency Matrix v. Adjacency Lists

Note that computer algorithms might store the edges of a graph as an adjacency matrix, or as adjacency lists, depending on the graph being dense or sparse. The decision is made in the interests of an algorithm's space-complexity or time-complexity, or both. As far as the implementation of a model of graphs is concerned, it does not matter one bit from the statistical point of view how a graph is stored, although the choice may well affect the speed or memory usage of an implementation of the model's operations.

11.3 Models of Graphs

When analysing graphs a datum is an individual graph, G, and a data-set, Gs, contains zero or more graphs. For a particular problem the graphs come from some data-space, some population, of graphs and all graphs in the data-space have the same type: directed or undirected, loops allowed or not, unlabelled or labelled.

Ideally an implementation of a fully parameterised statistical model of a data-space of graphs has the usual properties and abilities of a statistical model (Chap. 1), particularly probability `pr(G)` and negative log probability `nlPr(G)`, sufficient statistics `stats(Gs)` and negative log likelihood `nlLH(stats(Gs))`, `random()`, `estimator(.)` and so on. In addition, the probability of `random()` generating a particular graph `G` should be equal to `pr(G)`. Unfortunately not every would-be "model" of graphs fulfils this ideal, for example, it may provide a way to generate its idea of `G = random()`, but not provide a feasible way to calculate `pr(G)`, or vice versa.

11.4 Gilbert, Erdos and Renyi Models

Gilbert [40] and Erdos and Renyi [27] gave descriptions of closely related, simple models of graphs through the generation of random graphs. The former specified that for a given number of vertices, for each pair of vertices the decision to join the two vertices by an edge be made with probability p independently of other such decisions. The latter specified that all graphs having a given number of vertices and a given number of edges are equally probable. Both models leave open the choice of $|V|$ but any distribution over positive integers (Chap. 3) will do. The second model also leaves open the choice of $|E|$ in $[0, maxEdges(|V|)]$. It can be seen that the first model involves exactly a two-state model (Sect. 2.2) with parameter p on the absence and existence of possible edges—the 0s and 1s, or equivalently the Fs and Ts, that are the entries in the graph's adjacency matrix.

It is possible to implement a model of graphs, `GERfixed`, based on the above ideas. It requires a model of positive integers (Chap. 3) to model $|V|$. It uses the `MultiState((0,1))`, that is the two-state model, for the existence of edges. The probability of a graph G depends on `mdlV.pr(|VG|)` and `mdlE.nlLH(ss)` where `mdlV` is the model of $|V|$, `mdlE` is the model of edge existence, and `ss` is the statistics of the entries in the graph's adjacency matrix—the numbers of non-edges (0s) and edges (1s). The `Estimator` of `GERfixed` accepts a parameter on behalf of the `Estimator` of `mdlV`. A `random()` graph is generated by having `mdlV` choose a random number of vertices $|V|$ and having `mdlE` fill in the adjacency matrix at random.

Because of the close relationship between `GERfixed`, `GERadaptive` (see below) and potentially other models, it is convenient to create the following class hierarchy:

```
UPModel                      UPModel.M
 |                            |
 |-Graphs                     |-Graphs.M
    |{ upmV;                     |{ mdlV;   // *V for # vertices
    | ... }                      | ... }
    |                            |
    |-IndependentEdges           |-IndependentEdges.M
       |{ upmE;                     |{ mdlE; // *E for # edges
       | ... }                      | ... }
       |                            |
       |-GERfixed                   |-GERfixed.M
       |                            |
       |-GERadaptive                |-GERadaptive.M

UnParameterised Models       Parameterised Models
```

A `Graphs` model uses some model of positive integers for $|V|$. An `IndependentEdges` model uses some `Discrete.Bounded` model for the existence of edges. (`Graphs` and `IndependentEdges` are abstract.) The `GERfixed` model uses the two-state model with a fixed probability for the existence of edges, as mentioned, whereas the `GERadaptive` model of the next section uses the `Adaptive` discrete model.

11.5 Gilbert, Erdos and Renyi Adaptive

The fully parameterised Gilbert, Erdos-Renyi model, `GERfixed.M`, of the previous section assumes that the same fixed edge probability, p, is appropriate for every member of a data-set of graphs. This is overly restrictive in many cases. Sometimes we only want that the adjacency matrix of a graph be homogeneous—governed by some probability p—but do not require that the value of p be the same for every graph in a data-set. This is effected in the `GERadaptive` model which uses the `Adaptive((0, 1))` discrete model (Sect. 2.4) for the existence of edges rather than the "usual" two-state model. Recall that the `Adaptive` model assumes that each one of a *set* of discrete choices is governed by the same probabilities but does not state—does not care, if you will—what those probabilities are. `Adaptive` has a `Dirichlet` (Sect. 9.2.3) prior for the probabilities of those discrete choices. `GERadaptive` therefore requires the Dirichlet's $\langle\alpha, \beta\rangle$ as parameters of the prior on p and $\langle\alpha, \beta\rangle$ are included in its problem definition parameters. The `Estimator` for `GERadaptive` has only to estimate any parameters for the sub-model of $|V|$.

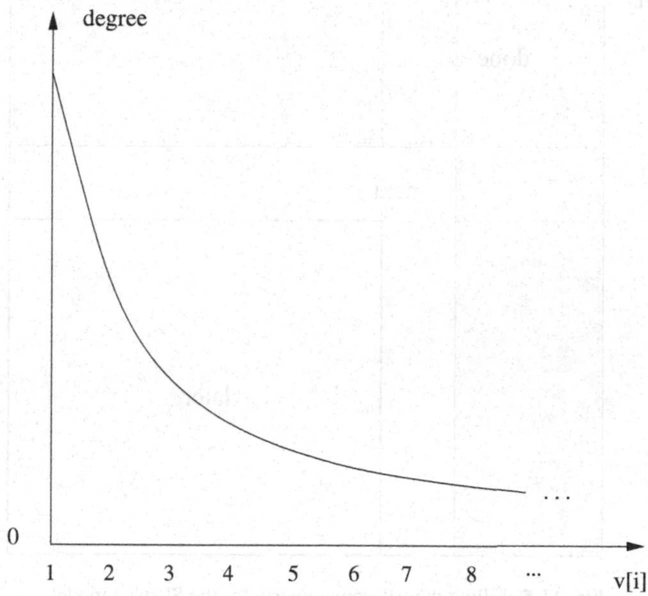

Fig. 11.4 Inverse power law ($\alpha = 1$)

`GERadaptive` generates a random graph by choosing a value of $|V|$, and a value of p from its prior, and then filling in an adjacency matrix at random according to these values.

11.6 Skewed Degree Model

A graph from a Gilbert, Erdos-Renyi model, fixed or adaptive, is expected to be statistically homogeneous—not identical in every region but sufficiently similar over regions that a uniform model of edges is the best description of all parts of the graph. However, it has been observed that some real world graphs have a skewed distribution of vertex degrees [23]. A few vertices have high degree while most vertices have low degree.

A power law distribution, $\sim 1/n^{\alpha}$, Fig. 11.4, is a special case of a skewed degree distribution that is of some interest in the literature. Processes have been described that can create a random graph, `R`, with such a degree distribution but unfortunately it is not clear how to calculate the probability, `nlPr(R)`, of such a graph in a feasible way.

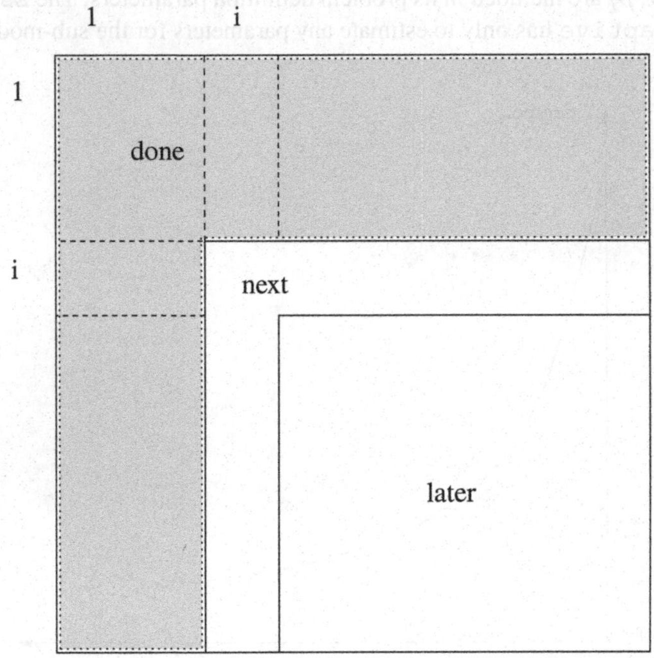

Fig. 11.5 Filling the adjacency matrix for the Skewed model

It is possible to implement a model, `Skewed`, of graphs with a skewed degree distribution. A skew in the distribution can be used to compress the graph and so calculate `nlPr(G)`. The vertices are sorted on descending degree so that degree $v_1 \geq$ degree $v_2 \geq \ldots$. The edges and non-edges of v_1, that is row_1 and, if directed, column_1, of the adjacency matrix are encoded, Fig. 11.5. This also puts an upper limit on degree v_2, and in fact some of v_2's edges may already be encoded—

any involving v_1. This knowledge allows v_2's edges and non-edges to be encoded more efficiently. In general, when v_i is being dealt with degree $v_i \leq$ degree v_{i-1} and any edges involving v_i with v_j where $j < i$ are already known.

If it were only required to encode the structure of an unordered graph then encoding $|V|$ followed by the adjacency matrix of the graph vertex-sorted on degree as above would be sufficient, but it does not allow recovery of the vertex numbering of an ordered graph. To recover a given *ordered* graph it is necessary to also encode *a* sorting permutation so that the adjacency matrix can be inversely permuted back to its original, given numbering. A full permutation takes $I(\pi_{|V|})$, which is approximately $|V|.\log_2|V|$ bits. Typically however many vertices in a skewed graph have the same degree so many permutations can achieve the desired sort. For every run of length k of vertices having the same degree one can save $I(\pi_k)$. As a special case, when *all* vertices have the same degree there is zero cost for the inverse permutation.

It is not obvious how to generate a random graph, `R=random()`, from the `Skewed` model in such a way that the probability of `random()` producing `G` exactly corresponds to `pr(G)`. It is however possible to come close by generating target vertex degrees, generating edges and non-edges for $v_0, \ldots, v_i, \ldots$ in turn, and finally randomly renumbering the vertices. But firstly just how the target degrees should decrease is not clear, and secondly the target degrees could be inconsistent—they are not independent of each other. Currently the target degrees are drawn according to an inverse distribution although, as mentioned previously, it is not obvious how to make full use of this in `nlPr(G)`. And, when generating edges to try to reach v_i's target degree, checks are made to ensure that v_j, where $j > i$, is not taken past its own target degree.

The `Estimator` for the `Skewed` model has only to estimate any parameters for the sub-model of $|V|$. `Skewed` fits into the class hierarchy as follows:

```
Graphs                         Graphs.M
 | { upmV; ... }                | { mdlV; ... }
 |                              |
 |-IndependentEdges             |-IndependentEdges.M
 |  |...                        |  | ...
 |                              |
 |-Skewed                       |-Skewed.M
```

UnParameterised Models — Parameterised Models

11.7 Motif Models

Our brains have to be trained - Pavloved - into logic. Culturally constructed, if you like. But our brains very naturally seek patterns. That's what they do best. [41]

Many data compression algorithms in various fields are based on exploiting frequently occurring *motifs*, that is patterns of some kind, in data. Frequent substrings can be used to compress strings of text, and frequent subgraphs can be used to compress graphs. Motifs within data can also reveal information of scientific value.

It has been claimed that some graphs derived from biological data exhibit frequent motifs (subgraphs) and that these motifs have a biological explanation [77]. There are also contrary views, for example [49].

```
Graphs                          Graphs.M
 | { upmV; ... }                 | { mdlV; ... }
 |                               |
 |-Motifs                        |-Motifs.M
    { mdlNMotifs;                   { motifs;
      mdlMotif;                       ...}
      ... }
```

UnParameterised Models Parameterised Models

Graph motifs are usually required to be connected in undirected graphs, and weakly connected in directed graphs.

An implementation of an unparameterised Graph Model, `Motifs`, based on motifs must contain a Model, `mdlNmotifs`, of how many distinct motifs (patterns) there are likely to be, and a Graph Model, `mdlMotif`, of individual motifs in general. These allow it to cost a fully parameterised Model, `Motifs.M`.

11.8 A Simple Motif Model

A motif model of graphs can be based on the idea of using *instances* of the motifs in a graph G to compress G's adjacency matrix although many design decisions must be considered to make this real. For a motif M, an instance of M in G is a subgraph M' of G that is isomorphic to M. The first design decision is what kind of subgraph isomorphism to consider, and the simplest choice is vertex-induced subgraph isomorphism: If injective function f maps vertices of M onto vertices of M' then $e(v_i, v_j) \in E_M \iff e(f(v_i), f(v_j)) \in E_{M'}$.

A random graph can be generated as follows. First, starting with an empty adjacency matrix, place instances of the motifs, $M_{i_0}, M_{i_1}, \ldots$, adjacent to each other along the diagonal. The instances cover a certain number of entries of the matrix. Next, use a `GERadaptive` model (Sect. 11.5), say, to generate the remaining entries. Finally, renumber the vertices uniformly at random.

Given a set of motifs, the adjacency matrix of a given ordered graph G can potentially be compressed by finding instances of the motifs in G. First, encode

$|V_G|$. Then state which motifs, $i_0, i_1, \ldots$, are used. Finally, give a renumbering of the vertices to exactly reconstruct G. If there are m motifs, it costs $\log m$ nits to choose one but note that any sequence of choices is possible provided the renumbering is consistent with it. And, as for `Skewed` model, the renumbering is not unique in general and so some saving may be possible.

Consider a directed graph, say, that is sparse and has an average vertex out-degree of d. An edge costs roughly $c = \log(|V|/d)$ to state under a GER-like model and the cost of stating the outgoing edges of a vertex v is roughly c.outDegree(v). If k of v's outgoing edges are instead encoded as part of an instance of a motif, one might hope for a saving of up to $k.c$. However, the renumbering can reduce that by up to $\log |V|$. It is a good thing if $k \geq 2$ for some vertices in the instance.

Given a set of motifs and G, the heart of the `nlPr(G)` calculation is to find a set of instances that gives the best compression of G. This is not an easy problem, and a simple greedy search has been implemented: Subgraphs of G in the range of motif sizes are enumerated and checked for isomorphism with the M_i. (Graph isomorphism is in general a far from trivial problem [56, 57], but a simple implementation is sufficient for small motifs.) A set of disjoint instances is built up as they are encountered.

```
Graphs                          Graphs.M
 | { upmV;                       | { mdlV;
 |   ... }                       |   ... }
 |                               |
 |-Motifs                        |-Motifs.M
    | { mdlNMotifs;                 | { motifs;
    |   mdlMotif;                   |   ...}
    |   ... }                       |
    |                               |-MotifD.M
    |-MotifD
```

UnParameterised Models   Parameterised Models

The implemented model of graphs, `MotidD`, takes upper and lower bounds on motif sizes and a model of positive integers, `mdlV`, as its problem definition parameters. The 'D' in `MotifD` stands for disjoint. It takes statistical parameters of `mdlV` and a set of motifs as statistical parameters. A `geometric` (Sect. 3.4) model is used for the number of motifs and a `GERadaptive` model is used to encode each individual motif. The latter uses a `Discrete.Uniform` model over the allowed motif sizes. The `estimator` for `MotifD` tries to find a good set of motifs for a given data-set of graphs (this is even harder than compressing a single graph given motifs). It does this by enumerating subgraphs of allowed size in the data-set. As a heuristic that is quick to compute, each candidate motif is ranked by the number of disjoint instances of the candidate found multiplied by the number of edges in the candidate; the reasoning behind the heuristic is that most of the cost of encoding a *sparse* graph comes from encoding edges and an instance may encode several edges at once. A short list of highly ranked candidates is then passed to a greedy algorithm which selects zero or more of them on the basis of compression. Clearly this is not necessarily optimal but evaluating all subsets of a realistic list of candidates would be much more time consuming.

The encoding described earlier is straightforward to implement provided that the instances of motifs are *disjoint*. One could entertain a model where any two instances could share at most one vertex (thus no shared vertex-pairs, no shared edges or non-edges), but the encoding would become more difficult: The second instance of a motif might share one vertex with the first and, if so, that fact and the vertex would need to be encoded. The third instance might share a vertex with the first instance and/or a vertex with the second. And so on.

One might even consider models where two instances of motifs could share one or more vertex-pairs. The question would then arise of whether overlapping instances would be required to be consistent or whether they would instead vote on the existence of edges between any shared vertex-pairs. Whichever, the encoding would be yet more difficult.

The implemented `MotifD` model, with its requirement for disjoint instances of motifs, is well-defined, straightforward to understand and implement, and its restrictions while being strict do prevent double counting. A more flexible model, `MotifA`, which side-steps some of `MotifD`'s restrictions is discussed next.

11.9 An Adaptive Motif Model

The `MotifD` model of the previous section ignores overlapping motif instances in the interests of simplicity and the prevention of double counting. This does, for example, mean that any Star_j instance (see Fig. 11.6) is completely separate from any Star_{j+1} instance, and any $K_{j,k}$ instance is necessarily completely separate from any $K_{j+l,k+m}$ instance. The `MotifA` graph model described here is an attempt to relax this restriction while remaining fairly straightforward to implement and acceptably efficient.

```
Graphs                              Graphs.M
 | { upmV;                            | { mdlV;
 |   ... }                            |   ... }
 |                                    |
 |-Motifs                             |-Motifs.M
    | { mdlNMotifs;                      | { motifs;
    |   mdlMotif;                        |   ...}
    |   ...}                             |
    |                                    |
    |-MotifD                             |-MotifD.M
    |                                    |
    |-MotifA                             |-MotifA.M
```

UnParameterised Models   Parameterised Models

Like `MotifD`, `MotifA` takes upper and lower bounds on motif sizes and a model of positive integers, mdlV, as its problem definition parameters. And it takes statistical parameters of mdlV and a set of motifs as statistical parameters.

Given a graph G, `nlPr(G)` encodes G's adjacency matrix a column, and if directed, a row at a time, that is the edges involving $v_0, v_1, \ldots$ in turn. When considering v_i, all edges between v_a and v_b where $a, b < i$ are already encoded. Suppose the next *possible* edge is $e(v_i, v_j)$ which may or may not exist. The encoder and decoder both maintain "background counters" for the number of edges that do not, and that do, exist absent the influence of any motif instance. They also each pose the hypothetical question, "if edge $e(v_i, v_j)$ were to exist in G would the known (encoded) part of G plus the hypothetical $e(v_i, v_j)$ contain a subgraph that includes v_j and $e(v_i, v_j)$ and that is (vertex-induced) isomorphic to a motif?" If so, it is *some* evidence for $e(v_i, v_j)$ to exist in G. Encoder and decoder each maintain per-motif counters for the non-existence and existence of edges in such circumstances. After the v_i, v_j entry is encoded (decoded), either under the background (no isomorphism) or motif (isomorphism) hypotheses, the encoder (decoder) update the relevant counters. The counters of the encoder and decoder at each stage are therefore always in synchronisation. The use of counters recalls the `Adaptive` multistate model (Sect. 2.4).

It can be seen that in contrast to `MotifD`, `MotifA`'s encoding of G does not identify any *explicit* instances of motifs, so there is no overhead for such identifications. Each motif instance is instead *implicit* and is only used for the final edge of the instance at that (this is in the interests of running time). Nevertheless, for every factor of 2^k that the ratio of edges to non-edges upon isomorphism exceeds the background ratio, k bits are saved. In the presence of multiple motif instances, the ratio upon isomorphism tends to increase during the encoding and, as a side-effect, the background ratio tends to decrease. Also note that the background counters effectively operate a `GERadpative` model and `MotifA` behaves as `GERadaptive` in the absence of motif instances.

Suppose that `MotifA` is given Star_j as a known motif and that G contains a $\text{Star}_{\text{k+l}}$ subgraph. `MotifA` may be able to recognise and make use of up to $l + 1$ instances of the motif. This is not double counting of overlapping instances, at least it is not improper double counting. The model is quite explicit that this is allowed, that parts of G may be covered with overlapping instances of motifs.

It has been observed that `MotifA` gets better compression of G when it deals with "high degree" vertices later—presumably because it more often encodes edges for which strong evidence is available. To take advantage of this, a renumbering gives higher numbers to vertices with degree > 8 say, the renumbered adjacency matrix is encoded as described above, and sufficient information for the inverse numbering is included.

A method of generating a `random` graph has not been implemented.

The `estimator` for `MotifA` faces a similar challenge to that for `MotifD`. A heuristic is again used to give an initial ranking of candidate motifs but in this case it is the number of *distinct* edges covered by instances (overlapping or not) of the candidate. Twice this quantity is the sum of the degrees of distinct vertices covered by instances of the motif.

11.10 Comparisons

The various models of graphs, and more yet to be implemented, can be seen as competitors in a contest to be recognised as the best model of a given population of graphs.

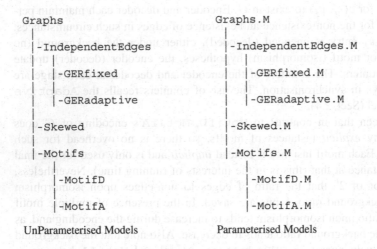

```
Graphs                          Graphs.M
 |                               |
 |-IndependentEdges              |-IndependentEdges.M
 |  |                            |  |
 |  |-GERfixed                   |  |-GERfixed.M
 |  |                            |  |
 |  |-GERadaptive                |  |-GERadaptive.M
 |                               |
 |-Skewed                        |-Skewed.M
 |                               |
 |-Motifs                        |-Motifs.M
    |                               |
    |-MotifD                        |-MotifD.M
    |                               |
    |-MotifA                        |-MotifA.M
UnParameterised Models          Parameterised Models
```

In a necessary sanity check, random graphs are generated by fully parameterised `GERfixed`, `GERadaptive`, `Skewed`, and `MotifD` models and the message lengths of these graphs are calculated using the same models and also `MotifA`. Returning a short message length is "good" and the shortest one wins.

`GERfixed` wins on `GERfixed` random graphs with `GERadaptive` close behind; the latter has to adapt to the edge density which the former knows in advance. `GERadaptive` almost always wins on `GERadaptive` random graphs unless a generated graph just happens to have the right edge density for `GERfixed` in which case it can win, rarely and narrowly. `Skewed` wins on `Skewed` random graphs. `MotifD` wins on `MotifD` random graphs provided that the motifs are dense enough, and that the generated graphs do indeed contain more than zero instances of the motifs; when there are no instances of motifs in a graph `GERadaptive` wins because it is the background model for `MotifD` without the latter's overheads. (It is not clear how to generate random graphs from `MotifA` in proportion to `pr(G)` but presumably it would win on them if we could.)

11.11 Biological Networks

It has been suggested [53, 77] that certain motifs occur frequently in biological networks. These include the hub, feed forward loop (FFL), and dense overlapping regulon, Fig. 11.6.

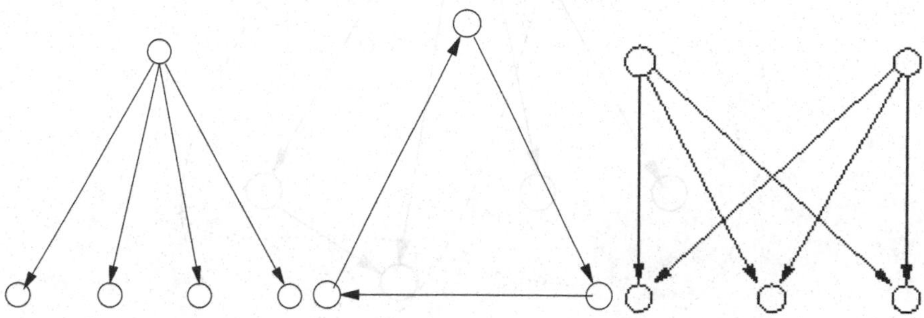

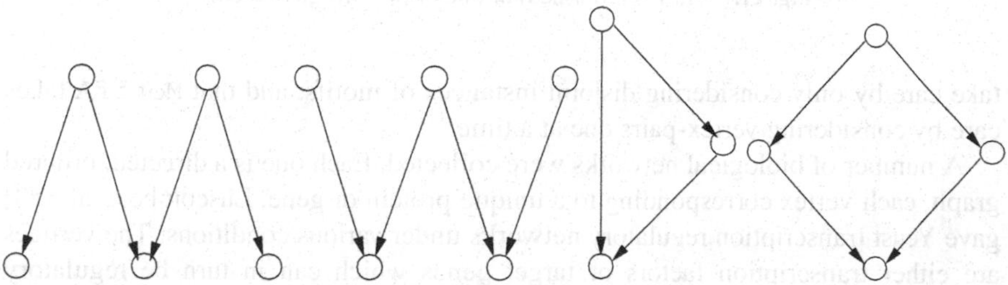

Fig. 11.6 **(a)** Candidate motifs: $Star_5$, C_3, $K_{2,3}$ **(b)** More candidate motifs: M_5, W_5, FFL, and FFL_4

Only the feed forward loop corresponds exactly to a single specific graph, namely $FFL = \langle\{a, b, c\}, \{\langle a, b\rangle, \langle a, c\rangle, \langle b, c\rangle\}\rangle$. A 4-vertex variation on FFL is sometimes mentioned:

$FFL_4 = \langle\{a, b, c, d\}, \{\langle a, b\rangle, \langle a, c\rangle, \langle b, d\rangle, \langle c, d\rangle\}\rangle$, a kite. A *hub* is described as a vertex with "several" out-edges regulating other vertices; it could be said to be a $Star$. But hub is not a graph with a fixed size, and if any two of the regulated vertices were connected in an instance it would contain a feed forward loop, and the instance would not be a vertex induced sub-$Star$ (Fig. 11.7). If $Star_j$, for some j, is taken to represent hub, care is needed because $Star_i$, $i > j$, contains ${}^iC_j$ instances of $Star_j$. A dense overlapping *regulon* involves "several" regulator vertices controlling "several" other vertices. The complete bipartite graph $K_{i,j}$, for some i and j, can be taken to represent regulon but care is needed, as with hubs. Note that `MotifD` does

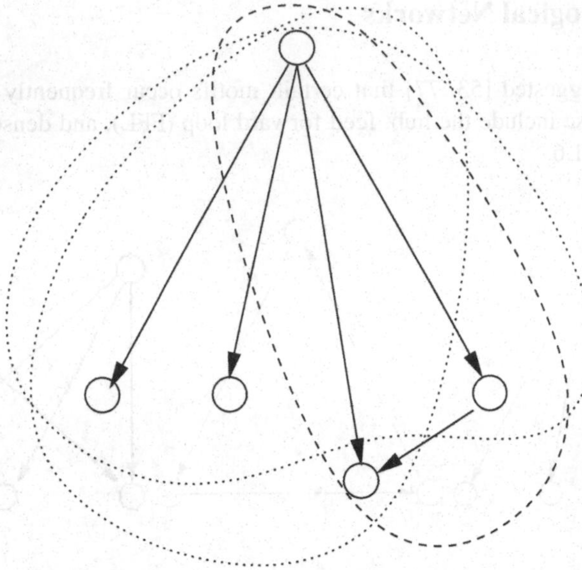

Fig. 11.7 An FFL (dashed) or one of two $Star_4$s (dotted)?

take care by only considering disjoint instances of motifs, and that `MotifA` takes care by considering vertex-pairs one at a time.

A number of biological networks were collected. Each one is a directed, ordered graph, each vertex corresponding to a unique protein or gene. Luscombe et al. [53] gave Yeast transcription regulatory networks under various conditions. The vertices are either transcription factors or target genes which can in turn be regulatory factors in further cascades. The endogenous (stress-free) cell-life cycle yields the graph *YeastCC* which contains 296 vertices and 550 edges. The diauxic-shift condition yields the graph *YeastDi* which contains 783 vertices and 1217 edges. The transcriptional regulatory network of Escherichia coli [77] gives the graph *EcoliTR* of 436 vertices and 530 edges. The signalling pathways of the (mammalian) hippocampal CA1 neuron [54] gives the graph *MammCN* of 594 vertices and 1421 edges.

The various graph models were run on the biological networks described above. `MotifD` and `MotifA` (Sect. 11.7) were both run in two modes. In the first mode they were given $Star_3$, $Star_4$, $Star_5$, C_3, C_4, $K_{2,2}$, $K_{2,3}$, W_5, M_5, FFL and FFL_4 as candidate motifs from which to choose zero or more motifs. In the second mode each used its search heuristics to discover motifs (having $3 \leq |V| \leq 5$) without assistance (Table 11.2).

	YeastCC	YeastDi	EcoliTR	MammCN	
|V|	296	783	436	594	
|E|	550	1217	530	1421	
GERadaptive	4822	12689	5271	13360	bits
Skewed	4443	10313	4902	13541	
				bits(#motifs)	
MotifD+	4827 (1)	12611 (1)	5230 (1)	13340 (1)	
MotifD-	4830 (0)	12611 (1)	5230 (1)	13368 (0)	
MotifA+	3961*(5)	9014*(3)	4310*(2)	12349*(4)	
MotifA-	4017 (4)	9014*(3)	4317 (1)	13046 (3)	

('+': given the list of candidates. '−': discovery.)

Table 11.2 Models × networks

	0	1	2	3	4	5	6	7	8	9	10
	S3	S4	S5	C3	C4	K22	K23	W5	M5	FFL	FFL4
YeastCC	*		*						*	*	*
YeastDi	*	*							*		
EcoliTR	*					*					
MammCN			*			*				*	*

Table 11.3 `MotifA`'s picks from the given candidates

Among the non-motif models, `Skewed` (Sect. 11.6) beat `GERadaptive` (Sect. 11.5) on YeastCC, YeastDi and EcoliTR, but the tables were turned on MammCN. When considering all the models, `MotifA` gave the most compression.

When given candidates, `MotifD` consistently chose $K_{2,3}$. `MotifD` also discovered $K_{2,3}$ by itself on YeastDi and EcoliTR although it was beaten by the no-motif `Skewed` model on three graphs.

	YeastCC_R	YeastDi_R	EcoliTR_R	MammCN_R
GERadaptive	4822	12689	5271	13360
Skewed	4456	10301	4910	13711
MotifD+	4827 (1)	12672 (1)	5280 (0)	13368 (0)
MotifD-	4830 (0)	12698 (0)	5280 (0)	13368 (0)
MotifA+	4019*(3)	9018 (3)	4511*(1)	13160*(2)
MotifA-	4045 (3)	9004*(4)	4511*(1)	13184 (2)

('+': given candidates. '−': discovery.)

Table 11.4 Randomised graphs, Models × networks

When given candidates (Table 11.3), `MotifA` always chose at least one $Star_i$. And it always chose either $K_{2,2}$ or M_5; the latter is a slightly broken $K_{2,3}$.

In discovery mode, `MotifA` generally discovered at least one $Star_i$ and often discovered M_5 or a close variant.

There is some support for hubs, or at least for some vertices having high fan-out, in `MotifA`'s choice of $Star_i$. There is some support for exact or approximate bipartite subgraphs in `MotifD`'s choice of $K_{2,3}$ and in `MotifA`'s choice of $K_{2,2}$ or M_5. There is also some support for feed forward loops in `MotifA` sometimes picking FFL and FFL_4. If `Skewed` is taken to be the null model then these conclusions are significant. It has been suggested [49] that graphs created by *preferential attachment* (PA) naturally give rise to FFLs. `Skewed` does compress PA graphs well, but a genuine PA model—that is a model that could calculate the probability of a graph to match the probability of generating the graph at random—should compress PA graphs better. But how much better?

Researchers who use frequentist statistics do not have a score with which to compare models directly and evaluate candidate motifs. In that case, the usual strategy is to compare the number of occurrences of subgraphs in (1) a given graph and (2) a random graph with similar properties. What is a random graph, and what is a random graph similar to a given graph are a pair of moot points. One option is to randomise the edges of a given network while maintaining the in- and out-degrees of each vertex. The biological networks were randomised in this way.

The randomised networks (Table 11.4) are rather less compressible than the originals. Fewer motifs are chosen (Table 11.5), or discovered, and mostly they are $Star_j$s.

	0	1	2	3	4	5	6	7	8	9	10
	S3	S4	S5	C3	C4	K22	K23	W5	M5	FFL	FFL4
YeastCC_R	*		*						*		
YeastDi_R	*								*	*	
EcoliTR_R		*									
MammCN_R		*						*			

Table 11.5 Randomised graphs, `MotifA`'s picks from the given candidates

Note that randomising a graph's edges while preserving vertex in- and out-degree is quite limiting, particularly in a graph with a skewed degree distribution (and `Skewed` beats `GERadaptive` except on MammCN): A vertex with high degree will remain a vertex with high degree and will remain the centre of a hub. $K_{i,j}$ may be broken up but it is likely that some part of it—some $K_{i-,j-}$—will remain and hence the randomised graph is likely to retain bipartite subgraphs. The results are not inconsistent with this.

Chapter 12
Bits and Pieces

> Take care of the bits and the hypotheses will take care of themselves.

It is one thing to have an awareness of a subject but it is another to be an active and able worker in it. This chapter describes experiences, pitfalls, hints and tricks that may help the reader to get started at putting MML into practice. "Probability theory is nothing but common sense reduced to calculation" (Laplace) but data analysis software is numerical software and the results of computations need to be checked with scepticism, common sense and cunning.

There can be different reasons to perform an MML analysis of a statistical model. If the method is applied "by hand," hopefully this is done with common sense, all necessary assumptions are satisfied, and there is a reasonable amount of data for the number of parameters to be inferred. Often however, a model that has been MMLed is implemented in a computer program.

If a model is implemented in a one-off, specialised program, perhaps the user of the program can be relied upon to use it in a sensible way and the computer code need not include too many safety checks such as, for example, MML87's assumptions (Sect. 1.6) being satisfied.

Sometimes a model is implemented as part of a general software `package` (Chap. 13) of statistical machine-learning tools. It is likely to be used by someone other than the library's author, by someone who might not pay attention to implicit or even explicit limitations on its use. In that case an individual model can face challenges that might be avoided in the situations above. The computer code must check that any necessary assumptions are satisfied and act appropriately if not—at the very least a warning should be issued.

L. Allison, *Coding Ockham's Razor*, https://doi.org/10.1007/978-3-319-76433-7_12

12.1 Priors

The use of a *prior*—that is a prior probability distribution over a model's parameters—is argued against by non-Bayesian, *frequentist* statisticians as being "subjective." The long running debate [29] on this topic is not entered into here. It is just noted that MML requires the use of priors and that there is a theoretical argument [88, 91] that it is impossible to learn anything at all in the total absence of priors. Moving on, if little is known about the true prior a bland prior should be chosen (but whatever is known should be used). A maximum-entropy (MaxEnt) distribution might be a good choice. A conjugate prior sometimes simplifies the mathematics. If there is enough data, the choice of one bland prior over another eventually makes little difference.

In requiring the use of a prior, MML makes explicit any preconceptions. If you do not like the prior used in an MML analysis, use a different one. The new estimator can be put into competition with the other and whichever wins in terms of shortest average message length on real data-sets is probably the better model, the difference in message lengths being the negative log posterior odds ratio. In an implementation (Chap. 13) it is sufficient to subclass (`extend`) the first implementation, overriding the `Estimator` with a new one that uses your preferred prior.

12.2 Parameterisation

MML is invariant to monotonic transformations of the parameters of a model—to reparameterisation. That is to say, if $\phi = f(\theta)$ then $\hat{\phi}_{MML} = f(\hat{\theta}_{MML})$. It does not matter whether the model is parameterised by θ or by ϕ, provided of course that equivalent priors are used on θ and ϕ.

As an example, the Exponential distribution (Sect. 4.2) is sometimes parameterised by A and sometimes by $\lambda = 1/A$,

$$\mathrm{pdf}_A(x) = \frac{1}{A} e^{x/A},$$

$$\mathrm{pdf}_\lambda(x) = \lambda e^{\lambda x}, \text{ where } \lambda = \frac{1}{A};$$

the mean is A and the variance A^2. Note that

$$\frac{\partial \lambda}{\partial A} = \frac{-1}{A^2}, \text{ and} \frac{\partial A}{\partial \lambda} = \frac{-1}{\lambda^2}.$$

Suppose for the sake of argument that a uniform prior density is put on A,

$$h(A) = \frac{1}{A_{max} - A_{min}}, \forall A \in [A_{min}, A_{max}],$$

We obviously require

$$\mathrm{pr}(A \in [A_1, A_2]) = \mathrm{pr}(\lambda \in [1/A_2, 1/A_1]),$$

$$\int_{A_1}^{A_2} h(A)\, \partial A = \int_{1/A_2}^{1/A_1} h(\lambda)\, \partial\lambda, \text{ when } A_{min} \le A_1 \le A_2 \le A_{max}.$$

Well,

$$h(A)\, \partial A = \frac{1}{A_{max} - A_{min}} \partial A = \frac{1}{A_{max} - A_{min}} . \frac{1}{\lambda^2}\, \partial\lambda = h(\lambda)\, \partial\lambda,$$

(the -1 can be dropped because it just shows that λ decreases as A increases) so

$$\int_{A_1}^{A_2} h(A)\, \partial A = \frac{A_2 - A_1}{A_{max} - A_{min}}, \text{ and}$$

$$\int_{1/A_2}^{1/A_1} h(\lambda)\, \partial\lambda = \int_{1/A_2}^{1/A_1} \frac{1}{A_{max} - A_{min}} \cdot \frac{1}{\lambda^2}\, \partial\lambda$$

$$= \frac{1}{A_{max} - A_{min}} \cdot \left[\frac{-1}{\lambda}\right]_{1/A_2}^{1/A_1}$$

$$= \frac{A_2 - A_1}{A_{max} - A_{min}}.$$

A uniform prior on A over $[A_{min}, A_{max}]$ is equivalent to a prior of $\frac{1}{\lambda^2}$ on λ over $[\frac{1}{A_{max}}, \frac{1}{A_{min}}]$ in the case that $\lambda = \frac{1}{A}$. The MML estimators for the Exponential model, with these priors, are $\hat{A}_{MML} = \frac{\sum_i x_i}{N-1}$ and $\hat{\lambda}_{MML} = \frac{N-1}{\sum_i x_i}$.

12.3 Estimators

An MML estimator minimises the length of a two-part message (Sect. 1.5) of an inferred model and the data given that model. However, the calculation of the accuracy with which a parameter estimate should be stated is valid even for a non MML estimate, for example, for the maximum likelihood estimate should it be different. A two-part message based on a non MML estimate corresponds to a *valid* code, even if it is longer than optimal. If it is too difficult to find the MML estimate, it is *valid* to use a different estimate.

12.4 Data Accuracy of Measurement (AoM)

The accuracy of measurement (AoM) (Chap. 4) of the continuous data in a data-set may be the same for every datum but it need not be so. For example, historic lengths might be in Imperial measurements to the nearest inch (2.54 cm) and more recent metric values to the nearest centimetre. These can be combined by multiplying the former data values by 2.54, giving them an AoM of 2.54, and appending the metric data with an AoM of 1.0. The former might have more influence than the latter on the complexity of a fitted model without that adjustment to the AoM. In some data-sets the AoM is a fraction of the data value, say ±5%. In principle the AoM could even vary unsystematically from datum to datum.

There seems to be an inclination for some scientists to over-state the accuracy of measurement of continuous data. Sometimes this is seen as harmless—"it is just a data formatting issue, everyone knows that the measurements are not really that accurate." For example, the three dimensional coordinates of atoms in a protein as derived by X-ray crystallography are recorded to 0.001 Å in the Protein Data-Base (PDB) [10] even though 0.1 Å, or greater, is probably closer to the mark in most cases [50]. Or, suppose that some data are integer quantities and a certain model applies to continuous data, for example the populations of towns and cities, some of which might only be known to the nearest thousand at best, are to be modelled by a Mixture (Chap. 7) of Normal distributions (Sect. 4.3). In the tail of the data there might be many small repeated values like 4000, 5000, and so on. If the AoM is set to 1.0 the search algorithm may decide whoopee, the mixture includes component classes such as $\mathcal{N}_{4000,0.5}$ and $\mathcal{N}_{5000,0.5}$ that give tremendous compression, but this is obviously ridiculous. The use of a sensible value for AoM solves this problem.

Although it may seem an easy matter to avoid the traps described above, they are nevertheless regularly fallen into, particularly when data are measured by one individual, collated by a second, and analysed by a third using a program written by yet another.

12.5 Small or Big Data

The MML87 [96] (Sect. 1.6) approximation to Strict MML assumes that the prior varies little across the parameter's uncertainty region and that the region lies within any bounds on the model's parameters. This is usually the case if the likelihood *is* somewhat sensitive to each parameter and there are more data than there are parameters to be estimated. If the assumptions do not hold it is possible that the simple "probability equals prior density times width" recipe might give probabilities greater than one and hence a negative length to the first part of the message. A person applying the recipe by hand would hopefully stop at this point.

An implementation of a certain model might be used as the leaf model of a classification-tree function-model (Sect. 8.4), say. A classification-tree works by dividing the data into smaller and smaller subsets as the data pass through fork nodes and input fields (variables) are tested. Eventually some fraction of the data-set arrives at each leaf node of the tree where the output field is modelled. It is possible for some leaves to capture little—even one or none at all—of the data. The leaf model must return a valid message length even in such a situation. It often seems that half of the computer code in an implementation is concerned with returning something sensible in supposedly unlikely cases.

At the other extreme, some problems require the analysis of very large data-sets and "big data" has become a thing. MML is agnostic about small versus big data. A particular algorithm for a particular model might have difficulty with a large data-set but that is down to the algorithm not MML. If you have an algorithm to efficiently calculate, or approximate, the sufficient statistics of a model and to calculate a valid message length from a big data-set, MML is amenable to that.

12.6 Data Compression Techniques

If a certain statistical model is a plausible model of some data and has a precise mathematical definition and its MML analysis is tractable, you are in luck and implementing the desired model may not be too hard. If not, there are techniques in data-compression that can sometimes be used to construct a model that gives a valid code—in principle data could be encoded and decoded according to it.

It has been said [60] that

$$\text{compression} = \text{modelling} + \text{coding}.$$

A statistical model calculates the probability, $\text{pr}(E)$, of each successive event E. Arithmetic coding [64, 70] essentially solves the coding part of the equation as it encodes E in a code-word of length arbitrarily close to the theoretical limit, that is $-\log \text{pr}(E)$. The best model gives the most compression. But another way of looking at it is that any valid (lossless, decodable) data compression method corresponds to some kind of model.

Work in data compression, including compression of files, text and images, has created various algorithms that give good compression but do not always directly correspond to a classical statistical model. For example, the Adaptive code for multistate data, never breaking down with small amounts of data and having as it does a known relationship with the MML code (Sect. 2.4), gives a safe and reliable way of calculating message lengths; the adaptive code is also a staple of data compression. It adapts the probabilities of symbols based on their observed frequencies from the start of the data-set upto and including the previous symbol—all known to both transmitter and receiver. Variations on the technique are common on data compression. If symbol probabilities are thought to change in different parts of a data-set, that is it is not homogeneous, this can be modelled by using symbol frequencies in a sliding window of recent symbols. The variable precision method of transmitting cut-points (median, quartiles, ...) in classification-trees [98] (Sect. 8.4) is a valid code and so a model.

12.7 Getting Started

It can be very daunting to have to write a computer program to model an unfamiliar kind of data in a new way. Often the degree of difficulty can be reduced by approaching the problem in the following order.

First get some real data and look at it! If you are not the experimenter, ask a lot of questions. Consider what form an *answer* to the inference question would take—what distributions (Sect. 13.7) can apply to parts or aspects of the data and what ranges of values are acceptable for their parameters. This shows what a fully parameterised model looks like; do not worry about how to find a good one, yet. Next, write routines to display a known model; these are necessary to present inferred answers to an end user and, well before that, to use in debugging.

Implement the message-length calculations for a known model and for data assuming that the model is true. If your kind of model consists of known, previously MMLed sub-models (Sect. 13.7) the message length can be taken as the sum of the message lengths of the sub-models, otherwise some MML analysis along the lines of earlier chapters may be necessary first. This is now enough software to run some useful tests on small hand-crafted examples: Does it give sensible results on less data compared to more data, on easier data compared to harder data, for a better model compared to a worse model?

Then, how can `random` data be generated from an answer, from a known fully parameterised model? When you have some, does the random data look plausible? The above might seem to be a distraction from the main task—from the original inference problem—but it puts the often difficult search problem to one side for a while as familiarity is gained. And, when a search method is implemented finally, it is necessary to test it on cases where the true model is known, that is on artificial test-data generated from a fully parameterised model. Once output routines and data-generation routines have been written it only(!) remains to devise a search method that will find an optimal model of given data, or at least a good model.

The testing of software that performs data analysis has all the usual problems of testing plus the challenges of numerical computing, numerical stability and perhaps very large data-sets. Reproducibility is an issue if (pseudo-) random numbers are involved. Make sure that you can set, record, and not set, the seed of the random number generator.

Start small with hand-crafted test-data. Go on to test-data generated from a known model; the model inferred from such data is unlikely to be identical to the true model (Sect. 12.8) but it should be close, and closer with more data, with a bigger "N".

Extra sanity checks may be possible: If the data are modelled as being independent and identically distributed (IID) then all permutations of a data-set should give the same results. Do they? Are there any other symmetries in the data? If there two parts to the data modelled as p_1; $(p_2|p_1)$ should that be equivalent to p_2; $(p_1|p_2)$? Is it? If $p_1 = p_2$ makes sense, what should happen then?

12.8 Testing and Evaluating Results

When you seemingly have a working computer program that can analyse data and make inferences, that can fit a model to data, how do you evaluate it? Applied to real-world data, the program surely produces models that are wrong [13] but are they useful, are they any good? Using data generated by, sampled from, a known true model gives something to compare an inferred model against. It is unlikely to be identical to the true model so one needs a measure of how close they are, and this must be taken several times to get an average and perhaps a variance.

The Kullback-Leibler divergence [51], $D_{KL}(M_T, M_I)$, of M_I from M_T, going from M_T *to* M_I, is a natural way to compare the true and inferred models, if you can implement it. A plot of the KL divergence against the size, N, of the data-set often makes an informative graph. If the KL divergence is not implemented, a rather noisy approximation to it is the average per-datum difference between the negative log likelihoods, nlLH(.), under the true and inferred models. Generally more data means better inferences; does the quality of inferences fall off dramatically below some value of N? Often it is the "order of magnitude" of N that matters most—10 to 100 is as 100 to 1000 and so on—so maybe choose values of N from a geometric series.

A plot of the inferred value of an important parameter against the true value as the latter changes may be interesting; include error bars if possible. There can be surprises and traps, for example, *sequence alignment* is used to compare DNA sequences [75]. We have good mathematical models of how sequences mutate so it is possible to simulate this and to produce pairs of diverged sequences a given "distance" apart. However, if two such sequences are compared on the basis of an *optimal* alignment they appear to be closer than we know them to be! A plot of inferred distance against true distance is not a straight line, not even a noisy straight line. The solution to this conundrum is to estimate distance from a weighted *average* over all alignments [102]. It turns out that optimal alignment is not the true model here.

The true model can be "exercised" in various ways to explore its parameter space. Perhaps some values of some parameters make for data-sets that are harder or easier to analyse. If the true model has several parameters, it may be impractical to take them all through a range of representative values in all combinations; it may be necessary to vary one parameter at a time while holding the others fixed. For a setting of the true model's parameters, the way in which inferences vary in response to changes in N, is often interesting.

It must be said that testing a machine-learning program on artificial data is like shooting fish in a barrel: The true model is known to lie in the family of models that the program can return. It is important that the program can pass such tests and they do give important information on variability against amount of data and areas of parameter space but the program should also be tested on real-world data.

So-called *gold-standard* data is real-world data for which the inference problem has already been solved—by the passage of time, by human experts or by some other means. For example, a mixture model on measurements of Irises can be compared (pages 73, 108) against the known, but previously withheld, species determined by an expert, but recall the not atypical doubts over the latter. A disadvantage, or maybe it is an advantage, of real-world data is that no-one can be completely sure of the true model.

12.8.1 Evaluating Function-Models

If we are inferring function-models (Chaps. 5, 8), the true and inferred function-models can still be compared on KL-divergence—on the divergence of conditional models, condModel(.), of output values given input data. Other testing methods are also seen.

Given input value `id`, a function-model can use the *mode* of its `condModel(id)` as a "hard" prediction of the value, `od`, of its output variable. It is common to compare function-models—inferred against true, or one candidate against another—on right-wrong scores, on the number of correct and incorrect output predictions for given inputs. This is simple to implement but it has inadequacies that are often overlooked: Suppose that the output variable is Boolean, $\{false, true\}$, and that for some case the correct output is $true$. Probabilistic predictions of $\{0.9 : 0.1\}$ and of $\{0.51 : 0.49\}$ both have a mode of $false$ and they are both wrong, but the former is obviously *much* worse than the latter: Imagine for a moment that you are a patient and the doctor is investigating whether or not you have appendicitis. It is a bad thing to be over-confident, particularly when wrong. This can be seen in information terms: $-log_2(0.1)$ is more than three bits but $-log_2(0.49)$ is only slightly over one bit.

When it comes to using gold-standard data *gs* (Sect. 12.8) to test a program that infers function-models, the training-set and the test-set must be different otherwise the program will have an improper advantage much like having prior knowledge of the questions on an exam paper. It is common practice to train the program on part of *gs* and to test it, by whatever measure, on the rest of the data. However, if the examples in *gs* are not independent, say due to bias in collecting them, then the training-set and the test-set may not be independent either, unless great care is taken, and the program may still have an improper advantage.

12.9 Programming Languages

If a model is to be used as a component of other structured models, it must satisfy some standard specification or interface. A programming language with a type-class system as in Haskell [67], Java [42] or C++ [82], is helpful in catching many errors as early as possible, that is at compile-time. A strong polymorphic type system with type inference as in Haskell is good here [1], generics as in Java and C++ slightly less so. A dynamic, run-time type system is very general, but type errors show up at run-time rather than at compile-time. With a little care, MML can of course be implemented in any computer programming language.

The probabilities of many fully parameterised models, and of much data, can be very small indeed risking numerical problems such as floating-point underflow. For example, assuming a uniform model over the four DNA bases, human chromosome 1 has a tiny probability of approximately $4^{-249,000,000}$ but a manageable message length of 5×10^8 bits. It is often safer to calculate message lengths, to work with $-\log$ probabilities, and to convert a message length to a probability only when necessary. Double precision (8-byte) floating-point arithmetic is generally preferred over single precision.

12.10 logSum

A message length m_i corresponds to a probability, $p_i = e^{-m_i}$ and $m_i = -\log p_i$. The probability of a data-set or of a complicated data value can be a tiny quantity and may even underflow, but message lengths are generally of a reasonable magnitude. It is often better to compute with message lengths, m_is, rather than with probabilities, p_is. The negative log of the sum of two probabilities can be computed from their negative logs, without converting them into probabilities, by logSum:

$$\begin{aligned}
\text{logSum}\; m_1\; m_2 &= -\log(p_1 + p_2)\\
&= -\log_e(e^{-m_1} + e^{-m_2})\\
&= -\log_e(e^{-m_1}(1 + e^{-(m_2-m_1)}), \qquad \text{if } m_1 \le m_2,\\
&\qquad\qquad \text{i.e., } e^{-m_1} \ge e^{-m_2},\\
&= m_1 - \log_e(1 + e^{-(m_2-m_1)}),\\
\text{logSum}\; m_1\; m_2 &= \text{logSum}\; m_2\; m_1, \text{ if } m_1 > m_2
\end{aligned}$$

This may avoid numerical problems. If $m_1 = m_2$, so $p_1 = p_2$, then logSum $m_1\; m_2 = m_1 - \log_e 2$ nits, that is one *bit* less than m_1, twice as probable as p_1. If $m_2 > m_1 + 30$ bits, say, then logSum $m_1\; m_2 \approx m_1$.

Mathematics generally calls for natural logarithms to base e, so do all internal negative log probability calculations in natural logarithms (nits) and only convert to base two if a user wants to print a message length in bits.

12.11 Data-Sets

When manipulating data-sets, it can be convenient to use operations that are familiar in functional programming—operations such as:

append joins two data-sets sequentially,

concatenate appends several data-sets,

zip converts a tuple of data-sets into a data-set of tuples,

unzip is the inverse of zip,

columns selects certain columns of a data-set of tuples,

map applies a function to every element of a data-set,

filter returns those elements that satisfy a predicate,

take returns the first n elements,

drop returns all but the first n elements.

slice returns elements from i to j.

They can also be easily implemented in non-functional programming languages.

Many estimators (and sufficient statistics, `ss = stats(ds)`), require only a single sequential pass through a data-set, for example, the MultiState (Sect. 2.3) and Normal (Sect. 4.3) estimators. In that case a data-set type or class could be based on an `iterator`, `Series` or `stream` class or similar—on something providing operations such as `has_some()`, `current_element()`, and `next()`. It is not essential to hold all of the data in main memory. There is also potential to use more than one processor on different parts of a very large data-set, combining the partial results.

The Intervals model (Sect. 5.3) needs to consider sections from i inclusive to j exclusive, of the data-set: $ds[i..j)$. The model's simple dynamic programming algorithm iterates, changing i or j by one at each step. The classification-tree function-model (Sect. 8.4) can take advantage of random access to a data-set, splitting arbitrary sections, $ds[i, j)$, of the data-set sorted on an input attribute (variable). To deal with these various requirements, models and estimators need to be able to calculate sufficient statistics for all or part of a data-set `ss = stats(ds, i, j)`, and to combine two sets of sufficient statistics `ss = stats(add, ss1, ss2)` and `ss = stats(add, ss1, ds, i, j)` by "addition" or "subtraction". Some models are able to implement some of these operations particularly efficiently.

To calculate a probability, not just a probability density or a likelihood density, models of continuous data need the sum of the negative log accuracies of measurement, AoM (equivalent to the negative log of the product of individual AoMs, over the whole data-set. If, as is often the case, all elements have the same AoM that sum can be calculated in constant time.

Mixture modelling (Chap. 7) deals with weighted data—the fractional memberships of each datum in the component classes of a mixture. A datum has a weight in the context of a data-set. Weights can also be used to represent compactly values that are repeated in a data-set, and to turn individual data "on" (1) and "off" (0), for example, to be used as training or test data. It is the sum of the elements' weights that is the size, the "N", of a data-set, not the number of records in some data-structure, although the sum is easily calculated if all data have the same weight. Weights must also be considered in the sum of the negative log AoMs.

Chapter 13
An Implementation

Software based on the minimum message length (MML) principle can be implemented in any reasonable computer programming language. The original version of the MML mixture modelling program *Snob* [93] was written in ALGOL-60 and later versions were written in FORTRAN and in C [92]. Prototype libraries or packages of more general MML code, as opposed to individual application programs, were written in Java [18, 34] and in Haskell [1]. A Java package, `mml`, of classes and methods for inductive inference using MML accompanies this book and can be found at https://www.cantab.net/users/mmlist/MML/A/.

13.1 Support

Package `mml` contains statistical models—the main subject of this book—but it requires utility and mathematical, classes and methods to support it and make it a practical proposition. Package `la` provides such support and contains sub-packages of utilities, `la.util`, and mathematics, `la.maths`. The most basic class is `Value` for data values, in sub-package `la.la`. Partly for historical reasons, `la.la` (after `la.λ`) also contains a lexical analyser, `Lexical`, a parser, `Syntax`, and an interpreter, `eval(.)`, for a simple functional programming language based on Church's λ-calculus [16].

L. Allison, *Coding Ockham's Razor*, https://doi.org/10.1007/978-3-319-76433-7_13

`package la`:

- `package la.la`
  - Includes `Lexical`, `Syntax`, `eval(.)` for a simple language.
    Also see classes `Value` and `Function`, and see (Sect. 13.2).
- `package la.util`
  - Some basic utility classes and routines.
    Also see class `Util` and see (Sect. 13.3).
- `package la.maths`
  - Includes mathematical constants and functions.
    Also see classes `Maths` and `Vector`, and see (Sect. 13.4).
- `package bioinformatics`
  - Place-holder for bioinformatics applications.

There should be little if any necessity for a user of `mml` to delve into the language `la.la` but the language might be useful and some of its classes, over and above `Value`, pop-up elsewhere in the documentation generated by `javadoc`. For example, `la.la` contains class `Function`, and the class of unparameterised models, `UPModel`, is a subclass of `Function`—because it is possible to `apply` an unparameterised model to statistical parameters—to parameterise it—to produce a fully parameterised statistical `Model`. In addition, some *simple* numerical methods such as `f.d_dx()`, `f.root(x0)` and `f.turning(x0)` are implemented on suitable instances of class `Function` and may be useful if an estimator, say, lacks a closed form.

13.2 Values

All data values are instances of class `Value`. `Value` is divided into `Atomic` and `Structured`, `Atomic` is divided into `Discrete` and `Cts` (continuous), and so on. `Enum` is for enumerated (categorical) data.

`package la.la`

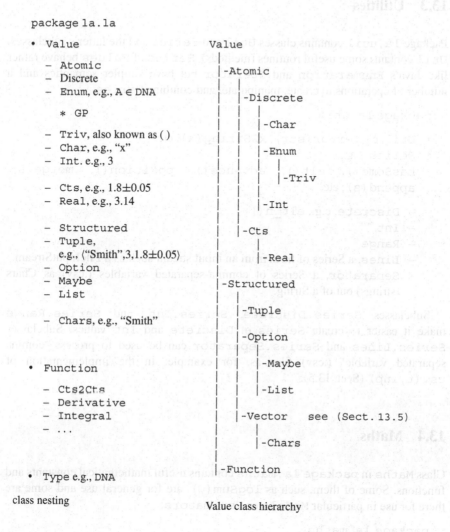

- `Value`
  - `Atomic`
  - Discrete
  - Enum, e.g., A ∈ DNA
    - `GP`
  - `Triv`, also known as ()
  - `Char`, e.g., "x"
  - `Int`. e.g., 3
  - `Cts`, e.g., 1.8±0.05
  - `Real`, e.g., 3.14
  - `Structured`
  - `Tuple`, e.g., ("Smith",3,1.8±0.05)
  - `Option`
  - `Maybe`
  - `List`
  - `Chars`, e.g., "Smith"
- `Function`
  - `Cts2Cts`
  - `Derivative`
  - `Integral`
  - ...
- Type e.g., DNA

class nesting

```
Value
 |
 |-Atomic
 |  |
 |  |-Discrete
 |  |  |
 |  |  |-Char
 |  |  |
 |  |  |-Enum
 |  |  |  |
 |  |  |  |-Triv
 |  |  |
 |  |  |-Int
 |  |
 |  |-Cts
 |     |
 |     |-Real
 |
 |-Structured
 |  |
 |  |-Tuple
 |  |
 |  |-Option
 |  |  |
 |  |  |-Maybe
 |  |  |
 |  |  |-List
 |  |
 |  |-Vector   see (Sect.13.5)
 |     |
 |     |-Chars
 |
 |-Function
```

Value class hierarchy

The most important property of a `Discrete` value is its `n()`. For a `Cts` value important properties are its `double x()`, accuracy of measurement, `AoM()`, and negative log AoM, `nlAoM()`.

`Option` is for `Values` that have one of several alternative forms, for example, a `List` which is either empty (`NIL`) or else a `Cell` containing a head element (`hd`) and a tail List (`tl`). Class `Maybe` can be used to represent optional values, values that may be either present or *missing* (Sect. 8.9)—something that is quite common in statistical data-sets.

13.3 Utilities

Package `la.util` contains classes `Util` and `Series` and the latter's subclasses. `Util` contains some useful routines (methods). `Series` of `Values` behave rather like Java's `Enumeration` and `Iterator` but have simpler semantics and a number of operations to create, manipulate, and combine `Series`.

package `la.util`

- `Util`, e.g., `error(str)`, `x2String(x)`, etc.
- `Series`, e.g., `hasSome()`, `elt()`, `advance()`, `position()`, `merge(s)`, `append(s)`, etc.
  - `Discrete`, e.g., `elt_n()`
  - `Int`
  - `Range`
  - `Lines`, a Series of lines from an input stream such as a FileInputStream.
  - `Separator`, a Series of comma-separated variables (.csv) as Chars (strings) out of a String.

Subclasses `Series.Discrete`, `Series.Int`, and `Series.Range` make it easier to create `Series` of `Discrete` and `Int` values. Subclasses `Series.Lines` and `Series.Separator` can be used to process 'comma separated variable' (.csv) files as, for example, in the implementation of `csv(t,inp)` (Sect. 13.5).

13.4 Maths

Class `Maths` in package `la.maths` contains useful mathematical constants and functions. Some of them, such as `logSum(,)`, are for general use and some are there for use in particular `Models` or `Estimators`.

package `la.maths`

- `Maths`, e.g., `twoPI`, `logSum(m1,m2)`, `logFactorial(x)` etc.
- `Vector`, see (Sect. 13.5)
- `Matrix`, –"–
- `Q`, –"–

As mentioned before (Sect. 13.1) there are also one or two *simple* numerical methods on `Functions` in package `la.la`.

13.5 Vectors

A `Vector` is a `Value`, a `Matrix` is a rectangular `Vector` of `Vectors`, and a quaternion, a '`Q`', is a `Vector` of four reals with certain semantics that can be used to define rotations of `Vectors` in $\mathbb{R}^3$. (Note that `la.maths.Vector` is distinct from `java.util.Vector`; the word "Vector" was just too good to pass up).

`v.nElts()` gives the number of elements in a `Vector`, `v`, but this is not necessarily the size of a data-set (the number of data) represented by `v`. An element, `v.elt(i)`, has a *weight* `v.wt(i)` in the context of `v`. The default weight is 1.0 but the weight can be used to represent a duplicated datum (`wt(i)>1`), to turn a datum "off" (`wt(i)=0`), and to indicate fractional membership (`0<wt(i)<1`) in a component class of a mixture model (Chap. 7). The *size* of the data-set `v` is instead `v.wts()` which could be larger or smaller than `v.nElts()`. It is true that `v.wts()` = $\sum_i$ `v.wt(i)` but the former can often be calculated much more quickly.

`package la.maths`

- `Vector`, e.g., `nElts()`, `shape()`, `elt(i)`, `wt(i)`, `normalised()`, `scaled(s)`, `append(v)`, `zip(v)`, `csv()`, etc.
  - `Ints`
  - `Doubles`
  - `Slice`, e.g., see `take(n)`
  - etc.
- `Matrix`, e.g., `elt(i)`, `elt(r,c)`, `nCols()`, `transpose()`, `times(M)`, `times(v)`, `inverse()`, `eigen()`, etc.
  - Ints
  - Doubles
  - Also see fromLexical(lex)
  - etc.
- `Q`, quaternions, e.g., `i()`, `conjugate()`, etc.
  - Also see `Vector.rotate(q)`, `Vector.match(v)`

A multivariate data-set can be read from a comma separated (`.csv`) file by `Vector.csv(...)`. A separator other than "," can be specified. The Type of a row—a `Tuple`—must be given. Various options may be given for trimming white-space from the head or tail of items. As an example, the Iris data-set (Sect. 7.4) can be read from `filename` by the following code:

```
Type.Enum Species =                  //   there are 3 Species
  new Type.Enum("Species",
    new String[]{"Iris-setosa", "Iris-versicolor",
                 "Iris-virginica"});

                                 // a 5-Tuple of R^4 & Species
Type.Tuple R4Species = new Type.Tuple.GP("R4Species",
  new Type[] {Type.CTS, Type.CTS, Type.CTS, Type.CTS,
              Species});

try{ inp = new java.io.FileInputStream(filename);
   }catch(Exception e)
   { Util.error("file "+filename+":"+e); }

                                   // ds, a Vector of 5-Tuples
Vector ds = Vector.csv(R4Species, inp);
```

However note that "the CSV file format is not standardized. The basic idea of separating fields with a comma is clear, but that idea gets complicated when the field data may also contain [special characters] ..." [20].

The four dimensions, the first four attributes of the data, can be separated out with `Vector ds4 = ds.cols(new int[]{0,1,2,3})`.

A `Slice` is a segment of a `Vector`. Two compatible `Vectors` can be appended but if they are both `Slices` of the same parent `Vector` and they abut, the results is also a `Slice` of the parent.

There are subclasses `Vector.Ints` and `Vector.Doubles` for `Vectors` constructed from `ints` and `doubles` and which may be implemented especially efficiently.

A `Matrix` is a rectangular `Vector` of `Vectors` (in general a `Vector` of `Vectors` can be irregular) so an element, `elt(r)`, of a `Matrix` is a `Vector`. Method `elt(r,c)` returns the "element" at column `c` of row `r`. As for `Vectors`, there are subclasses `Matrix.Ints` and `Matrix.Doubles`.

13.6 Graphs

Mathematically, a graph (network) (Chap. 11) consists of a set of vertices, V, $|V| > 0$, and a set of edges, E, $|E| \geq 0$. In code, a `Graph g` is a `Value`, `g.vSize() > 0` and `g.eSize() ≥ 0`. Subclasses such as `Directed` and `Directed.Dense` exist to make it easier to create `Graphs` in various ways. They should not be relied upon (`instanceof...`) to test a `Graph's` properties. For such purposes use `eSize()`, `isDirected()` and so on.

package graph

- Graph, e.g., vSize(), eSize(), isEdge(i,j), vLabel(i), eLabel(i,j), A(), arrayA(), canonical(), isomorphic(g), etc.
  - Vertex
  - Edge
  - Dense
  - Sparse
  - Contraction
  - Induced
  - Renumbered
  - SubGraphs
- Type (of a Graph)

- Directed
  - Dense
  - Sparse
  - C, cyclic graph C_n
  - etc.
- Undirected
  - Dense
  - Sparse
  - K, complete graph K_n
  - etc.

For a given Graph g, g.new SubGraphs(m,n) is a Series (Sect. 13.3) of the weakly connected, vertex-induced subgraphs of g that have between m and n vertices. This is useful in writing motif-based graph models (Sect. 11.7) such as MotifD (Sect. 11.8) and MotifA (Sect. 11.9). Other models of Graphs are described in Chap. 11.

13.7 Models

A fully parameterised Model is a Value, and an unparameterised model, an UPModel, is a Function is a Value. An Estimator is also a Function and hence a Value.

The main purpose of a Model is to assign a probability pr(d) to a datum d, also a negative log probability nlPr(d) to d, and a negative log likelihood nlLH(ss) to a data-set ds having sufficient statistics ss = stats(ds). The minimum message length principle requires that a Model has two-part message lengths msg1() and msg2 for the Model itself and the training data respectively. msg() = msg1() + msg2() allows two or more competing Models to be compared on a fair basis—the Model having the shorter total message length wins.

Given a data-set `ds` an `Estimator` estimates (fits) a `Model`. This involves two steps, first getting sufficient statistics `ss = stats(ds)`, and then `ss2Model(ss)`.

Most `Models` are instances of `UPModel.M` produced by the estimator `UPModel.Est` inside an unparameterised model, a `UPModel`. Often the `stats(ds)` defined in such nested `UPModel`, `Est` and `M` are identical but there are exceptions. Such an example occurs in `R_D.ForestSearch` where the *structure* of the model is undecided in the unparameterised model and the estimator so the statistics must be enough to cover all possibilities. The structure is fixed in the fully parameterised model so the statistics needed there, for `nlLH(ss)`, are fewer.

`package` mml

- MML, e.g., `logPI`, `Normal`, `Laplace`, etc.
- `Model`, e.g., `msg()`, `msg1()`, `msg2()`, `statParams()`, `pr(d)`, `nlPr(d)`, `stats(ds)`, `nlLH(ss)`, `random()`, etc.
- `Estimator`, e.g., `stats(ds)`, `ss2Model(ss)`, etc.
- `UPModel`, e.g., `defnParams()`, `estimator(ps)`, `stats(ds)`, `sp2Model(m1,m2,ss)`, etc.
  - `M`
  - `Est`
- `FunctionModel`, Models of id→od, e.g., `condModel(id)`, `condPr(id,od)`, `random(id)`, etc. see (Chap. 5)
- `UPFunctionModel`
  - `M`
  - `Est`
- `SeriesModel`, Models of Series (*experimental*)
- `UPSeriesModel`, UnParameterised Models of Series (*experimental*)
  - `M`
  - `Est`

A function-model models the relationship between an input-datum (independent variable) and an output-datum (dependent variable) (Chap. 5). `FunctionModel`, `UPFunctionModel`, `UPFunctionModel.Est`, and `UPFunctionModel.M` are related in the same way as `Model`, `UPModel`, `UPModel.Est`, and `UPModel.M`.

A number of statistical models are implemented in package `mml`:

```
UPModel
 |
 |-BestOf
 |
 |-Missing (see (Sect.8.9))
 |                                    .
 |-Discretes (see (Chap.2))           .
 |  |                                 .
 |  |-Discretes.Bounded               |
 |  |                                 |-Discretes.Bounded
 |  |-Discretes.Shifted                      (see (Chap.2))
 |  |                                    |
 |  |-Geometric0UPM (see (Sect.3.4))     |-Discretes.Uniform
 |  |                                    |
 |  |-Poisson0UPM                        |-MultiState
 |  |                                    |
 |  |-LogStar0UPM                        |-Adaptive
 |  |
 |  |-WallaceInt0UPM
 |
 |-ByPdf                              .
 |  |                                 .
 |  |-Continuous                      .
 |  |                                 |
 |  |-R_D (see below)                 |-Continuous (see (Chap.4))
 |                                       |
 |-Multivariate                          |-Continuous.Bounded
 |  |                                    |  |
 |  |-Dependent                          |  |-Continuous.Uniform
 |  |                                    |
 |  |-Independent                        |-ExponentialUPM
 |                                       |
 |-Mixture (see (Chap.7))                |-LaplaceUPM
 |                                       |
 |-Graphs  (see below)                   |-NormalUPM
 |                                       |
 |-Permutation                           |-NormalMu
    |
    |-Permutation.Uniform
         { Mdl; ... }
```

UPModel class hierarchy, continued . . .

```
.
.
|-R_D (see (Chap. 9))
   |                                    .
   |-R_D.NrmDir                         .
   |                                    .
   |-Simplex (see (Sect. 9.2))|
   |  |                       |-Graphs  (see (Chap. 11))
   |  |-Simplex.Uniform          |
   |  |                          |-Graphs.IndependentEdges
   |  |-Dirichlet                |  |
   |                             |  |-Graphs.GERfixed
   |-Direction (see (Sect. 9.3)) |  |
   |  |                          |  |-Graphs.GERadaptive
   |  |-Direction.Uniform        |
   |  |                          |-Graphs.Skewed (see (Sect. 11.6))
   |  |-vMF                      |
   |                             |-Graphs.Motifs (see (Sect. 11.7))
   |-R_D.Forest                     |
   |                                |-MotifD
   |-R_D.ForestSearch               |
                                    |-MotifA
```

UPModel class hierarchy

Package mml also contains some useful function-models:

```
UPFunctionModel (see (Chap. 5))
  |
  |-UPFunctionModel.K (see (Sect. 5.1))
  |
  |-Multinomial (see (Sect. 5.2))
  |
  |-Intervals (see (Sect. 5.3))
  |
  |-CPT (see (Sect. 5.4))
  |
  |-NaiveBayes (see (Sect. 8.1))
  |
  |-Tree (see (Sect. 8.4))
  |
  |-Linear1 (see (Sect. 10.1))
  |
  |-LinearD (see (Sect. 10.3))
```

UPFunctionModel class hierarchy

13.8 Example Programs

Package `eg` contains example application programs that generate some of the inference results in this book.

```
package eg
```

- `Iris`
- `Musicians`
- `Ducks`
- `Graphing`

`Iris` applies the `Mixture` (Sects. 7.4 and 10.2) and classification-`Tree` (Sect. 8.8) models to the Iris data-set. `Musicians` explores the 27-Club hypothesis (Sect. 7.5). `Ducks` is an example of Naive Bayes (Sect. 8.2). `Graphing` exercises the models of graphs (Sect. 11.10). In addition, `mml.Test` runs some rudimentary and far from exhaustive tests on most models.

Glossary

Adaptive In general a code with implicit parameters that adapts as it progresses through a data-set, in particular the adaptive code for multistate data (Sect. 2.4).

Adjacent Vertices u and v are adjacent in an undirected graph (Chap. 11) if (u, v) is an edge, and in a directed graph if $\langle u, v\rangle$ is an edge or $\langle v, u\rangle$ is an edge.

AoM The accuracy of measurement, ϵ, of a continuous (Chap. 4) datum, $x \pm \frac{\epsilon}{2}$, also `AoM()`; see nlAoM.

Arc An *edge* in a graph.

Arithmetic coding A method of encoding data [64, 70] $d_1, d_2, \ldots$, that can get arbitrarily close to the theoretical limit $-\log \mathrm{pr}(d_i)$, that is to the entropy per symbol on average if $pr(.)$ is the true model (but note that MML usually only requires calculating the *lengths* of hypothetical messages).

ban Unit of information, $-\log_{10}(\mathrm{pr}(.))$, also deciban equals one tenth of a ban, used by Alan Turing and the breakers of the Enigma code and other codes during WWII [43]; one ban equals $\log_2(10)$ bits, approximately 3 bits; see information.

L. Allison, *Coding Ockham's Razor*, https://doi.org/10.1007/978-3-319-76433-7

Bayes The Reverend Thomas Bayes (1702–1761) is buried at Bunhill Fields, London, *An essay towards solving a problem in the doctrine of chances* (Bayes's theorem) was published posthumously [8].

Bayes's theorem [8] $\text{pr}(ds \ \& \ H) = \text{pr}(H) \cdot \text{pr}(ds|H) = \text{pr}(ds) \cdot \text{pr}(H|ds)$, for data-set ds and hypothesis (model) H (Chap. 1), also Laplace [52] later and probably independently [81].

bit Unit of information, $-\log_2(\text{pr}(.))$; one bit equals $\log_e 2$ nits. Note, $-\log_2 0.5 = \log_2 2 = 1$; see information.

Box George Edward Pelham Box (1919–2013) a prominent statistician, remembered for the aphorism "all models are wrong but some are useful" [13], which is an important observation.

Class Various meanings—a component class of a mixture model (Chap. 7) and the reason for the name of the *Snob* program [92, 93]; a class in object-oriented programming (Chap. 13); a model class is a family of statistical models.

Classification-tree A kind of function-model (Sect. 8.4), also `Tree`.

Coding (i) Turning an algorithm into a computer program in some programming language; (ii) turning data into a string of symbols in some representation language, possibly for storage or transmission.

Conditional The conditional probability, $\text{pr}(Y = y|X = x)$, of Y equalling y given that $X = x$, or just $\text{pr}(y|x)$, "the conditional probability of y given x;" see function-model (Chap. 5).

Connected Vertices u and v in an undirected graph (Chap. 11) are connected if there is a *path* of one or more edges between u and v; also see *strongly* and *(weakly)* connected of directed graphs.

csv Comma-separated variable [20] file, `foobar.csv`, often from a "spread-sheet", and often separated by other than commas.

d A datum (often), also see *ds*.

Data-set Zero or more data, $ds = [d_1, d_2, \ldots, d_N]$.

Data-space The set / domain / type of which data values are members.

Datum A single item of data, but may be multivariate.

Decision-tree See *classification-tree*.

Direction A direction in $\mathbb{R}^D$ is a *normalised*, *D*-dimensional Vector (Sect. 9.3).

Dirichlet A probability distribution over the K-Simplex (Sect. 9.2.3) after Peter Gustav Lejeune Dirichlet (1805–1859).

ds More than one *d*, a data-set (often); also see *d*.

Edge A direct connection of vertices u and v in a graph G, unordered (u, v) if G is unordered, ordered $\langle u, v\rangle$ if G is ordered (Chap. 11).

Entropy The entropy of a probability distribution is the expected information per datum (Sect. 1.4).

Estimate A value for the parameter(s) of a model inferred from a data-set.

Estimator A mapping from data-sets to parameter estimates / models, also `Estimator`.

Exponential A probability distribution over $\mathbb{R}_{\geq 0}$ (Sect. 4.2).

F The Fisher information (Sect. 1.6.2) (often).

Fisher Sir Ronald Aylmer Fisher (1890–1962) [33] (Fisher's remains are in St Peter's Cathedral, Adelaide, South Australia); it is said that statisticians know him as the famous statistician, and biologists know him as the famous geneticist, also infamous for maintaining that smoking might not be a cause of lung cancer; see the Fisher information matrix (Sect. 1.6.2) and the von Mises–Fisher distribution (Sect. 9.3.2).

Fisher information The determinant of the Fisher information matrix.

(Fisher) information matrix The matrix of expected second derivatives of the negative log likelihood with respect to the model's parameters; it shows how sensitive the likelihood is to changes in the parameters (Sects. 1.6, and 1.6.2).

Function-model Model of relationship between id and od, of (dependent) output od given (independent) input id (Chap. 5), also `FunctionModel`; also known as *regression*.

Gaussian Normal or Gaussian probability distribution over $\mathbb{R}$ (Sect. 4.3).

Geometric A probability distribution over $\mathbb{N}_{\geq 0}$ (Sect. 3.4).

Graph $G = \langle V, E \rangle$ for vertices V and edges E, also known as a network (Chap. 11).

H A hypothesis (often).

$h(\theta)$ The prior distribution on parameter θ (sometimes).

Hypothesis Estimate / guess / model / hypothesis / explanation / theory.

$I(E)$ The information, $-\log(\mathrm{pr}(E))$, due to learning of event E, also known as $msg(E)$.

IID Independent and identically drawn.

Information $-\log p$, the number of nits (or bits, etc.) required to state (to transmit) the occurrence an event of probability p (Sect. 1.4).

Information matrix See *Fisher information matrix*.

Joint Joint probability of parameter(s) and data, $\mathrm{pr}(\theta \,\&\, ds)$.

K_n The complete graph (network) over n vertices, directed or undirected from context; it contains all possible edges, but no loops (Sect. 11.11).

$K_{m,n}$	The complete bi*part*ite graph (network) over two *parts* of m vertices and n vertices respectively, directed or undirected from context (Sect. 11.11).
KL	See Kullback-Leibler.
Kullback-Leibler divergence [51]	$D_{KL}(M_1, M_2)$ from Model M_1 to Model M_2; see Sect. 1.4.
L	The likelihood (often).
Lambda, λ	As in λ-calculus [16] (Sect. 13.1), the basis of functional programming.
Laplace	A probability distribution over $\mathbb{R}$ (Sect. 4.5), after Pierre Simon Laplace (1749–1827).
Lattice constant	κ_D [19], see Sect. 1.6.2.
Likelihood	$\text{pr}(ds\|\theta)$, the probability of a data-set ds given θ, but it is often considered to be a function of θ, $L_{ds}(\theta)$, given ds (Chap. 1); also see `nlLH`.
Linear regression	A function-model between continuous variables (Chap. 10); somewhat counter-intuitively not necessarily a linear function as x^2, say, may be taken to be a variable.
$logSum(m_1, m_2)$	The message length of an event of probability $p_1 + p_2$ where m_i is the message length of an event of probability p_i; also known as $logPlus$ (Sects. 12.10, and 13.4).
log*	$\log^*(x) = \log(x) + \log^2(x) + \log^3(x) + \ldots$, positive terms only (Sect. 3.1).
MAP	Maximum a Posteriori estimation—return the estimate $\hat{\theta}$ that has maximum posterior probability $\text{pr}(\theta\|ds)$; *not* the same as MML because the latter includes consideration of the optimum precision of estimates, even of discrete parameters, although one *might* say that MML is MAP done properly.
Mean	See bar, page 165, $\bar{}$, $\bar{x}$.

Median The median of a *sorted* list $[x_1, \ldots, x_N]$, where N is odd, is $x_{\lceil N/2 \rceil}$; if N is even then $(x_{\frac{N}{2}} + x_{\frac{N}{2}+1})/2$ but, particularly if that is not a proper value or does not make sense, the use of $x_{\frac{N}{2}}$ or of $x_{\frac{N}{2}+1}$ is not unknown.

Message Two-part message, (i) hypothesis H; (ii) data $ds|H$ (Sect. 1.5).

Mixture A weighted combination of two or more Models (distributions) (Chap. 7).

ML Maximum Likelihood, maximise the likelihood, equivalently minimise the negative log likelihood.

MML Minimum Message Length (Sect. 1.5), as in MML inference, say.

MML87 The c1987 formulation [96] of an approximation to Strict Minimum Message Length (SMML) (Sect. 1.6).

Mode The mode of a discrete probability distribution is the value d that has maximum probability $pr(d)$; for a continuous probability distribution *a* mode is a value x that has a *local* peak in $pdf(x)$ (which makes for a possible ambiguity with probability distributions of ordered discrete data); "bimodal" means twin peaks.

Model Estimate / model / hypothesis / explanation / theory (Sect. 1.2), also `Model`.

msg(E) Message length, the information, $-\log(pr(E))$, gained due to learning of event E, also known as $I(E)$.

Multinomial Model of the counts of the sides coming up in n rolls of a k-sided dice (Sect. 5.2); also see multistate.

Multistate Model over a Bounded Discrete data-space (Sect. 2.3), also `MultiState`.

Multivariate Multivariate model of a product data-space (Chap. 6).

$\mathbb{N}$ — The set (type, space) of natural numbers, the non-negative integers $\{0, 1, 2, 3, \ldots\}$; also see $\mathbb{Z}_{\geq 0}$.

$\mathbb{N}_{>0}$ — The set of positive integers, greater than zero; also see $\mathbb{Z}_{>0}$.

$\mathbb{N}_{\geq 0}$ — The set of non-negative integers (emphasising the inclusion of zero); also see $\mathbb{Z}_{\geq 0}$.

Naive Bayes — A kind of function-model (Sect. 8.1).

nat — See *nit*.

Negative log $\langle X \rangle$ — $-\log\langle X \rangle$, e.g., negative log Likelihood, $-\log L$; also see *bit* and *nit*.

Network — See *graph*.

nit — Unit of information, $-\log_e(\text{pr}(.))$; one nit equals $\log_2(e)$ bits, also known as *nat*; see information.

nlAoM — The negative log accuracy of measurement of a datum, also `nlAoM()`; see AoM.

nlLH — Negative log likelihood of a data-set; also see `nlLH(ss)`.

nlPr(d) — $-\log(\text{pr}(d))$, negative log probability of datum d; also see `Model.nlPr(d)`.

Node — A *vertex* in a tree or, less often, a graph.

Norm — The size (length, magnitude, $\|\vec{v}\|_p$) of a Vector, $\vec{v}$ (Sects. 9.1.2, and 13.5).

Normal — Normal or Gaussian probability distribution over $\mathbb{R}$ (Sect. 4.3).

Normalised — A Vector or a set of Vectors that have a norm of 1.0.

Null — As in null model or null hypothesis, a bland default model that could generate the given data-set, set up as a base-level competitor, a hurdle, to the kind of model that you are hoping to infer and to justify.

Ockham's razor — See William of Ockham.

Poisson A probability distribution over $\mathbb{N}_{\geq 0}$ (Sect. 3.5) after Siméon Denis Poisson (1781–1840).

Posterior *After* being given a data-set, for example, posterior probability of parameter(s) of a model given data ds, $\text{pr}(\theta|ds)$; note that posterior probability was known as *inverse probability* until the mid twentieth century [29].

pr(d) The probability of datum d; more fully, the probability that random variable D takes the value d, that is $\text{pr}(D = d)$, also `Model.pr(d)`.

Prior *Before* seeing a data-set, for example, prior probability of the parameter(s) of a model; also see *posterior*.

Product space $X \times Y = \{\langle x, y\rangle | x \in X \,\&\, y \in Y\}$. Similarly, $X \times Y \times Z$, etc.. $X^2 = X \times X$, $X^3 = X \times X \times X$, etc. (Chap. 6). Note that $X \times Y \times Z$, $(X \times Y) \times Z$, and $X \times (Y \times Z)$ are all different, although they are in obvious one to one to one correspondence.

$\mathbb{R}$ The set (type, space) of real numbers, positive, negative, and zero.

$\mathbb{R}_{>0}$ The set of positive real numbers.

$\mathbb{R}_{\geq 0}$ The set of non-negative real numbers.

Regression Reference [37], see *function-model* (Chaps. 5, and 8).

Shannon Claude Elwood Shannon (1916–2001), as in Shannon information theory [76], see Eq. (1.2).

Simplex (Standard) K-Simplex (Sect. 9.2).

slice Select part of a Vector (data-set), v.slice(i,j) (Sect. 6.3).

SMML Strict Minimum Message Length (Sects. 1.5, and 2.2).

ss Sufficient statistics of a data-set (often).

$star_k$	A graph with one "hub" vertex connected to the other $k-1$ vertices, no other edges (Sect. 11.11).
Strongly connected	Vertices u and v in a directed graph (Chap. 11) are strongly connected if there is a path of one or more edges from u to v or from v to u; a directed graph is strongly connected if every pair of vertices is strongly connected; also see weakly connected.
Sufficient statistics	Some quantity or quantities computed from a data-set `ds` that contain information from which to estimate a model, in the best case a few numbers, in the worst case the data-set itself, see `stats(ds,i,j)`.
Tree	See tree code (Sect. 3.2) and classification-tree (Sect. 8.4).
Tuple	$t = \langle t_1, t_2, \ldots, t_k\rangle$ is a k-tuple where $t_i : T_i$ so $t : T_1 \times T_2 \times \ldots \times T_k$; in programming language terms a *record* or *struct* and the t_i are the fields, elements or members of t.
Universal code	A class of codes for the integers (Sect. 3.1).
unzip	Convert a Vector (data-set) of tuples (columns) into a tuple of Vectors (Sect. 6.3), inverse of zip.
`UPModel`	Unparameterised model, needing statistical parameter(s) to produce a parameterised model.
Vector	$\vec{v} = [v_1, \ldots, v_D]$ where the v_i are all of the same type, often of the type $\mathbb{R}$ (Sect. 9.1).
vMF	The von Mises–Fisher distribution over directions (Sect. 9.3.2).
von Mises	As in the von Mises distribution on S^1, that is on directions in $\mathbb{R}^2$, a special case of the von Mises–Fisher (vMF) distribution on S^K, that is on directions in $\mathbb{R}^{K+1}$ (Sect. 9.3.2).
Weakly connected	Vertices u and v in a directed graph (Chap. 11) are (weakly) connected if there is a path of one or more edges between u and v when the directions of the edges are ignored;

	a directed graph is weakly connected if every pair of vertices is weakly connected; also see strongly connected.
William of Ockham	William of Ockham (1285–1349) [78], known for *Ockham's razor* (Chap. 1), sometimes Occam.
X	A real-valued random variable (sometimes).
x	A real-valued variable, an unknown, a real datum (sometimes).
$\mathbb{Z}$	The set (type, space) of integers, positive, negative, and zero.
$\mathbb{Z}_{>0}$	The set of positive integers, greater than zero.
$\mathbb{Z}_{\geq 0}$	The set of non-negative integers, greater than or equal to zero; also see $\mathbb{N}$.
zip	Convert a tuple of Vectors (data-sets) into a Vector of tuples (Sect. 6.3), inverse of unzip.

Γ	$\Gamma n = (n-1)!$ (Sect. 13.4), for integer $n \geq 1$.
Γ	$\Gamma x = \int^{\infty} y^{x-1} e^{-y} dy$, for $x > 0$. $\Gamma(x+1) = x\Gamma x$.
θ	Parameter(s) of a model (often).
κ_D	Lattice constant, see Sect. 1.6.2.
μ	The mean of a distribution (often).
v	The variance of a distribution, that is the mean squared distance from the mean (often).
σ	The standard deviation, $\sqrt{v}$ (often).
Π	Product, $\Pi_{i=1}^{n} x_i = x_1 \times \ldots \times x_n$.
Σ	Sum, $\Sigma_{i=1}^{n} x_i = x_1 + \ldots + x_n$.
$\hat{}$	Hat, as in $\hat{\theta}$, an estimate of the parameter(s) of a model.
$\{x \mid P(x)\}$	The set of xs for which the predicate $P(x)$ is true.
$\vec{v} = [v_1, \cdots, v_D]$	The (row-) Vector of D components, all of the same type, often of the type $\mathbb{R}$ (Sect. 9.1).

$\vec{v}^T$	The column-Vector, the transpose of $\vec{v}$.
$\bar{}$	Bar, as in $\bar{x}$, x-bar, the mean of several xs, $(\sum_{i=1}^{N} x_i)/N$.
$\cdot$	Dot, dot product (Sect. 9.1) of two Vectors.
$\times$	See product space and tuple; also cross product of two Vectors in $\mathbb{R}^3$ (Sect. 9.1).
$\|x\|$	The absolute value of a real number, e.g., $\|3\| = \|-3\| = 3$.
$\|S\|$	The number of members of a set S.
$\|M\|$	The determinant of a matrix M.
$\\|\vec{v}\\|_p$	The $\mathbb{L}_p$-norm of a Vector (Chap. 9).
$[lo, hi]$	Closed interval, the set $\{x\|lo \leq x \leq hi\}$, lo inclusive to hi inclusive.
$[lo, hi)$	The set $\{x\|lo \leq x < hi\}$, lo inclusive to hi exclusive.
$(lo, hi]$	The set $\{x\|lo < x \leq hi\}$, lo exclusive to hi inclusive.
(lo, hi)	Open interval, the set $\{x\|lo < x < hi\}$, lo exclusive to hi exclusive.

Bibliography

1. L. Allison, Models for machine learning and data mining in functional programming. J. Funct. Program. **15**(1), 15–32 (2005). https://doi.org/10.1017/S0956796804005301
2. L. Allison, On the complexity of graphs (networks) by information content, and conditional (mutual) information given other graphs. Technical report 2014/277, Faculty of Information Technology, Monash University, 2014. http://www.allisons.org/ll/Publications/2014Graph/
3. L. Allison, C.S. Wallace, C.N. Yee, Finite-state models in the alignment of macromolecules. J. Mol. Evol. **35**(1), 77–89 (1992). https://doi.org/10.1007/BF00160262
4. E. Anderson, The Irises of the Gaspe Peninsula. Bull. Am. Iris Soc. **59**, 2–5 (1935)
5. E. Anderson, The species problem in Iris. Ann. Mo. Bot. Gard. **23**, 457–509 (1936). https://doi.org/10.2307/2394164
6. M. Anderson, R.D. Pose, C.S. Wallace, A password-capability system. Comput. J. **29**(1), 1–8 (1986). https://doi.org/10.1093/comjnl/29.1.1
7. L. Babai, Graph isomorphism in quasipolynomial time, in *Proceedings of the 48th Annual ACM SIGACT Symposium on Theory of Computing (STOC)* (ACM, New York, 2016), pp. 684–697. https://doi.org/10.1145/2897518.2897542
8. T. Bayes, An essay towards solving a problem in the doctrine of chances. Philos. Trans. 370–418 (1763). http://www.jstor.org/stable/2333180
9. R. Bird, P. Wadler, *Introduction to Functional Programming* (Prentice Hall, Englewood, Cliffs, NJ, 1988). ISBN 978-0134841892
10. A.J. Bleasby, J.C. Wootton, Constructing validated, non-redundant composite protein sequence databases. Protein Eng. **3**(3), 153–159 (1990). https://doi.org/10.1093/protein/3.3.153
11. D.M. Boulton, The information measure criterion for intrinsic classification. PhD thesis, Department of Computer Science, Monash University, 1975
12. D.M. Boulton, C.S. Wallace, The information content of a multistate distribution. J. Theor. Biol. **23**(2), 269–278 (1969). https://doi.org/10.1016/0022-5193(69)90041-1
13. G.E.P. Box, Robustness in the strategy of scientific model building. Robustness Stat. **1**, 201–236 (1979). https://doi.org/10.1016/B978-0-12-438150-6.50018-2. Includes, “All models are wrong but some are useful”
14. R.P. Brent, Some comments on C S Wallace’s random number generators. Comput. J. **51**(5), 579–584 (2008). https://doi.org/10.1093/comjnl/bxm122
15. M.D. Cao, T.I. Dix, L. Allison, C. Mears, A simple statistical algorithm for biological sequence compression, in *Data Compression Conference (DCC)* (IEEE, New York, 2007), pp. 43–52. http://dx.doi.org/10.1109/DCC.2007.7
16. A. Church, *The Calculi of Lambda Conversion*. Annals of Mathematical Studies (Princeton University Press, Princeton, NJ, 1941). https://press.princeton.edu/titles/2390.html

L. Allison, *Coding Ockham’s Razor*, https://doi.org/10.1007/978-3-319-76433-7

17. J.H. Collier, L. Allison, A.M. Lesk, P.J. Stuckey, M. Garcia de la Banda, A.S. Konagurthu, Statistical inference of protein structural alignments using information and compression. J. Bioinformatics **33**(7), 1005–1013 (2017). https://doi.org/10.1093/bioinformatics/btw757
18. J.W. Comley, L. Allison, L.F. Fitzgibbon, Flexible decision trees in a general data-mining environment, in *Intelligent Data Engineering and Automated Learning*. LNCS, vol. 2690 (Springer, Berlin, 2003), pp. 761–767. https://doi.org/10.1007/978-3-540-45080-1_102
19. J.H. Conway, N.J.A. Sloane, *Sphere Packings, Lattices and Groups* (Springer, Berlin, 1988). ISBN 978-0387966175. https://doi.org/10.1007/978-1-4757-6568-7
20. CSV, Comma-separated values. arXiv. Retrieved 2017. https://en.wikipedia.org/wiki/Comma-separated_values
21. H.B. Curry, R. Feys, *Combinatory Logic* (North Holland, Amsterdam, 1958)
22. H.A. David, First (?) occurrence of common terms in mathematical statistics. Am. Stat. **49**(2), 121–133 (1995). https://doi.org/10.2307/2684625. http://www.jstor.org/stable/2684625
23. D. de Solla Price, A general theory of bibliometric and other cumulative advantage processes. J. Am. Soc. Inf. Sci. **27**(5), 292–306 (1976). https://doi.org/10.1002/asi.4630270505
24. L. Devroye, *Non-Uniform Random Variate Generation* (Springer, Berlin, 1986). http://luc.devroye.org/rnbookindex.html
25. J.G. Dowty, SMML estimators for 1-dimensional continuous data. Comput. J. **58**(1), 126–133 (2013). https://doi.org/10.1093/comjnl/bxt145
26. P. Elias, Universal codeword sets and representations of the integers. IEEE Trans. Inf. Theory **IT-21**(2), 194–203 (1975). https://doi.org/10.1109/TIT.1975.1055349
27. P. Erdos, A. Renyi, On random graphs. Publ. Math. **6**, 290–297 (1959). http://www.renyi.hu/~p_erdos/1959-11.pdf
28. G.E. Farr, C.S. Wallace, The complexity of strict minimum message length inference. Comput. J. **45**(3), 285–292 (2002). https://doi.org/10.1093/comjnl/45.3.285
29. S. Fienberg, When did Bayesian inference become "Bayesian"? Bayesian Anal. **1**(1), 1–40 (2006). https://projecteuclid.org/download/pdf_1/euclid.ba/1340371071
30. R.A. Fisher, The use of multiple measurements in taxonomic problems. Ann. Eugenics **7**(II), 179–188 (1936). https://doi.org/10.1111/j.1469-1809.1936.tb02137.x
31. R.A. Fisher, The negative binomial distribution. Ann. Eugenics **11**(1), 182–187 (1941). https://doi.org/10.1111/j.1469-1809.1941.tb02284.x. David (First (?) occurrence of common terms in mathematical statistics. Am. Stat. **49**(2), 121–133 (1995). https://doi.org/10.2307/2684625. http://www.jstor.org/stable/2684625) attributes the "first (?) occurrence" of the term "information matrix" to this paper
32. R.A. Fisher, Dispersion on a sphere. Proc. R. Soc. Lond. A **217**(1130), 295–305 (1953). https://doi.org/10.1098/rspa.1953.0064
33. J. Fisher Box, *R. A. Fisher: The Life of a Scientist* (Wiley, London, 1978). ISBN 0471093009
34. L.J. Fitzgibbon, L. Allison, J.C. Comley, Probability model type sufficiency, in *Intelligent Data Engineering and Automated Learning*. LNCS, vol. 2690 (Springer, Berlin, 2003), pp. 530–534. https://doi.org/10.1007/978-3-540-45080-1_72
35. J.-L. Gailly, M. Adler, gzip (2003). http://www.gzip.org/
36. B.R. Gaines, Behaviour/structure transformations under uncertainty. Int. J. Man Mach. Stud. **8**(3), 337–365 (1976). https://doi.org/10.1016/S0020-7373(76)80005-3
37. F. Galton, Section H. Anthropology. Opening address by Francis Galton. Nature **82**, 507–510 (1885). https://doi.org/10.1038/032502a0. David (First (?) occurrence of common terms in mathematical statistics. Am. Stat. **49**(2), 121–133 (1995). https://doi.org/10.2307/2684625. http://www.jstor.org/stable/2684625) attributes the "first (?)" occurrence of the term "regression" to this address
38. F. Galton, Kinship and correlation. Stat. Sci. **4**(2), 81–86 (1989, reprinted). https://doi.org/10.1214/ss/1177012581. http://www.jstor.org/stable/2245330
39. M.P. Georgeff, C.S. Wallace, A general selection criterion for inductive inference, in *European Conference in Artificial Intelligence*, vol. 84 (1984), pp. 473–482
40. E.N. Gilbert, Random graphs. Ann. Math. Stat. **30**, 1141–1144 (1959). http://www.jstor.org/stable/2237458

41. P. Goldsworth, The biology of poetry. Judith Wright memorial lecture, Australian Poetry Festival, 2002
42. J. Gosling, B. Joy, G. Steele, G. Bracha, A. Buckley, *The Java Language Specification, Java SE 8* (Addison Wesley, Reading, MA, 2014). ISBN 978-0133900699
43. A. Hodges, *Alan Turing: The Enigma* (Simon and Schuster, 1983). https://en.wikipedia.org/wiki/Simon_%26_Schuster-and-https://en.wikipedia.org/wiki/Alan_Turing:_The_Enigma
44. N.K. Humphrey, The illusion of beauty. Perception **2**(4), 429–439 (1973). http://cogprints.org/1771/
45. P. Kasarapu, L. Allison, Minimum message length estimation of mixtures of multivariate Gaussian and von Mises-Fisher distributions. Mach. Learn. 1–46 (2015). https://doi.org/10.1007/s10994-015-5493-0
46. D.T. Kenny, Stairway to hell: life and death in the pop music industry. The conversation (27/10/2014), 2014. https://theconversation.com/stairway-to-hell-life-and-death-in-the-pop-music-industry-32735
47. D.T. Kenny, The 27 club is a myth: 56 is the bum note for musicians. The conversation (19/11/2014), 2014. http://theconversation.com/the-27-club-is-a-myth-56-is-the-bum-note-for-musicians-33586
48. D.T. Kenny, A. Asher, Life expectancy and cause of death in popular musicians: Is the popular musician lifestyle the road to ruin? Med. Probl. Perform. Art. **31**(1), 37–44 (2016). https://doi.org/10.21091/mppa.2016.1007
49. A.S. Konagurthu, A.M. Lesk, On the origin of distribution patterns of motifs in biological networks. BMC Syst. Biol. **2** (2008). https://doi.org/10.1186/1752-0509-2-73
50. A.S. Konagurthu, L. Allison, D. Abramson, P.J. Stuckey, A.M. Lesk, How precise are reported protein coordinate data? Acta Crystallogr. **D70**(3), 904–906 (2014). https://doi.org/10.1107/S1399004713031787
51. S. Kullback, R.A. Leibler, On information and sufficiency. Ann. Math. Stat. **22**(1), 79–86 (1951). https://doi.org/10.1214/aoms/1177729694
52. P.S. Laplace, Mémoire sur la probabilité des causes par les évènemens (1774). https://projecteuclid.org/download/pdf_1/euclid.ss/1177013621. Translated by S. M. Stigler (1986) (Laplace's 1774 memoir on inverse probability. Stat. Sci. **1**(3), 359–363 (1986). https://projecteuclid.org/download/pdf_1/euclid.ss/1177013620)
53. N.M. Luscombe, M.M. Babu, H. Yu, M. Snyder, S.A. Teichmann, M. Gerstein, Genomic analysis of regulatory network dynamics reveals large topological changes. Nature **431**, 308–312 (2004). https://doi.org/10.1038/nature02782
54. A. Ma'ayan, S.L. Jenkins, S. Neves, A. Hasseldine, E. Grace, B. Dubin-Thaler, N.J. Eungdamrong, G. Weng, P.T. Ram, J.J. Rice, A. Kershenbaum, G.A. Stolovitzky, R.D. Blitzer, I. Iyengar, Formation of regulatory patterns during signal propagation in a mammalian cellular network. Science **309**, 1078–1083 (2005). https://doi.org/10.1126/science.1108876
55. G. Marsaglia, Choosing a point from the surface of a sphere. Ann. Math. Stat. **43**, 645–646 (1972). http://www.jstor.org/stable/2240001
56. B.D. McKay, Computing automorphisms and canonical labellings of graphs, in *International Conference on Combinatorial Mathematics*. LNCS, vol. 686 (Springer, Berlin, 1977), pp. 223–232. https://doi.org/10.1007/BFb0062536
57. B.D. McKay, A. Piperno, Practical graph isomorphism II. arXiv: 1301.1493 (2013). http://arxiv.org/abs/1301.1493
58. G.R.G. Mure, Aristotle's posterior analytics, in *Aristotle Organon and Other Works*, ed. by W.D. Ross (1925). https://archive.org/details/AristotleOrganon
59. A. Narayanan, Algorithm AS 266: maximum likelihood estimation of the parameters of the, Dirichlet distribution. J. R. Stat. Soc.: Ser. C: Appl. Stat. **40**(2), 365–374 (1991). https://doi.org/10.2307/2347605. http://www.jstor.org/stable/2347605
60. M. Nelson, Arithmetic coding + statistical modeling = data compression. Dr Dobbs J. (1991). http://marknelson.us/1991/02/01/arithmetic-coding-statistical-modeling-data-compression/
61. R.T. O'Donnell, L. Allison, K.B. Korb, Learning hybrid Bayesian networks by MML, in *Australasian Joint Conference on Artificial Intelligence*. LNCS, vol. 4304 (Springer, Berlin, 2006), pp. 192–203. https://doi.org/10.1007/11941439_23

62. J. Oliver, Decision graphs – an extension of decision trees, in *4th International Conference on Artificial Intelligence and Statistics* (1993), pp. 343–350. http://citeseerx.ist.psu.edu/viewdoc/summary?doi=10.1.1.52.1476
63. J. Oliver, C.S. Wallace, Inferring decision graphs, in *IJCAI, Workshop 8* (1991)
64. R.C. Pasco, Source coding algorithms for fast data compression. PhD thesis, Stanford University CA, 1976
65. J.D. Patrick, An information measure comparative analysis of megalithic geometries. PhD thesis, Department of Computer Science, Monash University, 1979
66. J.D. Patrick, C.S. Wallace, Stone circle geometries: an information theory approach, in *Archaeoastronomy in the Old World*, ed. by D. Heggie (Cambridge University Press, Cambridge, 1982), pp. 231–264. https://doi.org/10.1017/CBO9780511898310.016
67. S. Peyton Jones et al., *Haskell 98 Language and Libraries, the Revised Report* (Cambridge University Press, Cambridge, 2003). ISBN 978-0521826143
68. J.R. Quinlan, Induction of decision trees. Mach. Learn. **1**(1), 81–106 (1986). https://doi.org/10.1023/A:1022643204877
69. J.R. Quinlan, *C4.5: Programs for Machine Learning* (Morgan Kaufmann, Los Altos, CA, 1992). ISBN 978-1558602380
70. J. Rissanen, Generalized kraft inequality and arithmetic coding. IBM J. Res. Dev. **20**(3), 198–203 (1976). https://doi.org/10.1147/rd.203.0198
71. J. Rissanen, A universal prior for integers and estimation by minimum description length. Ann. Stat. **11**(2), 416–431 (1983). http://www.jstor.org/stable/2240558
72. E. Sava, C. Twardy, R. Koester, M. Sonwalkar, Evaluating lost person behavior models. Trans. Geogr. Inf. Syst. **20**(1), 38–53 (2016). https://doi.org/10.1111/tgis.12143
73. D.F. Schmidt, E. Makalic, MMLD inference of the Poisson and geometric models. Technical report 2008/220, Faculty of Information Technology, Monash University, 2008. https://www.researchgate.net/publication/268057041_MMLD_Inference_of_the_Poisson_and_Geometric_Models
74. D.F. Schmidt, E. Makalic, Universal models for the exponential distribution. IEEE Trans. Inf. Theory **55**(7), 3087–3090 (2009). https://doi.org/10.1109/TIT.2009.2018331
75. P.H. Sellers, On the theory and computation of evolutionary distances. SIAM J. Appl. Math. **26**(4), 787–793 (1974). https://doi.org/10.1137/0126070
76. C.E. Shannon, A mathematical theory of communication. Bell Labs Tech. J. **27**(3,4), 379–423, 623–656 (1948). https://doi.org/10.1002/j.1538-7305.1948.tb01338.x
77. S.S. Shen-Orr, R. Milo, S. Mangan, U. Alon, Network motifs in the transcriptional regulation network of Eshericia coli. Nat. Genet. **31**, 64–68 (2002). https://doi.org/10.1038/ng881
78. P.V. Spade (ed.), *The Cambridge Companion to Ockham* (Cambridge University Press, Cambridge, 1999). ISBN 978-0521582445. https://doi.org/10.1017/CCOL052158244X
79. A. Spencer, *World of Numbers* (Xoum Publishing, Surry Hills, 2015). ISBN 978-1921134869
80. S. Sra, A short note on parameter approximation for von Mises-Fisher distributions: and a fast implementation of $I_s(x)$. Comput. Stat. **27**(1), 177–190 (2012). https://doi.org/10.1007/s00180-011-0232-x
81. S.M. Stigler, Laplace's 1774 memoir on inverse probability. Stat. Sci. **1**(3), 359–363 (1986). https://projecteuclid.org/download/pdf_1/euclid.ss/1177013620. Introduction to translation of Laplace (Mémoire sur la probabilité des causes par les évènemens (1774). https://projecteuclid.org/download/pdf_1/euclid.ss/1177013621. Translated by S. M. Stigler (1986) (Laplace's 1774 memoir on inverse probability. Stat. Sci. **1**(3), 359–363 (1986). https://projecteuclid.org/download/pdf_1/euclid.ss/1177013620)) pp.364–378 same issue
82. B. Stroustrup, *The C++ Programming Language: Special Edition* (Addison Wesley, Reading, MA, 2000). ISBN 978-0201700732
83. R. Subramanian, L. Allison, P.J. Stuckey, M. Garcia de la Banda, D. Abramson, A.M. Lesk, A.S. Konagurthu, Statistical compression of protein folding patterns for inference of recurrent substructural themes, in *Data Compression Conference (DCC)* (IEEE, New York, 2017), pp. 340–349. https://doi.org/10.1109/DCC.2017.46

84. R. Viaña, Quick encoding of plane graphs in $\log_2 14$ bits per edge. Inf. Process. Lett. **108**(3), 150–154 (2008). https://doi.org/10.1016/j.ipl.2008.04.017
85. C.S. Wallace, Suggested design for a very fast multiplier. Technical report UIUCDCS-R-63-133, Digital Computer Laboratory, University of Illinois, 1963
86. C.S. Wallace, A suggestion for a fast multiplier. IEEE Trans. Electron. Comput. **EC-13**(1), 14–17 (1964). https://doi.org/10.1109/PGEC.1964.263830
87. C.S. Wallace, An improved program for classification, in *Proceedings of the 9th Australian Computer Science Conference*, vol. 8(1) (1986), pp. 357–366
88. C.S. Wallace, How to do inductive inference using information theory. Seminar, Department of Computer Science, Monash University, 1993. http://www.allisons.org/ll/Images/People/Wallace/1993-08-10/
89. C.S. Wallace, Fast pseudorandom generators for normal and exponential variates. ACM Trans. Math. Softw. (TOMS) **22**(1), 119–127 (1996). https://doi.org/10.1145/225545.225554
90. C.S. Wallace, Multiple factor analysis by MML estimation. Technical report 218, Department of Computer Science, Monash University, 1998. http://www.allisons.org/ll/Images/People/Wallace/Multi-Factor/
91. C.S. Wallace, A brief history of MML. Seminar, Faculty of Information Technology, Monash University, 2003. http://www.allisons.org/ll/MML/20031120e/
92. C.S. Wallace, *Statistical and Inductive Inference by Minimum Message Length* (Springer, Berlin, 2005). ISBN 978-0-387-23795-4. https://doi.org/10.1007/0-387-27656-4
93. C.S. Wallace, D.M. Boulton, An information measure for classification. Comput. J. **11**(2), 185–194 (1968). https://doi.org/10.1093/comjnl/11.2.185
94. C.S. Wallace, D.M. Boulton, An invariant Bayes method for point estimation. Classif. Soc. Bull. **3**(3), 11–34 (1975)
95. C.S. Wallace, D.L. Dowe, Estimation of the von Mises concentration parameter using minimum message length, in *Proceedings of the 12th. Australian Statistical Society Conference* (1993)
96. C.S. Wallace, P.R. Freeman, Estimation and inference by compact coding. J. R. Stat. Soc. Ser. B Methodol. 240–265 (1987). http://www.jstor.org/stable/2985992
97. C.S. Wallace, P.R. Freeman, Single-factor analysis by minimum message length estimation. J. R. Stat. Soc. Ser. B Methodol. 195–209 (1992). http://www.jstor.org/stable/2345956
98. C.S. Wallace, J.D. Patrick, Coding decision trees. Mach. Learn. **11**(1), 7–22 (1993). https://doi.org/10.1023/A:1022646101185
99. C.S. Wallace, R.D. Pose, Charging in a secure environment, in *Security and Persistence* (Springer, Berlin, 1990), pp. 85–96. https://doi.org/10.1007/978-1-4471-3178-6_6
100. M. Wolkewitz, A. Allignol, N. Graves, A.G. Barnett, Is 27 really a dangerous age for famous musicians? Retrospective cohort study. Br. Med. J. **343**, d7799 (2011). https://doi.org/10.1136/bmj.d7799
101. A.T.A. Wood, Simulation of the von Mises Fisher distribution. Commun. Stat. Simul. Comput. **23**(1), 157–164 (1994). https://doi.org/10.1080/03610919408813161
102. C.N. Yee, L. Allison, Reconstruction of strings past. J. Bioinformatics **9**(1), 1–7 (1993). https://doi.org/10.1093/bioinformatics/9.1.1
103. P. Zador, Asymptotic quantization error of continuous signals and the quantization dimension. IEEE Trans. Inf. Theory **28**(2), 139–149 (1982). https://doi.org/10.1109/TIT.1982.1056490

Index

L. Allison, *Coding Ockham's Razor*, https://doi.org/10.1007/978-3-319-76433-7

Printed in the United States
By Bookmasters